# When the Senate Worked for Us

# When the Senate Worked for Us

*The Invisible Role of Staffers in Countering Corporate Lobbies*

**Michael Pertschuk**

VANDERBILT UNIVERSITY PRESS

NASHVILLE

© 2017 by Vanderbilt University Press
Nashville, Tennessee 37235
All rights reserved
First printing 2017

This book is printed on acid-free paper.
Manufactured in the United States of America

Cover design: Rich Hendel
Text design and composition: Dariel Mayer

Library of Congress Cataloging-in-Publication Data
LC control number  2016044846
LC classification number  KF373.P478 A3 2017
Dewey classification number  373.7307/1
LC record available at lccn.loc.gov/2016044846

ISBN 978-0-8265-2166-8 (cloth)
ISBN 978-0-8265-2168-2 (ebook)

Float like a butterfly,
sting like a bee.
—Muhammad Ali

# Contents

# Introduction

In a querulous conversation late in Richard Nixon's presidency, John Ehrlichman, Nixon's domestic policy director, bemoaned the torrent of new regulatory laws from Congress. These laws impinged on the freedom to harm, sicken, deceive, and pollute of the morally impaired business lobbyists to whom Nixon owed allegiance.

Signing progressive regulatory laws was hardly what Nixon had expected when he wrested the presidency from the liberal Democrats. It was as if John F. Kennedy or Lyndon Johnson were still president. Ehrlichman didn't dwell on the laws' contents, but he fingered the culprits: not the elected legislators, not even the Democrats who still controlled the Congress, but their unelected staff members. These young hellhounds, he insisted, were goading otherwise sober and reasonable legislators into inflicting Sisyphean regulatory burdens on the already overregulated. As I vividly remember, he scorned the more aggressive staff members as "bumblebees, hovering around the honey of power."

I was then serving as the majority Democratic staff director of the Senate Commerce Committee, chaired by Washington State senator Warren G. Magnuson. Ehrlichman was substantively right but semantically wrong: bumblebees pay no attention to honey; only honeybees do. But bumblebees do sting. Nixon felt that sting when he was forced to sign laws he disdained, many of which had been shepherded through Congress by liberal Democratic and several liberal Republican staffers. Failing to sign the bills would evoke broad public condemnation—fueled by the hated "liberal press"—or a veto override by the Democratic majorities and their liberal Republican allies in both houses of Congress.

Along with my fellow Magnuson staffers, I was bursting with pride over what we readily accepted as Ehrlichman's backhanded tribute to our role in incubating a good number of the laws that plagued Nixon. "Bumblebee" would become our badge of honor. My own Bumblebee pride was soon boosted by the ranking Republican on the Senate Commerce Committee, Norris Cotton of New Hampshire, a senator who steadfastly voted against much of Magnuson's consumer protection and regulatory public health legislation. Cotton proudly called himself a "mossback New England conservative" and was tight with the Republican Senate leadership and the Nixon White House, but he was also a close friend of his liberal Democratic counterpart, Senator Magnuson. Happily for me, their mutual affection trickled down to me and my Republican staff counterpart. Together with him, I often conferred collegially with Senator Cotton. The senator was always ready to tease me for my liberalism, and when we next met after Ehrlichman's rant, Cotton gleefully reported that during recent strategic conclaves in the White House I had been singled out for scorn.

Ehrlichman was right in crediting staff members with a role in toughening the liberal laws that reached the president's desk for signature. But he was wrong in implying that the impetus came only from staff. As James Q. Wilson points out in *Bureaucracy*, his examination of Congress, the liberal activism that we experienced was the product of "*entrepreneurial* politics."

"Elected politicians," he explains, "won reputations and power by leaping to the front of public enthusiasm for environmental protection" and other popular causes, not least consumer protection and public health.[1] Ira Shapiro, in his encyclopedic celebration *The Last Great Senate*, affirms what Wilson asserts, narrating how senators of both parties, serving together on one committee after another, transcended greed, ambition, and partisanship to join across party lines and successfully promote landmark legislation on a wide range of issues that served public needs.[2] His account of the collaboration of virtuous senators consumes nearly five hundred pages. These pages are so crowded with good deeds that even Magnuson's voluminous legislative accomplishments are squeezed into just two of them. The role of staff, however, is virtually invisible.

My own experience networking with staff members from other committees and senatorial offices taught me that behind almost every successful entrepreneurial senator was a team of facilitating staff. Many were simply doing the bidding of their bosses, but others were as ambitious as we were. Shapiro himself played vigorous roles in the 1970s as the highly respected staff director and chief counsel to the Senate Select Committee on Ethics, counsel to the majority leader, minority staff director, and chief counsel to the Governmental Affairs Committee. Yet he takes no credit for his part in the legislative achievements of the senators he chronicles and makes no attempt to convey the roles of other staff in those achievements. If he had done so, his book would be too heavy to lift. In one sense, then, this book is designed to complement Shapiro's narrative of bipartisan comity among many senators in the 1960s and 1970s. But my focus is far more narrow. I present a selection of stories about the staff of one high-achieving Senate committee, powered by Magnuson's Bumblebees. I believe that the multifarious roles we Bumblebees played are representative of the roles played by other staff members in the achievements of the senators and committees that Shapiro celebrates.

Our work, however, was unique. Between the early 1960s and the late 1970s, the number of progressive laws that came out of the Senate Commerce Committee bearing the invisible fingerprints of entrepreneurial staff comes close to the output of all the other Senate committees combined. As we shall see, the force that powered the Commerce Committee's productivity was a harmonic convergence of the strengths, strategies, and needs of two monumental figures: Chairman Magnuson and my predecessor as staff director, Gerald "Jerry" Grinstein.

Grinstein brought to bear his passion for enabling the committee to do good; Magnuson brought to bear his formal power, strengthened by decades of Senate seniority, and the informal power born of the affection in which he was held not only by his Democratic colleagues but by many Republican senators who liked and trusted him. That esteem helped bring stability and concord to both the committee and the full Senate.

One result of Magnuson's and Grinstein's combined strengths was the unmatched expansion of the committee's professional staff, most of whom were under their direct control. By the mid-1970s, the ranks of professional Magnuson Commerce Committee staff members had expanded to over forty, including several credentialed experts. In an effort to determine how to select Magnuson Bumblebee stories for this book, I turned to the work of David Price, who undertook an assignment from the consumer advocate Ralph Nader in the summer of 1970. With remarkable ambition, Nader had convened more than a hundred volunteers to produce unalloyed profiles of every member of Congress and every congressional committee. Price was assigned to the Senate and House Commerce Committees. He brought with him deep investigative skills and the experience of serving as a staff member for one of the Senate Commerce Committee's public interest advocates, Senator Edward Lewis "Bob" Bartlett of Alaska. Price was so perfectly attuned to the workings of the Congress that he went on to be elected to the House of Representatives from his North Carolina home for at least thirteen terms.

In his work for Nader, Price focused on staff members who were "concerned with consumer affairs" and who "exhibited independence and activism." He called them "entrepreneurial staff" almost two decades before Wilson adopted the label "entrepreneurial" for proactive senators. In his report, Price describes these staff members as "'second-level experts' with enough knowledge and sophistication to gain an overview of the areas with which they were involved, to be critical of information and recommendations received from other sources, to request and then apply information on their own terms, and to undertake translations into concrete policy proposals."[3] In an earlier book, Price argues that the interest these staff members have in legislative problems is sometimes "more lively . . . than that of their bosses." They are "engaged in a continual 'search' operation, seeking both gaps for policy initiatives and fledgling proposals that might be developed and made politically viable." They frame "alternative courses of action for the Chairman and sometimes for the members, paying considerable attention to the realities and possibilities of public and group support in the process." They devise hearings "to realize their maximum potential for publicity" and often leak "news of rumored defections and opposition efforts to the press."[4]

The staff members Price describes as "entrepreneurial" had the same qualities as those who evoked Ehrlichman's pique, the Magnuson Bumblebees whose stories I relate here. Not all of Magnuson's Commerce Committee staff members were Bumblebees. Some lacked the imagination and initiative to be entrepreneurial; others, while competent, had politically neutral administrative tasks or were assigned to work in the areas of committee responsibility that rarely permitted room for entrepreneurship. Still others proved passively apolitical.

Over the four years that I worked on this book, beginning in January 2013, I sought out a representative sampling of the most entrepreneurial of the Magnuson Commerce Committee Bumblebees. I interviewed them and continued to confer with them as the book progressed. Out of these interviews and exchanges I have sought to select stories that illustrate the full complement of Bumblebee strategies and actions and, at the same time, the comity, mutual respect, and frequent affection that prevailed among senators across party lines. I have attributed these activities to "Magnuson Bumblebees," since the perpetrators were all hired under Magnuson's imprimatur as committee chairman, but their assignments required that they also serve many of the other Democratic committee members. Some members were far more flexible and easy to work with than Magnuson, while others were more resistant to Bumblebee ambitions than he. I deeply regret that I am unable to include all the staff members who met Price's criteria and earned the badge of the Bumblebee. Records of the interviews as well as the full development of the book are available in the Michael Pertschuk Archive in the Library of Congress. The archive includes a folder for each interviewee that contains the voice recordings of the interviews, printouts of all e-mail exchanges, and copies of the evolving drafts of his or her story.

Price drew on what he had gleaned from interviews with committee senators and staffers of both parties to describe our work with uncanny insight. But he could not tell our full stories. Though what we told him was the truth, we could not tell him all of it. We certainly did not disclose such discomfiting details as Magnuson's testy resistance to offering the consumer protection bills that ultimately brought him prideful recognition. We avoided recounting the extent to which Magnuson delegated the details to us and how we took advantage of our long leash to tilt hearings to favor supportive witnesses, scheduling hostile witnesses in the late afternoon when the cameras and journalists had packed up. We did not tell him that we drafted bills that Magnuson presented but never read, as well as floor statements, also unread, that he delivered verbatim. We did not tell him that we wrote press releases, committee reports, and chastening letters to delinquent regulators and corporate heads bearing Magnuson's signature—which Magnuson never read or even knew about. Nor did we confess our blunders, deceptions, weaknesses, and failures.

Price also ran up against the creed of the successful staff member: Hide your name. The less the media and the electorate learn of your role in serving the politicians you work for, the more credit and reelection currency they accrue—and the more content they will be with you. The more you disappear, the better. This creed constrained us from going public for more than forty years, leaving the shadowy roles of staff largely untold.

Our boss, Magnuson, was among the least egocentric of the senators we worked for. Unlike many other senators, who were wary of staff members who threatened to outshine them, Magnuson appreciated able staff. But even he was loath to see our names in print, absorbing credit for his achievements. Thus, when he heard about "Bumblebees" (in contrast to the staff members who had seized on Ehrlichman's wrathful term as a compliment), Magnuson decided to wield it against us. During one of our informal afternoon "children's hour" sessions in his office,[5] Magnuson announced that henceforth he would bestow a "Bumblebee of the Week" award on any staff member who managed to get his or her own name in print. The prize would be tape across the errant staffer's mouth. Inspired by this decision, Magnuson's wife, Jermaine, who despised staff self-aggrandizement because it diminished her husband's public image, embroidered a bumblebee on a pillow that was thereafter plumped down obtrusively on a chair in Magnuson's office.

Magnuson never actually got around to bestowing a Bumblebee of the Week award. But his message to us was clear. To the best of my knowledge, no other senator adopted the label "Bumblebee" for his staff. Nor did any other former staff members spontaneously form an alumni group to gather, as we still do, to tell and retell stories of our boss's idiosyncrasies and our own. We cherished the label "Bumblebees." We owned it.[6]

Magnuson's iconic status in Washington State is secure. Those of us Bumblebees who have survived into our seventies and eighties are now safe from retribution. For many of us, the opportunity to serve Magnuson and the Commerce Committee remains the high-water mark of our professional lives. The stories we tell each other, again and again, of those treasured days with the committee are vivid, if somewhat altered by repetition and the passage of time. Along with Price and contemporaneous issue advocates such as Nader, those among us with the most intact memories hold the rest of us to the truth.

In Part I, I tell stories about my stumbles and the lessons I learned on the way to becoming a Bumblebee. In Part II, I offer a sample of Bumblebee stories I have drawn out of the extensive interviews with former colleagues whose memories are more trustworthy than mine. I include a cross section of the Bumblebees who played roles in a wide range of committee activities. Their stories introduce several entrepreneurial senators who took on the subcommittee leadership roles from which Magnuson had withdrawn.

Why might the Bumblebee stories be relevant today? In part because the powerful oppositional forces that existed then were not so different from those that exist now. We Bumblebees, like today's legislators and their staffs, commonly faced the oppressive influence of corporate money and its power. In particular our House counterpart, the House Commerce Committee of the 1960s and early 1970s, fueled our nightmares; they would have fit cozily alongside the worst of today's Congress. Then, as now, the majority of the House committee members, Democrats and Republicans alike, welcomed the money and took their orders from lobbyists seeking to gut or sink the public interest bills Magnuson and his Senate allies would maneuver through the Senate to the House. Their inclination to frustrate us was also fueled by what they scorned as inflated upper-chamber egos. We were forced to sharpen our tactical arrows to pierce the barriers they would erect.

In my interviews with Nader, he generously called Magnuson's Commerce Committee staff the "Grand Central Station" for public interest advocates and advocacy groups because we brought the "outside" "inside" by working with conscientious journalists and columnists—whom the right wing correctly tarred as left-leaning—as well as self-educated experts and those from academia who were free from the influence of moneyed interests. If "working with" meant "leaking to," so be it. They were all critical allies in opening the otherwise invisible machinations of dark lobbies to the light of public exposure.

This book also addresses an important lacuna in my own earlier books: all five recount the stories and strategies of individual advocates and organized citizenry to offset the economic and political power of corporate lobbies; but none focuses, as I do here, on the complementary role of staff, who alone held significant power to transform the objectives of the advocates working from outside Congress.

My fondest hope is that this book will awaken the interest of young people to the potential rewards of working in the federal government. I have encountered many young people who are determined to change the world for the better. Many seek the opportunity to serve dedicated non-government, nonprofit organizers of social justice movements or to help realize the promise for good in new technologies. I have been saddened by how few look to government as the answer for themselves or for the country. Having witnessed the dysfunction of Congress, they would not even consider working for the House or Senate. These young people could use a dose of inspiration and hope and, no less, the promise of experiencing the pleasures of mischief-making in the public interest such as they will find in these stories.

In my first interview with Nader for this book, he lamented:

> There's a whole generation of Americans who have accepted the belief
> that the Congress can't do anything, won't do anything, is beset by all
> kinds of conflicting interests and gridlock. They have no idea, even
> about the bills that were passed. When you don't have any mooring
> in the history of a time when the Senate was remarkably responsive

compared to today, although never up to our standards, then what happens: then ignorance turns into cynicism, cynicism turns into withdrawal, and you have millions of people who have convinced themselves they don't count, they don't matter, and they unwittingly shed their own self-respect.

Perhaps this book can help dispel that inertia and inspire a new generation of Bumblebees.

# PART I

# 1

# *An Accidental Bumblebee*

I was bred a New Deal Democrat. President Franklin Roosevelt was an icon in our family. But it never occurred to me to engage in politics, other than to vote robotically for Democrats. By high school, I wanted to be a poet. So troubled was my father by his conviction that a poet could never earn a living that he began pocketing Cuban cigars at social events and saving them for me in the hope that by habituating me to expensive smokes he would sabotage my determination to become a penniless poet and redirect me to a living-wage trade, such as the law.

My predilection for writing poetry, however, was seared into my psyche and reinforced in my freshman year at Yale College when I was pounced on by a fevered dorm neighbor from Groton, the elite and very conservative prep school. He was hell-bent on the United States dropping a preventive nuclear bomb on the Soviet Union. I begged to differ. I would rather see the Soviet Union conquer the United States, I told him, than blow up the world with nuclear mutual destruction. After all, like any historic conqueror, Soviet communism would collapse in time, our globe would remain intact, and democracy would have a fighting chance.

At the time, red-baiting McCarthyism was enjoying its apex. "You're a Communist," he charged. "I'm going to report you to the FBI." He never did; but the threat was so unnerving that I timidly vowed thereafter to confine my extracurricular activities to romantic poetry writing.

As for my vocational trajectory, my father succeeded. I would become a lawyer, though I still harbored a muted ambition to be a poet.

I never considered entering government. Despite our trust in Roosevelt, my family shared the collective Jewish immigrant wariness of governments, which had historically been our people's oppressors. This sentiment is best expressed by the rabbi in *Fiddler on the Roof* when a young man asks, "Is there a proper blessing for the Tsar?"

"Of course!" the rabbi exclaims. "May God bless and keep the Tsar—far away from us."

After a two-year detour to Fort Sill, Oklahoma, to serve out my military obligation as an artillery officer, I returned to Yale to attend law school. In 1959, with my new degree, I headed out west to Portland, Oregon, to clerk for a wise federal judge, appropriately named Solomon. Government service was far from my mind. I followed Judge Gus J. Solomon's firm guidance and accepted a junior position in the most prestigious corporate law firm in Portland. That year I voted for John F. Kennedy for president. It was the extent of my involvement in politics. In my mind, my future would be limited to climbing the rungs, ultimately reaching the heights of a safe, lucrative partnership within the law firm.

Judge Solomon's secretary, Helen Bradley, was a passionate activist Democrat with whom I had formed a warm friendship during my clerkship. She had worked hard for the Oregon State election to the US Senate of the liberal journalist Richard Neuberger, and then, after his sudden death, for the election of his wife, Maurine Neuberger.

In 1961, only a year and a half after I joined the law firm, I received a call from Bradley. She had heard from Senator Neuberger, who was seeking a new legislative assistant. Would I be interested? My answer was a quick, "Not for me."

Yet that night, as I talked over the possibility with my wife, my resistance softened. In those days, it seemed as if every other young lawyer in Portland was eager to get to Washington to bask in the glamour and excitement that surrounded the youthful President Kennedy. It would be a novel experience; it might even burnish my résumé. Perhaps I could arrange a one-year leave of absence from the firm, secure in the knowledge that I would return to the safe bosom of Davies, Biggs, Strayer, Stoel, and Boley (which was destined to grow into the seventeenth largest corporate law firm in the United States in the 1970s).

I decided to apply for the Neuberger job. My credentials were hardly impressive. I knew less about lawmaking in Washington than the average eighth grader: I didn't realize that the Capitol, where Congress resides, was in a separate building down Pennsylvania Avenue from the White House. Fortunately, Senator Neuberger had written Bradley that she had only one requirement for the job: the candidate must be able to write English. That I could do. I got the job without being interviewed by the senator, or even visiting Washington.

In February 1962, I arrived in Washington and began serving Senator

Neuberger as her legislative assistant. She was a tenacious, independent legislator, the ninth woman ever to serve in the US Senate. Among her predecessors, she was easily the least deferential to the institution's traditional male dominance—a fearless liberal and a seasoned consumer advocate.

On her way to the Senate, Neuberger had gained national attention as an Oregon State House member who had stood before television cameras and a state senate committee in an apron, with a mixing bowl and a package of margarine on the table before her. Her target was a mandate pushed through every state house in the nation by the dairy lobby that forbade the sale of butter-colored margarine. The margarine industry, in response, had made its product a law-abiding white, accompanied by a small packet of butter-yellow dye. Neuberger demonstrated the laborious effort required to mix the margarine and the dye just to deceive butter-habituated children. Her testimony was featured on national television news. Oregon soon repealed this indefensible law. Within five years, so had every other state except Minnesota and Wisconsin, which held out for another decade.

To please my new boss, I found I had to be aggressive in finding initiatives for her to champion that could burnish her political identity as a consumer protection advocate. But I had no idea how to go about doing it. I sorely needed guidance. My first stroke of luck was to be taken in hand by the senator's chief of staff, Lloyd Tupling. The former editor of an independent muckraking newspaper in Idaho, Tupling had effectively been driven out of the state when he fearlessly attacked the consumer-rate inflation of one of the state's most powerful corporate monopolies, the federal dam–created Idaho Power.

First, Tupling told me, comb through the Washington papers and watch the TV news. Second, never write a Senate floor speech on any initiative without simultaneously drafting a press release on it.

I was readily infected with the populist spirit that had inspired Tupling to challenge the energy companies, and I began poring over the *Washington Post* and the *Washington Star* every day with an eye out for issues that would appeal to Neuberger. I bumped into an opportunity almost immediately. On March 8, 1962, the back pages of the *Washington Post* carried a story about the publication of a report issued by a distinguished panel of the Royal College of Physicians in London. The panel had concluded that smoking is a major cause of sickness and death and proposed regulatory restraints on cigarette advertising.

I knew that the senator had struggled to give up smoking and that any action to curb smoking would fit within her consumer protection commitment. That day I set about drafting a Senate floor statement for her that began with a summary of the panel's report, but I had no idea how to finish it. In desperation I wrote, "Within the next few days, I expect to introduce legislation to deal with this tragic problem."[1] Senator Neuberger read the statement into the *Congressional Record* as I had drafted it, giving it no more forethought than I had.

That afternoon, a *Washington Star* reporter called me and asked, "Exactly what action will the senator call for?" Nonplussed, I promised to get back to him and again sought counsel with Tupling. He suggested the time-worn response to issues one has no idea how to solve: have the senator introduce a congressional resolution directing the president to name a national panel of experts. I promptly drafted the resolution. (As if the British were a different species, it called for a review of research on the impact of cigarette smoking on US smokers.) Neuberger's resolution attracted only six cosponsors and went nowhere. The media paid attention, however, and the resolution gained Neuberger unaccustomed public exposure, which pleased her. She began to have some confidence that I could do the job.

I had never before thought about smoking as a public health issue. I had smoked a pipe in law school because I thought it made me look like a sober lawyer, though I soon gave it up since every fourth or fifth pipeful left me so queasy I had to lie down. My motivation in pursuing tobacco control legislation on behalf of Neuberger was primarily the desire to please her and secure my new livelihood. But as I set about learning more about the science and public policy research on cigarette marketing strategies, I developed an intense revulsion to the tobacco industry's disingenuous insistence on the safety of cigarettes and their aggressive marketing targeted at children. Philip Morris was proving to be the most rapacious of cigarette marketers. I woke up almost every morning scheming: What can I do today that will make Philip Morris executives squirm?

Media attention to the Neuberger resolution had brought me together with several dedicated tobacco control advocates, each of whom helped educate me. Among them were Michael Shimkin, a cancer researcher from the National Cancer Institute who opened my eyes to the substance and politics of health science; Morton Mintz, the most irrepressible reporter on corporate abuse and consumer protection the *Washington Post* had ever turned loose; Stanley Cohen, a veteran Washington columnist and editorial writer for the advertising industry trade journal *Advertising Age*, who turned out to be an unexpectedly harsh critic of cigarette advertising; Philip Elman, a brilliant legal scholar and aggressive consumer protector who was one of the five commissioners on the Federal Trade Commission (FTC); and David Cohen, who showed me what a skilled public interest lobbyist could provide a staff rookie.

Knowing little about health science, I had made a blind call to the National Cancer Institute, seeking a researcher who specialized in tobacco and health research. I was learning that government bureaucrats responded even to junior staff telephone calls. That call led me to Michael Shimkin. He hardly fit the stereotype of the neutral scientist. His first question when he came to my office was, "Do you smoke cigarettes?"

"No. Why?" I responded.

"Because smokers are incapable of hearing the bad news," he said. "They are all members of the Flat Earth Society."

Shimkin told me there was no scientific doubt that cigarettes cause cancer and heart disease but that his colleagues at the Cancer Institute, many of whom were smokers, had scorned the evidence because they were determined to prove that their own focus, air pollution, was the only cause of lung cancer. Though they would later be proven wrong, at the time they provided soothing balm to the tobacco lobby. Shimkin's crusade was a lonely one, but he was a disciplined scientist, and I learned from him the basics of the scientific case against smoking—and the answers to the claims of tobacco companies' hired scientists that the science condemning cigarette smoking remained "controversial," rendering regulatory action as yet unwarranted.

As I intensified my focus on the aggressive cigarette advertising that dominated nighttime television, I began to get regular calls from Stanley Cohen. At first I was on my guard. I assumed that a writer for the advertising industry would be sympathetic to the commercial interests of the cigarette companies that advertised heavily in *Ad Age*. I could not have been more wrong. In an editorial Cohen wrote for *Ad Age*, he made the journal one of the first publications to call editorially for a ban on cigarette advertising. Imagine a trade journal's publisher allowing a reporter, much less an editorial writer, to risk offending lucrative advertisers today. In an interview shortly before his death, Cohen, at age ninety-two, explained why *Ad Age* was different:

> You were doing something that was new and important, and I sensed that it would be a good thing for *Advertising Age* to get into this story early. At that stage in my life, I was essentially just a reporter. I was a loose cannon, and I simply wrote anything I felt like writing. I was

supported because the philosophy of the Crane family [owners and publishers of *Ad Age*] was that you serve your readers best if you give them information that they can rely on to make sound decisions. And so they told me when they hired me, "We expect you to call it like you see it. And if you try to anticipate what will please the advertisers or the readers, we'll fire you."

Later, I would draft statements for the senator, noting disingenuously that even the advertising industry's "mouthpiece" (which it truly was not) "supported a ban on cigarette advertising." My conscience gave me only a twinge when Cohen began to treat me to lunch and counsel me almost weekly at the august National Press Club.

Through Stan Cohen, I met federal trade commissioner Philip Elman, with whom I soon developed a close working relationship. He schooled me in the need for Senator Neuberger to pressure Paul Rand Dixon, the weak-kneed chair of the FTC. She readily agreed, and I drafted a letter for her urging the FTC "to hold as inherently deceptive all [cigarette] advertising that failed to include a warning on the health hazards of smoking." Dixon was characteristically reluctant to take this stand, but Neuberger continued to press him for a response while Elman pushed him from inside the FTC.

After months of silence, Dixon finally responded to Senator Neuberger: "If the Commission is able to secure competent probative scientific evidence including that furnished by the Public Health Service" (a mandatory FTC requirement for such warnings), it would likely "be upheld in appellate courts."[2] That, at least, seemed like progress toward action by the FTC.

Morton Mintz was an inquisitorial investigative reporter who drove his editors at the *Washington Post* mercilessly, demanding ever more space for his exposure of corporate wrongdoing without excluding *Post* advertisers, for whom negative coverage soured their enthusiasm for enriching the paper. Though his sentiments were always with the wrongdoers' victims, he was scrupulous in his investigations. A Bumblebee I later worked with, Leonard Bickwit, told me: "Morton would always write stories that were beneficial to us and hostile to our enemy. But he was not easy to deal with. He would say things to me like, 'Let's not manage the news here.' If all you had heard was our discussion, you wouldn't have expected the story to be favorable to our side—as it almost always ended up."

Then there was David Cohen, still a young man, lobbying for progressive nonprofit organizations such as Americans for Democratic Action. He was almost as green as I was, but over the next fifty years he would come to be known informally as the "dean of public interest lobbyists." He would also become my closest ally outside the government, and my friend and partner in public interest advocacy. In 1962 he came to visit me to help support Senator Neuberger's consumer protection initiatives. Unlike the other public interest lobbyists I had begun to meet, most of whom were smokers blinded by their addiction, Cohen welcomed Neuberger's initiatives on tobacco control. He helped guide me to a strategy that would make Neuberger effective. Among the tools available even to a junior senator, he counseled me, were openly publicized letters to all the potential decision-makers who could move tobacco control forward, from President Kennedy on down to the surgeon general of the Public Health Service.

President Kennedy, however, had plenty of other headaches with a Congress in which southern senators from tobacco-growing states held positions of power. The last thing he needed was an issue that would only intensify his already strained relations with them. They had served so long in one-party Democratic states that they chaired almost every important committee vital to his agenda.

On May 23, 1962, a reporter asked Kennedy at a press conference what he intended to do about the growing evidence that smoking is harmful. He waffled elegantly: "That matter is sensitive enough and the stock market is in sufficient difficulty without my giving you an answer which is not based on complete information, which I don't have."[3] The president's solution was almost exactly what Neuberger had advocated: a call for a study by the surgeon general, Luther Terry. But Kennedy had another objective: to kick the issue down the road to avoid alienating his tobacco-state Democrats.

Two weeks later, Terry announced that he planned to appoint a committee of experts to review all the evidence and report back to him. It soon became clear that the tobacco lobbyists and their friends on Capitol Hill were already at work to weaken the study. In a concession doubtless dictated by an intimidated White House, Terry agreed that the tobacco industry could have veto power over the naming of members to this committee.

Despite complaints, the most forceful by Neuberger, that the committee would contain no scientist who had actually studied the risks of smoking, the veto held. Every nominee to the committee was vetted by tobacco industry lawyers and every nominee they objected to was dropped. Senator Neuberger was outraged. She kept up with letters and telephone calls to Terry, pressing him to appoint competent and truly neutral members to his committee. In that, she succeeded. Charles A. LeMaistre, a physician who was perhaps the committee's most distinguished member, later wrote, "It is not surprising that Surgeon General Terry listed [Neuberger's] interest in the subject as one of the seven reasons he decided the study should be done."[4]

I spent the next year and a half monitoring the progress of the surgeon general's committee for Senator Neuberger, noting rumors of tobacco-industry access and lobbying and what we viewed as unconscionable delays. Calls and letters flowed ceaselessly from the senator's office: What is taking so long? What contacts are committee members having with industry representatives? Is there White House or congressional pressure to whittle down the severity of the committee's conclusions? We also coordinated spurs to the surgeon general from Mintz and other equally concerned journalists. Still, no committee report arrived.

Shortly after Memorial Day 1962, Congress, in its customarily leisurely manner, recessed and went home. The staff were free to indulge in aimless pastimes, such as bridge. I had always yearned to be an author, so I eagerly took up the task of drafting a book for Senator Neuberger, designed to pressure the committee with her own recitation of the strong science and failed government policy on tobacco. For substance, I turned to my mentors, particularly Shimkin on the science and Elman on the policy.

One year after the formation of the committee, May 1, 1963, we sent out a flamboyant press release announcing the publication of *Smoke Screen: Tobacco and the Public Welfare*. I had again been schooled by Tupling. In the release, Neuberger declares that the book's primary purpose is to detail a comprehensive program for the control of diseases related to cigarette smoking and to present to the public and the Surgeon General's Advisory Committee on Smoking and Health the product of several years of research and investigation she and her staff had conducted. She refers to the tobacco industry's "callous and myopic pursuit of its own self-interest" and "the bleak tableau of defaulted public responsibility." Recalling Neuberger's sole requirement for the job of legislative assistant, I took quiet pride in a one-sentence review in a letter to the senator by the famously literate economist Kenneth Galbraith (a good friend of hers): "This book is written from beginning to end in English." (With the experience of age, the cynical possibility occurs to me that Galbraith, unimpressed with the book, had contrived a comment that appeared supportive to his friend Neuberger but could hardly be deployed as a promotional blurb.)

## The Front Pages

The Surgeon General's Advisory Committee went public with its report on Saturday morning, January 11, 1964. Its conclusions were strong, clear, and unanimous: cigarette smoking kills from lung cancer, probably from heart disease, and possibly from other diseases. The publicity in all the major media of what came to be known as the Surgeon General's Report was extraordinary. The definitive story led the evening news on every TV network (which, back then, almost everyone watched). A front-page story in the *New York Times* the following day labeled the report "a severe blow to the new rearguard action fought in recent years by the tobacco industry."[5] The *New York Herald Tribune*'s story was headlined, "It's Official—Cigarette Smoking Can Kill You." It judged the report "far harsher than anticipated," adding that "the burden of disproof" now fell on the industry. The *Washington Post* also gave the story top billing under the headline "Smoking and Health." Ironically, what we had most protested in the formation of the committee—the tobacco industry's veto power over the committee's membership—became Neuberger's oratorical weapon and greatly validated the authority of the committee's judgments.

## Time for Action

It was time for the FTC to act against cigarette advertising. However, I received an alarming call from Elman, who told me that Dixon had received a heavy-handed call from President Lyndon Johnson. Johnson—most likely put up to it by his longtime lawyer and current adviser, Abe Fortas—ordered Dixon to hold off on regulating cigarette advertising. Dixon, already waffling, was intimidated. I drafted a strong note for Neuberger to send Dixon, insisting that the time for FTC action against cigarette advertising had come.

After allowing Dixon time for Neuberger's letter to sink in, Elman called to tell me that he had arranged to meet the commission chair in his office so that they could read through the Surgeon General's Report together. Elman recalls Dixon's response as they read: "'Jesus, Phil, listen to this,' . . . and before long he stubbed out his smoke and said, 'That's my last cigarette— I've got to talk to my boys,'" who were heavy smokers. When Dixon read out the part of the report calling for "appropriate remedial action," he said, "They're talking about us."

Elman was primed for action. Even if the tobacco industry claimed the FTC had inadequate statutory authority to regulate this issue, Elman believed the commission would prevail in the Supreme Court under its activist chief justice, Earl Warren. Furthermore, the FTC was an independent body and need not bother consulting Congress—or, at least technically, obeying the president. Dixon gave Elman the nod to develop proposed FTC action against cigarette advertising.

What came next offers an ironic footnote to judicial history. Elman had a brilliant young attorney adviser named Richard Posner. Posner would later become a famed federal appeals court judge and judicial libertarian with an aversion to overregulation. All weekend after Elman's meeting with Dixon, Posner hammered out a report for Elman to present to the other four federal trade commissioners. Posner had developed a radically liberal interpretation of the FTC's powers. He argued that the FTC had the implicit rule-making power to regulate whole industries—rather than its previously perceived power, which could be exercised only by pursuing each individual company and proving that it had committed "unfair or deceptive" practices. The report concludes with a proposal that the FTC mandate an industrywide rule requiring strong health warnings in every cigarette commercial and printed advertisement.

Although the tobacco lobby would forestall FTC and congressional action for several years, this FTC effort, as we shall see, became a stalwart building block for accomplishing the same goal. Senator Neuberger's relentless tobacco control advocacy had left a mark, and I had taken a step toward Bumblebeehood.

### A Taste of Power Beckons

To senators, the Commerce Committee ranked among the least preferred assignments. Hence Neuberger, a junior senator with no seniority who also bothered her senior male colleagues by her refusal to do the toadying that was then expected of a woman, was shuffled off to Commerce by the committee of aging male Democrats who made the committee assignments.

As chairman, Senator Magnuson had rarely used the Commerce Committee's inherent powers to advance consumer protection legislation. Neuberger tried, and I, now staffing her Commerce Committee work, labored for her. Predictably, she introduced bills to mandate the strong warnings in cigarette advertising that Elman had proposed. They went nowhere. She also supported the efforts of committee member Philip A. Hart of Michigan, an equally strong consumer advocate. Hart had long fought for a fair packaging and labeling bill to bring order out of the deliberate chaos of food packaging. Labeling had long since been artfully designed by the giant processed-food marketers to deceive consumers and make it nearly impossible for them to make healthful choices and compare prices.

In a closed committee session debating Hart's fair packaging and labeling bill in the mid-1960s, Neuberger used the packaging of potato chips in five dozen different sizes by competing brands to illustrate how nearly impossible it was for the consumer to quickly compare prices. A grocery manufacturers' shill on the committee, Tennessee senator Ross Bass (aka "Big-Mouth Bass"), argued back that any woman who fed her kids potato chips did not deserve protection. While he was speaking, a late-arriving committee member sat down next to Neuberger and asked her what was going on. Her stage-whispered response resounded throughout the room, "Kindergarten!"

Neuberger annoyed Magnuson. She was not only a rare freshman female senator (from whom he expected quiet) but one whose persistence bordered on contempt. Fortunately, Magnuson had never noticed me. His staff director, Jerry Grinstein, however, had paid attention to Neuberger's effective advocacy on smoking control and my role therein. Though he and I had been classmates at Yale, we had barely known each other then. Jerry, an extrovert, was an editor for the *Yale Daily News*; I, an aspiring poet, was what would later be called a "nerd." As soon as I arrived in Washington, I had sought Jerry's counsel in navigating Neuberger's path to effective consumer advocacy. He, too, had become a mentor and we had drawn closer as friends.

I had been with Senator Neuberger for two years when Jerry offered me a staff position on the Commerce Committee, part of a new consumer protection subcommittee he had dreamed up, to be chaired by Senator Magnuson himself. In our interview for this book, Jerry insisted that what had stood out most in his memory of me at Yale was my running breathlessly up the stairs of our shared dormitory, reveling in having discovered a hitherto unknown off-color pun in Chaucer's "The Wife of Bath's Tale." He said that the notion of having a poet on the committee staff had appealed to him and that he had been tickled by my opening sentence in the Neuberger book: "Dogs are unenthusiastic smokers."

I preferred to think that my work with Senator Neuberger was at the root of Jerry's judgment. It made sense to me that since consumer protection, including public health, had become a hot issue, such legislation merited its own subcommittee. I was grateful for all I had learned from my experience in Neuberger's office, but Jerry was offering me an opportunity to participate in actually shepherding consumer protection bills to enactment into law with the power of Chairman Magnuson behind them. Serving as a midwife to consumer protection legislation could become my métier. Jerry's offer, a whiff of power, was irresistible. I greedily accepted.

# 2

# *Jerry and Maggie*

For the next five years, until 1969, Jerry Grinstein was my boss. At first I bristled internally, since we were the same age. But my ego was swiftly quieted. Jerry never pulled rank. He would become my mentor and model and an increasingly close friend. More than that, Jerry quickly revealed a caring disposition that has characterized him as long as I have known him.

Soon after I moved into my new Commerce Committee role and office, Jerry asked me to draft a floor statement for Magnuson on a minor bill. I did so. In keeping with what I had been taught in Senator Neuberger's office, I also prepared a press release on the statement. In response, I was verbally assaulted by a long-serving committee curmudgeon. He stormed into my office, demanding to know how I had had the effrontery to draft a Magnuson press release. He always prepared Magnuson's committee press releases, he proclaimed. So offended was he that he announced he would report the outrage to Jerry. I was undone. I had screwed up my very first assignment. I slunk home that evening in great distress. Then Jerry called with a cheery three-word message: "Pertsch, forget it." This was a small gift—but it loomed larger as I came to appreciate Jerry's uncommon concern for those who worked with and for him.

Jerry was—and is—a formidable figure. Emanuel Rouvelas—a canny Bumblebee whom Jerry recruited early in his career—recalls Jerry in his element, weighing "about 230, 240 pounds, smoking cigars, and walk-ing up and down the corridor," in striking contrast to the aging Warren Magnuson, who was hardly prepossessing. Jerry's laugh "would boom out. It just would fill the place," allowing him to "keep a light touch under stress." I thought I could top his witticisms. I never could. He invariably one-upped me with a sly quip. Yet there was no doubt who Jerry's boss was, and who would be mine when I succeeded Jerry as Democratic committee staff director.[1]

Without Magnuson's status and influence, Jerry and I would have been powerless. But Magnuson was much more to us than the boss. He was our enabler, though not always aware of the consequences. He was also our obstacle, a fluctuating source of frustration. He delighted us; he disappointed us. He saved us from the brink of defeat when we had least hope, and he left us with stories of his idiosyncrasies so entertaining that we ancient Bumblebees still recite them endlessly to each other whenever we get together to share memories. He earned our deep affection and undying devotion, and as he came to know us and became comfortable with us, he offered us in turn his friendship.

When I so eagerly jumped from Neuberger to Magnuson, my disloyalty was fueled by ambition. Neuberger was among the most junior members of the Senate, Magnuson among the most powerful. Magnuson could get things done. Having been a member of the Senate since 1944, he enjoyed the benefits of formal Senate power gained through the automatic processes of seniority. By the time I joined the staff of the Senate Commerce Committee in 1964, Magnuson had been chairman of the committee for nine years. When I left in 1977, he had been chairman for twenty-two years, longer than any other Commerce Committee chair in the history of the committee. In 1964, Magnuson was also a senior member of the Senate Appropriations Committee —a powerful position because most senators were always hungry for their home-state funding.

In these capacities Magnuson was in position to earn the gratitude of many Senate members of both parties by accommodating their pleas for funding projects and programs that benefited their constituents. He was a longtime member of the bipartisan Senate Committee on Committees with the critical power to set the size and number of each party's seats on each committee. He was a founder and continuing member of the Democratic Policy Committee, which played a strong role in setting policy priorities for Senate Democrats as a whole and appointing senators to committees, some of which were highly desirable for the power they conferred, others highly undesirable. He was also, during my first years, chairman of the Senate Democratic Campaign Committee, which meant that he could raise—or divert—the vital funding of his colleagues' and prospective colleagues' election campaigns.

But Magnuson's influence with his fellow senators stretched far beyond these formal powers. Yet his "soft power" was the motivational reverse of what the bullying Lyndon Johnson had notoriously exercised in his many years as Senate Democratic leader. Where Johnson had inspired fear of reprisal, Magnuson inspired trust, gratitude, and affection.

He was also acutely attuned to the culture of the Senate, as Jerry recalls, able to sit in the office of the Senate sergeant at arms and drink vodka "with the boys who had power." Magnuson's effectiveness was enhanced by his modesty about his own powers. He had, Jerry says, "terrific natural talent" and was "incredibly successful."

Magnuson had served under five presidents. He was especially close to Lyndon Johnson; they had both come to Washington as members of Congress in the early New Deal and were drawn to each other. Soon after Johnson became president, Magnuson went to visit him at the White House. At the time, Magnuson had been living with Jermaine Elliott Peralta for several years without the benefit of a marriage certificate. "For God's sake," Johnson told him, "*marry* Jermaine." He did, at an intimate wedding in the White House presided over by Johnson.

Magnuson's loyalty, however, was to the Senate. According to Jerry, Magnuson attributed much of his success there to luck. Jerry captures this humility by describing him as often wondering, "How the hell did I get to be a senator?" In his study for the Ralph Nader Congress Project, David Price identifies in Magnuson what sociologists call "social" leadership—"the maintenance of an atmosphere of cooperation and harmony, the promotion of group solidarity." Price quotes interviews with Magnuson's colleagues on the Commerce Committee, most of whom list traits in Magnuson that contribute to group cohesion, calling him "easy to work with . . . tolerant and understanding . . . an incredible man." James Pearson, a Republican, says, "I love the man; he's a great big bear. . . . His strong point is his ability to bring people together."[2]

Central to Magnuson's ability to work with Republicans was the nonpartisan consideration and respect he gave them. No Republican was more responsive than Senator Norris Cotton, who shared leadership on the Commerce Committee and the Appropriations Committee. "I've often said," Cotton told Price, "there are two people I have to get along with in this world, my wife and Magnuson. And I do get along. We manage to work together well."

Among the many stories in this book, none so well highlights the nearly universal trust and respect Magnuson inspired as the story of the mistakenly delivered fund-raising lists. In 1966, Magnuson chaired the Senate Democratic Campaign Committee; Thruston Morton of Kentucky chaired its counterpart, the National Republican Senatorial Committee. One day, a befuddled staff member of the Democratic Campaign Committee mistakenly delivered a package to Morton's office that was intended for Magnuson's. In it were the secret Democratic fund-raising lists. Morton's staff was jubilant over this feast of political intelligence. But Morton ordered them to put the lists back in their boxes without reading them. "Send them back to Maggie," he said, using the nickname most senators used. "That's what he would do if our lists came to him."

As a token of our affection, we Bumblebees also called him "Maggie," but only among ourselves. I always addressed him directly as "Mister Chairman." I use the more respectful "Magnuson" throughout this book, except where the context calls for "Maggie." He accepted the nickname, his political sense telling him that it made him seem more human and accessible. But whenever we received a phone call from an unknown supplicant who insisted that he was a close friend of "Maggie's," we knew he wasn't. His good friends knew that he preferred "Warren." If the caller said he was an old friend of "Warren's," we jumped to attention. Jerry told me that when Magnuson was invited by President Harry S. Truman for an evening of poker and dinner at the White House, the honored guest was British prime minister Winston Churchill. As Magnuson later told Jerry, on being introduced to Magnuson, Churchill said to him, "I understand you're known as Maggie. Well, I'm known as Winnie in every pub in England, and that's how I get to stay prime minister."

### The Mystery of Magnuson

Magnuson was very well known, but little understood. His archives at the University of Washington library contain mountains of articles and doctoral theses and a book written by an astute Washington State journalist, Shelby Scates, who covered Magnuson for decades.[3] These sources portray Magnuson variously as idealistic, shady if not corrupt, eloquent, tongue-tied, imperious, and insecure. They call him a drunk, a stumblebum, and a canny and strategic legislator. Very few of us Bumblebees really knew him deeply. Among those few who did was Jerry, who complained to me that Scates "really didn't get Maggie." The rest of us came to know him as a legislator who often disappointed us and who, when we most expected to be disappointed, stunned us by his passion and strategic wisdom.

One persistent perception of Magnuson by too many of his Senate colleagues in his later years was that he was bordering the onset of senility. Whatever his flaws, this perception was incorrect. True, by the mid-1960s his rounded figure, his lumbering gait, even his occasional displays of bewilderment led many of his colleagues to wonder whether he was over the hill. These diminishments of Magnuson were fueled by the common knowledge that he drank copious amounts of vodka.

As I developed a senior role with Magnuson, Jerry and I would meet with him in his inner office first thing in the morning, around ten o'clock. Magnuson's first action was to wander into the small bathroom attached to the office and emerge with a full glass of water. Except that it wasn't water, it was vodka. I never saw Magnuson drunk, though I almost never spent evenings with him. If we had a complex issue to discuss with him, we chose the morning to raise it, when his mind was clearest.

Even we, his own staff, enjoyed and privately parroted his seemingly unconscious, often outrageous mispronunciations. To this day, when the Bumblebees convene in fond memory of our time with him, we revisit cherished examples of Magnuson's malaprops. Jerry insists, however, that they were a manifestation of his guile, a conscious tactic. I once watched Magnuson mangle the name of an aggressive House conferee during a tense Senate-House conference over a bill for which the Senate and House versions differed on important provisions. The most insistent House conferee could barely stifle his laughter over Magnuson's mispronunciation—so much so that he was distracted from his arguments and the House gave in to Magnuson's priorities for the final bill.

Terry Lierman, a Magnuson staff member on the Senate Appropriations Committee, was a keen observer of Magnuson's behavior. He is a fount of good stories. Magnuson so trusted Lierman that when Magnuson became chairman of the full committee in 1977, he leaped over many older committee staff members to appoint Lierman the full committee staff director, though he was only twenty-five at the time. Lierman still holds the record as the youngest staff director of any Senate committee. He told me:

> There was a senator named Lawton Chiles from Florida—not a good person to work with. Maggie always called Lawton "Lawson." And that became a deliberate pattern. Everyone just thought he was this bumbling person, but I caught onto the fact that if he didn't like somebody he deliberately mispronounced their name. Lawton Chiles would sit [in Appropriations Committee meetings] and lecture us about the correct thing to do. And Maggie would say, "Thank you, Lawson, thank you." I mean, it was perfect. That's Maggie.

Jerry recalls another example of Magnuson's conscious or subconscious deployment of mispronunciation to indicate disdain. Magnuson was holding a committee hearing investigating difficulties that the International Olympic Committee had been facing in organizing US participation in the upcoming 1972 Olympics. The Olympic Committee's austere, aristocratic president, Avery Brundage, was testifying before him. Magnuson addressed him as "Average Bundy," inspiring yet another snicker from the Bumblebees. The source of Magnuson's disdain, Jerry later told me, was Brundage's efforts to bar Jewish athletes from the 1936 Olympics in Germany.

Lierman also witnessed Magnuson as a strategic actor:

> What always amazed me was that he would walk out from the backroom private Appropriations Committee office into the Appropriations hearing room as the members were gathering, and he would sometimes act confused, as if he just plain wasn't there. I could see people look at me, and they'd look at him, and then look back at me with looks that said, "Is he totally out of it?" What they would do was give him anything he wanted. And then he would go back into the backroom and change, just like that. And he would talk lucidly and candidly and very forcefully about the issues. I came to the conclusion that it was his act. It was his way of getting something that he wanted.

### What Drove Jerry

Jerry had no dreams of turning the Senate Commerce Committee upside down when he joined the committee staff in 1959. He had finished Harvard Law School after Yale and returned to his family home in Seattle. His goal was to practice conventional law in Seattle, but he was not quite ready to begin. Though he had thought about applying for a clerkship with a federal judge, he was drawn to Washington, DC, because it was "a place where interesting things were happening." And so, he says, "I decided I'd like to take a look, and I came down to Washington and talked to Irv Hoff," Magnuson's senior and ablest staff member, the administrative assistant in his Senate office, and his closest political adviser.

There were no Magnuson jobs available at the time, but Hoff was impressed with Jerry. He was also troubled that too many of Magnuson's Commerce Committee staff members were neither energetic nor competent. At the first opportunity, he invited Jerry to return to Washington and take on a short-term job researching a complex transportation problem that the two assigned Commerce Committee staff members could not handle.

Six months later, Jerry had fixed the problem and was ready to go back to Seattle to practice law, but Hoff asked him to stay and take on another project. By then, Jerry was hooked: "It was history spreading open for you. It was a different view from what you and I ultimately had—that we could do something significant and important. At the beginning, it was mainly, 'Jesus, this is how the Constitution works. This is how government works. This is all the stuff that we've studied all these years.'"

After completing a few short-term projects, Jerry accepted a key committee staff job: Merchant Marine Subcommittee staff counsel. Because ocean shipping and the economic health of Washington's ports were vital to the economy of the state, and federal regulation of ocean shipping was a significant part of the committee's work, Magnuson was closely involved in the issues for which Jerry was now responsible.

For the first six or seven months, Jerry confesses, he fell into the laissez-faire habits of his fellow committee staffers. The lobbyists for the shipping interests and the maritime labor lobbyists wooed him ceaselessly. The typical phone call, he remembers, would begin, "Let's have a bite," which meant lunch and a lot of drinking that left Jerry unable to function effectively in the afternoon. After several months, Jerry said to himself, "Oh shit, I can't live like this." He gave up drinking, though he continued to accept lunch invitations from those lobbyists whose concerns affected Washington State interests. He ate their lunches, but he never swallowed their arguments.

Jerry took his work seriously and applied his developing skills to the issues. In the process, he developed a warm, easy working relationship with Magnuson. Magnuson trusted him increasingly. Beyond the sober work, their personalities were compatible. Hoff took note of Jerry's success and Magnuson's comfort with him. He also noted Jerry's finesse in dealing with sensitive issues. He seemed to be in tune with Magnuson's political interests and able to deftly moderate between often competing constituent concerns.

At the same time, Hoff had begun to suffer doubts about Magnuson's upcoming 1962 campaign for reelection. In this, he was virtually alone. Magnuson's last reelection campaign against a formidable Republican had turned into an electoral rout. All the political pundits in both Washington State and Washington, DC, predicted that 1962 would follow the same pattern. Magnuson seemed unbeatable. Even the Republican Party leaders believed this to be true; they chose a political novice, a sacrificial goat, to oppose him: a dour Lutheran minister who had never before run for political office.

Despite the nearly universal conviction that Magnuson was a shoo-in for reelection, Hoff's political antenna detected signs that Magnuson's long-term popularity had begun to fade. President John F. Kennedy had set the new model for political leadership, and whatever political virtues Magnuson had, charisma and glamour were not among them. Confidential early campaign polls had warned Hoff that Magnuson was in trouble. Hoff had little confidence that Magnuson's long-term political operatives, out of touch with the changing political environment, were capable of responding to this changing constituency.

In October 1961, Hoff invited Jerry back to Seattle to observe a gathering of Magnuson's campaign team to discuss the strategy for the 1962 campaign. Jerry agreed with Hoff that the old guard lacked the required insight and ability to change. So too did Magnuson, who interrupted the meeting to exclaim: "It's the same old story of dams and jobs and transportation—we just aren't telling them anything new!" The campaign managers nonetheless continued to pursue outdated strategies. Hoff's fears were verified. Magnuson squeaked by in 1962, winning with only 51 percent of the vote, compared with almost 62 percent in the previous (1956) election.

In the wake of this close call, Hoff and Howard "Mac" MacGowan, a longtime friend of Magnuson's and a skillful operator at the blurred interface between private enterprise and public largess, shared Hoff's conviction that Magnuson needed to make a drastic change in his political identity in Washington State before his next reelection campaign in 1968. One early step they suggested was to exploit Magnuson's chairmanship of the Commerce Committee in ways that would appeal to voters. They urged Magnuson to appoint Jerry as committee staff director. Jerry was only twenty-nine; this appointment would mean jumping over a half dozen seasoned committee staff members. Magnuson took their advice, and Jerry became staff director in 1963.

The committee had broad potential jurisdiction over issues that were emerging on the public agenda. Jerry immediately set to work looking at ways to persuade Magnuson to address the issues that would appeal to Washington State voters and through which Magnuson could benefit by taking a leadership role. Among them was a crisis in the nation's (including Washington State's) economically essential railway system. Jerry found other such opportunities that enhanced Magnuson's public identity, but consumer protection was not yet among them.

Hoff and MacGowan's vision for Jerry was to help secure Magnuson's reelection in 1968. Jerry was determined to meet that goal. But that alone could not satisfy him. He told me in our interview that one of his first acts as staff director was to sit down with his formal counterpart, minority staff director Jeremiah Kenney, newly appointed by Senator Cotton.[4] The two men became partners in finding common ground between the committee's Democrats and Republicans—especially between Magnuson and Cotton—despite their ideological differences. Jerry and Kenney talked about doing something worthwhile together. Jerry recalls:

> We never thought that what we had been doing was useful at all. We thought we were always rearranging existing things, but not changing anything. It became a very close working relationship. Each of us was totally transparent to the other. I would write drafts of concepts and bills and share them with him. We shared a sense of what was right and wrong, a terrific set of values. We both recognized that his boss wanted to work with Magnuson. That had to work. . . . [Kenney] could have been brittle, he could have been sleazy, but he wasn't. He was a terrific asset.

Jerry is most proud of the role he played, just before I joined the committee staff, in helping advance the goals of the civil rights movement. It was the first major test of his working relationship with Kenney and their "first opportunity to really do something great."

The Commerce Committee had jurisdiction over Title II of the civil rights bill that President Kennedy had proposed on June 11, 1963. Hoping to fulfill the vision of the slain president, Magnuson had introduced Title II, proposed by Johnson, to be added to the other Johnson civil rights proposals in Title I, as the public accommodations bill in 1964. It would broadly prohibit segregation in interstate activities, such as on trains and buses and in restaurants and motels. It was reported out to the Senate favorably on a vote by the Democratic majority of the Commerce Committee. Senator Cotton, however, expressed the Republican minority's opposition in a separate addendum to the committee's majority report.

On the Senate floor the bill faced formidable opposition from the alliance between southern segregationist holdouts and conservative Senate Republicans. The fate of the bill rested heavily on the position of the Senate Republican leader, Everett Dirksen of Illinois. Dirksen had signaled that he was inclined to oppose the bill. When Jerry learned that Attorney General Robert Kennedy of New York, carrying the weight of his brother's legacy, had arranged a private session to persuade Dirksen to support the public accommodations bill on the Senate floor, he met with Kennedy and suggested that his appeal to Dirksen could be strengthened if he and Kenney joined him in the meeting. Kennedy agreed. In the meeting, Kennedy made a fervent argument. His plea was strengthened by Jerry and Kenney's presence, which signified that the Commerce Committee Democrats and Republicans jointly supported the bill. Jerry recalls that Dirksen reluctantly agreed. "'Okay,' he finally said, 'I've got to do it my way,' but 'I'll go to bat for you.' And he did." The public accommodations provisions were added as Title II to the Civil Rights Act, which was enacted in July 1964, having passed in undiluted strength with bipartisan support.

I asked Jerry recently what inspired him growing up. He thought for a while, then answered, "I'm probably largely influenced by my mother. Selma was one of about two early Seattle liberal activists. I can remember when they were talking about building the Alaska pipeline. She was worried sick about the caribou. One day she said, 'Oh God, they're going to kill all those caribou.' I said, 'Mother, what the hell do you know about the caribou?' And she said, 'Oh, I've been reading about it. It's just horrible what they're doing up there.'"

Jerry remembers her saying once that she was going to vote for Norman Thomas, the Presbyterian minister who became a socialist pacifist and six-time presidential candidate for the Socialist Party of America. "I thought, '*Norman Thomas?* My God!'" Jerry was shocked, but her passion for justice inspired him. "She had an enormous amount of compassion for people."

### Why Me?

Although Jerry and I had been casual acquaintances as undergraduates at Yale, we grew closer during the time I worked for Senator Neuberger. When I arrived, Jerry was already wise in the ways of the Senate, and I drew on his counsel as I stumbled along. He had been impressed by the favorable media coverage Senator Neuberger had received on her tobacco control and other consumer initiatives, a rarity for a freshman senator. Jerry had also observed, to his surprise, that Magnuson himself took umbrage at what he viewed as consumer exploitation by business wrongdoers.

"Little things used to irritate him," Jerry told me. "The jacked-up prices the concessionaires in the airport charged, it used to drive him crazy. And he'd complain and complain about it. I was in an airport with him once, and he said [to a concessionaire], 'You guys are just robbing us.'"

The Commerce Committee's jurisdiction over consumer protection was broad and flexible. Jerry had begun to muse about Magnuson's taking the lead in promoting consumer protection legislation. He would make consumer protection the center of Magnuson's campaign for reelection in 1968 by providing him with a new identity as the consumer's champion, shedding that of an aging, pork-barrel pol, out of tune with the emerging youthful Washington State electorate.

### What Drove Jerry to Distraction

Jerry's task in harnessing Magnuson's power for the public good was complicated by Magnuson's insecurity, his resistance to change, his need to ingratiate himself even to Republican conservatives, and his preference for compromise driven by his aversion to conflict and confrontation. Thus, he refused to let Jerry rid the staff of his old cronies, who resented Jerry's roiling of their comfortable sinecures.

Worst among the staff cronies was Fred Lordan, who had long served as Magnuson's link to Washington State's special interests, especially the establishment business and labor leaders. Because Magnuson could not bring himself to confront Lordan and fire him as Jerry sought, Lordan remained as administrative assistant, with an office adjoining Magnuson's. As Jerry developed the aggressive consumer protection agenda, Lordan became deeply envious of his growing closeness to Magnuson. He retaliated by filling Magnuson's ears with the complaints of his old business buddies, who felt threatened by Jerry's efforts to institute reforms that would rein in their freedom.

Magnuson's aversion to conflict was no boon to us. When confronted by a Senate colleague or a lobbyist friend with an action one of us had taken in his name, Magnuson would plead innocence. He couldn't keep track of what all his staff members were up to, he confessed, and shook his head in disbelief and disapproval. The truth often was, as Jerry told me, "He didn't want to know. But he did know." This tactic deflected potential wounds that Magnuson might have suffered, but it hardly improved attitudes toward Jerry and later me, whom many saw as arrogant, unelected staff run amok.

Jerry was finally successful in persuading Magnuson to embrace a broad public interest agenda; but he had to proceed in incremental steps. One step that was discomforting for me was the delayed creation of the Consumer Protection Subcommittee. The promise of that subcommittee was the bait Jerry had dangled to lure me onto the committee staff. What Jerry had neglected to tell me was that he had not yet approached Magnuson with his bold campaign plan to provide him with a new identity as a consumer advocate, much less to create such a subcommittee.

So Jerry pursued a step-by-step strategy to engage Magnuson as a leader for consumer protection one bill at a time. Even when he simply asked Magnuson to sponsor a consumer protection bill that was enjoying popular support, Magnuson would hesitate. It often took two or three attempts to persuade the reluctant Magnuson to attach his name to such a bill. When he did, and when even the introduction of such bills began generating favorable media coverage, especially in Washington State, Magnuson became more likely to accept Jerry's suggesting another. Finally, almost a year after I joined the staff, Magnuson was ready to agree to the creation of the new Consumer Protection Subcommittee that he himself would chair.

# 3

# *A Bumblebee's Crucible*

After two years with Senator Neuberger, I still knew little about the process of legislating. Neuberger had never managed a bill in the Senate, much less for the Commerce Committee. My experience with consumer issues gave me a start, but it would be a while before I worked on a project I knew anything about.

Only after I had quit Neuberger's office and joined the committee staff did I learn that Jerry Grinstein, sensitively attuned to Magnuson's resistance to change, had not yet found the right moment to reveal his grand plan to achieve the senator's reelection in 1968—which involved, as one skeptical observer, James Ridgeway of the *New Republic*, later commented, "changing his image from corporation stooge to consumer champion"[1]—or his plan to create a consumer protection subcommittee. Or his hiring me. I'd never met the chairman before joining the committee staff, and in our brief early encounters I was so intimidated that I could barely respond to his brusque questions without stammering. That didn't help. He plainly thought me an effete Easterner, which, of course, I was.

Jerry assigned me first to work on cattle marketing. I was to staff committee member Senator Gale McGee of Wyoming, who wanted to create a national commission to investigate the gap between the historically low prices Wyoming ranchers were receiving for their beef and the record-high prices consumers were paying for it. We ended up in the Wild West town of Rock Springs, taking testimony from outraged ranchers. When it came time for dinner, I ordered steak, having learned cattle-country decorum from a gaffe during my brief spell as a junior lawyer in Oregon (holding the briefcase of our senior trial lawyer, who was trying a case in remote cattle country, I alone had ordered fried shrimp for dinner). McGee's joint resolution received uneventful, unanimous passage by both houses of Congress.

The House, however, added a few noncontroversial amendments, requiring that the bill be returned to the Senate and approved as amended before it could be sent to the president for signature. As the staff member assigned to the bill, I sat next to Magnuson on the Senate floor, ready to help him. When he asked me whether the bill was "ready to be called up," I assured him it was, and so he called it up. He then turned to me and said, "Have you got the papers?" What papers? Magnuson gestured impatiently in the direction of the Senate clerk. I assumed that, whatever he meant, "the papers" were ready. I approached the Senate clerk at the podium and asked if he had "the papers." Only then did I learn that a piece of legislation is a tangible object, not a concept. When a bill is introduced to the Senate, a physical copy ("the papers") is produced and entrusted to the care of the clerk. If the bill passes the Senate, the copy is delivered to the House clerk's office. If the House adds amendments to the Senate bill, it delivers the amended bill back to the Senate clerk. The Senate cannot approve the House-amended bill unless it is securely in the hands of the Senate clerk. It was not.

The House clerk's office had not yet sent the bill over. It was late on a Friday afternoon. Magnuson, sitting alone on the Senate floor, impatient to get on with whatever the evening's social calendar had in store, grunted. I took off running through the Capitol corridors to find the House clerk's office. When I arrived, the House clerk's staff took one look at the breathless greenhorn from the Senate and announced that I was too late; they were closing for the weekend. They'd get to it Monday. I ran back to the Senate floor with the news that the Senate could not act on the bill today. Magnuson growled again and stormed off the Senate floor.

I still have nightmares about that episode. I was sure Magnuson would fire me. But Jerry's guile came to my aid. He told Magnuson that I was Senator McGee's chosen staff person, which was not precisely true—I was Jerry's chosen staff member, though McGee was comfortable working with me. Because Magnuson was softhearted and loath to fire anyone, and because he was inclined to keep his committee members happy, I survived. At least for the time being.

### Smoke in My Eyes

One morning in late spring 1965, I walked across the hall of the old Russell Senate Office Building, from my office to Magnuson's, to see Alma Hostettler, the chairman's secretary of many years. I was still finding my way within the Senate Commerce Committee and had at best a tentative relationship with its chairman. By now I had learned to pop in for a report from Hostettler on the senator's temperature for the day, especially whether he might be receptive to annoying news or questions. Jerry had recently assigned me staff responsibility for developing the Senate cigarette labeling bill Magnuson was sponsoring, and now our bill and the House version awaited a Senate-House conference to settle the differences. Without comment, Hostettler handed me a pink telephone slip that awaited the chairman's arrival. It read: "Abe Fortas called. 'We want you to accept the House version of the cigarette-labeling bill.'"

The cigarette manufacturers had formed a united front to combat any congressional effort to regulate their advertising, and among those leading the charge was Fortas, a lawyer for the tobacco company Philip Morris and the most influential attorney in the capital. He had been for many years one of President Lyndon Johnson's closest friends and advisers. (Johnson would soon nominate him to the Supreme Court.) Fortas had masterminded Johnson's victory in his notoriously corrupt 1948 Texas Senate election, stealing just enough votes to win by a suspect seventy-eight votes and earning for Johnson the smirking Texas label "Landslide Lyndon." The "we" in Fortas's note was neither an editorial formality nor a reference to his client, Philip Morris. "We" implied the president's imprimatur.

I was appalled at Fortas's arrogance. He was so secure in the power of his closeness to the president that he felt no need to pay the chairman the courtesy of a visit or even a telephone conversation. I wondered how many thousands of dollars Fortas would charge Philip Morris for leaving this one-sentence message. Still, I knew Magnuson was very close to the president and responsive to him. I could hardly count on Magnuson to ignore Fortas's note. And who was I to stop him?

During my first year on the committee staff, Jerry had not allowed me to get near any committee business that had to do with regulating the tobacco industry. He felt that my aggressive work with Neuberger on smoking and health made me vulnerable to the tobacco lobby's cry that they were victims of staff bias. But once it was clear that the committee had to develop legislation to constrain cigarette advertising, Jerry assigned me to staff the process.

I was thrilled to work on an issue I knew something about, but I was also wary. As the lead committee staff member on smoking, I knew I needed to demonstrate at least a semblance of fairness in dealing with the tobacco lobby. I also knew from having watched Neuberger's tobacco control bills repeatedly fail that no bill the tobacco industry opposed would ever pass.

The industry's power combined the seniority of tobacco-state senators with the tobacco lobby's campaign largess to non-tobacco-state senators.

Then along came Earle Clements. Clements, another Johnson intimate, was an old warrior who knew where all the levers were that operated Washington's political machinery. A former Kentucky governor and US senator who had been Majority Leader Johnson's whip and most trusted lieutenant, he was a marvel of soft-covered iron, known for such maxims as "Never ask a man to vote for something that isn't good for him." Ousted from office in the 1956 Eisenhower landslide, Clements was called back to Washington to work for the Democratic National Committee during the 1960 election. As a lobbyist, Clements was buoyed by Johnson's sudden ascension to the White House, where his daughter began serving as the First Lady's appointment secretary and the old pol himself was still welcome at private White House movie screenings. For his influence and strategic cunning, Clements had been hired as president of the Tobacco Institute, the center of coordinated lobbying for all the tobacco companies.

As soon as Clements learned that I had been assigned to manage tobacco control legislation for the committee, he made it his business to woo me with a barrage of oily personal attention. His first step was to telephone me. He was ingratiating. He teased me about my mistaken notions of the risks of smoking. Then he invited me to lunch at the imposing International Club, where he entertained me with stories that featured his close association with legendary political figures, among them Governor Earl Long of Louisiana. Clements spoke of sitting in a hotel room at the Kentucky Derby, listening while the governor, stripped to his underwear, talked about the wild life of his brother, the infamous Huey Long. He also shared his insights into the behavior of senators, explaining, for example, that "membership on the Commerce Committee ensures the participation by many in one's campaigns for reelection." Lunch over, he insisted that I accept $4 to cover the cost ($1.50) of my taxi ride back to the Hill. Despite my better sense, I was snowed by him.

Clements was as canny a strategist as he was seductive a lobbyist. He saw that government regulation of cigarette marketing was inevitable. When the FTC threatened to require all cigarette advertising to display a strong warning about the risks of smoking, the tobacco company executives had panicked. Their lawyers told them that the notoriously liberal Supreme Court presided over by Earl Warren would almost certainly uphold the commission's power to do just that. Clements seized on this threat to persuade the tobacco company CEOs not to oppose enactment of a minimal package warning label: "Caution: Continual Cigarette Smoking May Be Hazardous to Your Health." To ease their fear of the FTC and other possible regulators, he oversaw the development of the fine print to accompany the pallid warning. Clements's draft bill did nothing to regulate cigarette advertising and would have preempted forever any restraint of cigarette advertising by any city, state, or federal agency, including the FTC and the Federal Communications Commission (FCC). To the tobacco industry, the bill amounted to a tap on the wrist. This well-honed corporate strategy for accepting what Ralph Nader would label a "no-law law," I learned, is known as "preemption."

Meanwhile, I realized that to fulfill my desperate need to undo Magnuson's early disdain for me, I needed to develop a bill that would bear his name, yet be tolerable to Clements's tobacco-industry clients. Clements recognized this opening. Knowing that his bill could not credibly be introduced by a tobacco-state senator but only by the widely trusted and powerful committee chairman, Magnuson, Clements asked me to meet with him and Robert Wald, the one tobacco company lawyer I had come to respect. Wald represented the P. Lorillard Company, which tobacco control advocates viewed as a shade more responsible than the others because, in an effort to make smoking less hazardous, they had developed tar-reducing filters in their Kent cigarettes.

Clements and Wald brought me the proposed bill and assured me that it could be history making for Magnuson—the first legislation passed by Congress to require a warning to smokers. I knew the bill's preemption of any government action on advertising was outrageous, but I was convinced that nothing better could pass. As Richard Kluger, author of *Ashes to Ashes*, a history of the tobacco control movement, put it, "Pertschuk was not entirely unwitting clay in the hands of Earle Clements."[2] Kluger was right: I knew full well that the preemption provisions were unconscionable. But my conscience was immobilized by my ambition to gain Magnuson's goodwill by handing him a bill that would be history making.

To my eternal gratitude, Stanley Cohen of *Advertising Age* and Jerry saved me from folly at the very last minute. The day before Magnuson was to introduce the bill, I leaked a copy of the draft to Cohen and then called him for his reaction, expecting his approval. "It's shocking!" he exclaimed. "It's a total sellout to the industry." I still recall my flush of shame as I hung up. That night, I couldn't sleep. When Jerry came to work the next morning, I was waiting in his office to unburden myself of my feelings of guilt. He had known nothing of the process by which the bill had been shaped, yet his reaction was calm and clear: "We'll just take out the preemption provisions."

Senator Magnuson introduced the bill on January 15, 1965. Clements called to express his deep hurt at the disappearance of the preemption provisions.

## A Posse of Lobbyists

Next came committee hearings on two bills, Magnuson's and a stronger labeling bill introduced by Senator Neuberger (with quiet help from me, though I knew it was going nowhere). Despite actively colluding in Clements's scheme for drafting Magnuson's bill, I played no role in organizing the committee hearings. My passivity, however, amounted to further collusion. I did nothing to ensure that there was strong testimony from highly credentialed scientists who had done the research that supported the evidence condemning smoking. I did not contact the members of the surgeon general's committee or the scientists I had met through the Neuberger initiatives. I did not try to find out early who would testify for the industry so I could arm Magnuson and Neuberger against them with questions challenging their credentials and what were sure to be their distortions of the scientific evidence. I did not know then that such preparation was my job. I was yet no Bumblebee.

The industry's legal team was led by another tobacco titan, H. Thomas Austern, managing partner of Covington and Burling, the one firm that rivaled Arnold, Fortas, and Porter for prestige in Washington. Austern was the legal counsel and lobbying force behind the Tobacco Institute and its "scientific" front, the Council for Tobacco Research, whose boundless coffers funded any researcher prepared to find causes for lung cancer and heart disease other than smoking, such as workplace pollution. A few years later, I learned that tobacco industry fees brought in ten million dollars a year, 10 percent of Covington and Burling's annual income.

While I was doing nothing to prepare for the hearings, Austern's minions had put out a nationwide dragnet for PhDs who had expressed doubt about the causal relationship between smoking and ill-health and recruited them as witnesses. Twenty-four hours before the hearings were to begin, in accordance with committee rules, thirty-seven identical boxes arrived at our offices, each one containing the requisite number of copies for committee members, staff, and reporters, in identical type, of prepared testimony for each one of Austern's recruited skeptics. It was simple to determine that these had been delivered from Covington and Burling, not, according to the usual practice, from the witnesses themselves. Most of the testimony came from scientists who had research credentials of a sort, but in fields other than medical research.

The full committee hearings, with Magnuson as chair, went on for six days between March 22 and April 2, 1965. The first two days were filled with testimony in support of the bill from witnesses such as the clinical physicians who were that year's rotating presidents of the American Cancer Society, the National Tuberculosis Association, and the American Heart Association, none of them a researcher, an expert, or a practiced witness. Republican senator Thruston Morton of tobacco-rich Kentucky, the natural lead tobacco-industry voice, bombarded them with technical questions they could not answer, weakening their credibility. I had prepared neither the chairman nor Senator Neuberger for a counterattack.

Next, Austern's thirty-seven "experts" enjoyed two days of prime media time to sow doubt and confusion about the scientific proof that smoking causes illness and death. The committee members who supported the legislation either fled the hearings or remained quiescent. No one thought to establish that the witnesses were recruited, tutored, edited, and paid handsomely by the tobacco lawyers for their testimony—either directly or through research grants. Robert C. Hockett, scientific director of the Council for Tobacco Research, summarized these witnesses' testimony: "In the absence of corroboratory clinical and experimental evidence, judgments that cigarette smoking is a health hazard would seem to go beyond the realm of *scientific* conclusions and to contain a considerable element of guess."[3]

Austern also prevailed by the numbers: eighteen witnesses in support of the science and the bills and thirty-seven in opposition. Of the wires, letters, resolutions, and written statements submitted to the committee, twenty-six supported the bills and fifty-one opposed them. By a two-to-one margin, the case against smoking appeared unproven.

I sat through the hearings tormented by helplessness. During a lunch break, Austern accosted me in the corridor. He was in avuncular mode, at once ingratiating and condescending. He urged me not to heed any premature indictment of smoking, pointing to the evidence established by his thirty-seven witnesses. I did not argue. A few minutes later, however, I confronted Clements: "I may have to sit through these hearings, but I don't have to listen to a lecture from Tommy Austern." To my glum satisfaction, that was the last I ever saw of Austern. Clements banished him.

The industry's goal was not to stop the bill. Their goal was to use the publicity surrounding the hearings to sustain their public relations campaign that the case against smoking remained unproven and "controversial," that the science was flawed, that it would require more research—decades and decades more—before any action other than the tepid warning they had drafted was warranted.

One day during a break in the hearings, I got fed up with the industry witnesses' scientific pap and took refuge in the small private committee office directly behind the public podium on which the senators sat. I wasn't the only unhappy participant in the hearing. The door opened and Senator Morton came in and closed it. He'd been smoking throughout the hearings. He stamped out his cigarette and said to me, "I can't wait until these damn hearings are over and I can quit smoking." I commiserated.

I had not been surprised to see Morton's requisite Kentucky need to discredit the witnesses in support of the bills with tricky questions artfully prepared for him by Austern's lawyers. But I was sickened to hear Democratic senator Vance Hartke of Indiana—where no tobacco grew—consistently mouth the industry line. Before the committee markup debate, I recall his saying that he had approached the hearings with an open mind, thinking that "there must be some connection between smoking and lung cancer." When he heard the testimony, he brazenly announced to his colleagues sitting in the markup session that he had been "shocked" to learn that such a connection was not proven at all. Hartke had been elected to office in a close race in 1958, when Clements was serving in the largely invisible and formally modest role of staff director of the Senate Democratic Campaign Committee. There Clements had raised stacks of campaign money that he lavished on successful Democratic candidates such as Hartke. Though I had admired Hartke for his early outspoken opposition to the escalating Vietnam War, he now seemed to be dancing to Clements's tune.

I remember a joke that was passed among Senate staff members at a breakfast table in the Senate cafeteria where several of us—from both parties—convened jovially several mornings a week. The joke went something like this: An innocent asks, "I didn't know they grew tobacco in Indiana." A wise friend answers, "It's not tobacco; it's the green lettuce." The second senator from Indiana was Birch Bayh, well liked and well respected. When the joke got to me, I observed with disdain, "There are two senators from Indiana, Bayh and Bought."

After the hearing, I was determined to do something useful to prepare for the committee meeting to mark up and vote on the cigarette labeling bill. I set out to write an analysis for the committee members, summarizing the most reliable scientific sources for and against smoking as a cause of debilitation and death. I had drafted this analysis for the committee's confidential use when the tobacco lawyers caught wind of my efforts—I suspected Senator Hartke or one of the older staffers, always eager to help a corporate lobby—and insisted that they had the right to review what I had written. I knew no better, and so I found myself one morning in the magisterial offices of the Fortas law firm. I sat alone, across a conference table from some of the most senior lawyers in Washington, behind them a phalanx of the latest bright law school graduates, including several former Supreme Court clerks, convened from the six or seven Washington firms representing each of the industry's giants. There must have been thirty lawyers around that table—or so it felt.

The senior Philip Morris lawyer from the Fortas firm, Abe Krash, opened by informing me that I had no right to include in my briefing memo to the committee any evidence or facts that had not been presented to the committee during its hearings. The lawyers began grinding away at virtually every sentence in support of the scientific case against tobacco. I was intimidated—as I was meant to be—and began to back away from some of my stronger assertions of scientific certainty.

Then Wald spoke up. "We can't do this to Mike," he said. "It's not right." That was the end of the meeting. Not long afterward, Wald and his small law firm resigned the P. Lorillard account—the only example I know of a law firm resigning so lucrative an account on principle.

When I returned to my office, I checked with Jerry. The tobacco lawyers had lied to me. There was nothing in the Senate or committee rules that limited me to the boundaries of the hearings themselves or prohibited me from preparing a memorandum based on research from any quarter. I made no cuts in my draft analysis on the strength of the scientific evidence against smoking that I had prepared for the committee markup of Magnuson's bill. I began to feel liberated.

Magnuson convened the Commerce Committee to debate and vote on the bill on May 19, 1965. A few minutes before the committee was scheduled to convene in closed session to deliberate on the bill—and while I and other staff members were preparing to brief them—Clements walked into the meeting room, exploiting a courtesy extended to former members of the Senate. He stepped into the telephone booth inside the room, ostentatiously leaving the door open so we could all hear his conversation. He then called Hartke and ordered him to get there immediately—a crude demonstration of his power over the senator.

When the committee convened and began deliberations, it was clear that Morton had persuaded all the committee's Republicans to follow his lead to weaken Magnuson's bill. Also opposed were three Democrats—two from tobacco states, plus Hartke. Morton offered the industry's amendment to restore the permanent and total preemption language that we had taken out of the bill. His amendment passed by a vote of 9 to 8, with Magnuson and the remaining Democrats voting in the minority.

Not for the last time, I had underrated Magnuson's commitment. With no prodding from me, Magnuson declared that he would vote against the amended bill and, furthermore, that he would not manage so weakened a bill on the Senate floor. The industry supporters on the committee were flummoxed. With Magnuson's opposition, and without his floor leadership, the bill would go nowhere and Clements's strategy would fail.

The committee took a break. Magnuson, Jerry, and I went into a huddle and devised a substitute for the Morton amendment. When the committee reconvened, Magnuson announced that he would support and manage the bill only if the committee agreed to substitute for the Morton amendment a three-year moratorium on FCC and FTC action on cigarette advertising and include a new requirement Jerry, Magnuson, and I had developed on the spot. The amendment would mandate that the FTC, in consultation with the Department of Health, Education, and Welfare (HEW), would within eighteen months and annually thereafter investigate and report to Congress on the health consequences of smoking, current information on the practices of cigarette advertising, and recommendations for legislation. Also, the fudging word "continual" would be dropped from the warning. It would now read: "Caution: Cigarette Smoking May Be Hazardous to Your Health." The committee members accepted Magnuson's amendment and voted unanimously to report the bill.

Magnuson's spontaneous tough stand had freed the repressed Bumblebee in me. I now had some leeway to do damage to the industry in writing the committee report to accompany the bill to the Senate floor; I would thus help establish part of the legislative history of the bill. Magnuson's floor statement in support of the bill as it was called up for a vote in the Senate drew from my report. The report asserts that while there remained a handful of individual physicians and scientists who did not believe that it had been demonstrated conclusively that smoking causes lung cancer or other diseases, no prominent medical or scientific body undertaking systematic review of the evidence had ever reached a conclusion opposed to those of the surgeon general's committee. Yet, "too many Americans, particularly teen-agers, are unaware of the extent of the potential hazard in smoking and . . . these people will not be convinced," the report concludes, "until the Federal Government . . . takes affirmative action" by enacting the bill.[4]

I also found a novel way to reinforce the scientific weight of the case against smoking. Through Michael Shimkin at the National Cancer Institute, I requested copies of every significant paper on which the scientific consensus that smoking is a health hazard was based. I then arranged for the Government Printing Office to produce a separately bound volume of all these papers as an appendix to the committee report. When the bill was brought up for a vote in the Senate on June 15, 1965, on every senator's desk was a copy of the committee report and a thick volume of scientific papers—the literal weight of the evidence.

I had neglected to inform Magnuson, however, that this tome was a mere theatrical prop. As he leafed through its pages while speaking in support of the bill, he noticed that many of the papers were written by foreign scientists in languages other than English. Pausing briefly in his presentation, he spontaneously asked for unanimous consent that the Library of Congress be instructed to translate all the papers into English. No objection. For the next year, until this new all-English volume surfaced, I guiltily entertained an image of Library of Congress staff members spending hundreds of hours bowed over their desks in the drudgery of translation, preparing a document I felt sure no senator would ever open.

### It Could Have Been Worse

The bill passed the Senate overwhelmingly the same day. In the Senate-House conference to reconcile their conflicting bills, Magnuson had ignored the phone message from Abe Fortas; he never mentioned it to me. He gave no ground to the House conferees on preemption of the FTC, except to move to give the House a modest face-saving concession to placate Clements and friends: the effective date to free the FTC to proceed with a rule to require warnings in all cigarette advertising was delayed for a few years, to July 1, 1969. Otherwise, the Senate bill's provisions prevailed in the conference report, the bill was ratified without opposition, and the Cigarette Labeling and Advertising Act was signed into law unobtrusively by President Johnson on July 17, 1965.

The 1965 labeling law was no public health triumph. FTC commissioner Philip Elman, Kluger reports, called it "one of the dirtiest pieces of legislation ever," and Democratic senator Frank Moss of Utah "remarked that in exchange for a few tepid cautionary words on the side of the pack, 'Congress exempted the cigarette industry from the normal regulatory process.'"

Kluger continues:

> Yet given the times and the realities of political power, a tougher law would not likely have been enacted. . . . And arguably, the substance of the labeling law mattered less than the fact of it: for the first time, the federal government had acted against the perils of cigarette smoking. The product now would bear the stigma of being officially labeled a hazard, and the lethal risk smokers ran had passed from the realm of folklore into state notification of their folly.[5]

The price that Magnuson, conferring quickly with Jerry and me, laid down for supporting and serving as floor leader of the bill in the Senate turned out to include a poison pill for the tobacco lobby: the mandate requiring the HEW secretary to report to Congress annually on the current science on smoking health and requiring the FTC to report on the status of cigarette advertising.[6] To the committee members at the time, this mandate seemed insignificant. Clements was undisturbed. We were all wrong.

Charles LeMaistre, a leading member of the US Surgeon General's Advisory Committee on Smoking and Health, the committee that produced the groundbreaking 1964 Surgeon General's Report, is a friend of longstanding. In a personal communication in February 2013, he told me that after the cigarette labeling bill passed, the surgeon general and the FTC had seized on Magnuson's amendment. Between 1967 and 2011, the surgeon general's office produced twenty-nine new reports documenting the scientific evidence on the consequences of smoking or breathing someone else's cigarette smoke. "Their interpretation through the media to the public," LeMaistre told me, "proved to be a major factor in the decline of tobacco use in the subsequent four decades. The tobacco lobby was no match for an informed American public." He also told me that the Institute of Medicine called the decline in smoking "one of the ten greatest achievements in public health of the twentieth century."

The national media response to the bill was broadly favorable. Senator Magnuson was delighted with the media attention and the credit he garnered for his leadership in enacting the first congressional law to force the cigarette companies to acknowledge the hazards of smoking on every package label. One of the few exceptions was a scathing *New York Times* editorial headlined "Cigarettes vs. F.T.C."

> Congress has now virtually completed action on a shocking piece of special interest legislation in this field. The bill forbids not only the F.T.C. but also state and local governments from regulating cigarette advertising in any way for the next four years. As a maneuver to distract attention from this surrender to the tobacco interests, the bill also directs that cigarette packages carry an innocuous warning that "smoking *may be* hazardous" (italics added). Contrary to an unctuous and misleading statement by Senator Magnuson, the bill is not "a forthright and historic step toward the responsible protection of the health of this nation's citizens." Rather, it is a bill to protect the economic health of the tobacco industry by freeing it of proper regulation.[7]

Yet Magnuson's image as the consumer's champion began to glow, and his initial chill toward me melted.

Basking in the light of bubbly media praise at home, Magnuson grew more comfortable with Jerry's vision of his role as a consumer advocate. Jerry was now freer and more able to free me and our staff colleagues to initiate (on Magnuson's behalf) a wide range of consumer protection and other public health and public interest initiatives, including waging continual guerilla warfare against the tobacco lobby—always ensuring that Magnuson received the credit and the media spotlight.

I was shaken by my initial caving in to Clements. Had it not been for Stan Cohen, Jerry, and Magnuson himself, the Clements bill I had swallowed for Magnuson might have derailed the curbing of cigarette advertising for decades—as Clements had planned. Once awakened, however, I had been able to contribute something useful by encouraging Magnuson to hold the line on preemption and by writing an unconstrained committee report along with Magnuson's Senate floor talking points. What is undeniable is that I learned several necessary lessons on my bumpy route to becoming a Bumblebee.

# 4

# *A Triumph of Passionate Truth over Power*

Jerry Grinstein launched the development of the Magnuson Bumblebees, but Ralph Nader contributed more than anyone else to our Bumblebee strategies to overcome the seemingly impregnable power of the corporate interests that still hound us today. In 1965, Nader launched a personal campaign to persuade Congress to enact new legislation to curb the automobile industry's unconscionable neglect of safety. Though totally unprepared to tangle with Detroit's political standing as one of the great corporate powers in the United States, Congress was obliged to deal with Nader and automobile safety.

Legislative responsibility fell to the Senate Commerce Committee, and a year later Congress passed the National Traffic and Motor Vehicle Safety Act. There is no doubt that Nader's passion and inexhaustible energy was the greatest moving force behind that law. In the process, Nader demonstrated the power of an alliance between Bumblebees and expert public interest advocates against corporate lobbies.

The stories in this chapter also contain a Bumblebee bonus: the tale of an inexperienced young woman, Joan Claybrook, who, though virtually unknown, was almost as responsible as Nader for the strength of the automobile safety law. She was the invisible leader in overcoming the very real threat that weakening amendments pursued by the auto industry lobby would enfeeble the regulations. Claybrook was not even employed by Congress. She was a one-year intern on a fellowship, the very lowest rung on Congress's ladder of power. Yet she led a trio of entrepreneurial legislators, one in the House and two in the Senate, and she led me to strengthen the bill so that it met Nader's uncompromising standards.

## Not a Great Start

In early 1965, Philip Elman, my guide, co-conspirator, and friend from the FTC, called and told me that a fellow named Ralph Nader was a man I needed to meet and listen to. He said Nader would call me but he didn't say why. Within a year, Nader would be a media sensation and a national hero. At the time, I'd never heard of him. At our first meeting, in the staff and visitors' cafeteria in what was then known as the New Senate Office Building, Nader launched into a compelling recital of the economic underpinnings of automobile-crash mayhem. The rising toll of dead and maimed, he argued, was the direct result of an unspoken conspiracy among four symbiotic commercial enterprises that benefited greatly from that toll: trauma surgeons, automobile repair shops, the automobile insurance industry (which had an excuse to escalate insurance premiums), and the automobile manufacturing industry (which pinched pennies on safety while sparing none for style and marketing). The Senate Commerce Committee, Nader insisted, had to deliver comprehensive automobile safety laws to reduce this toll. I expressed token sympathy with his cause but then told him, in effect, that there was no way in hell that Magnuson or the current Senate Commerce Committee would ever impose regulation on Detroit, the politically invincible economic fortress of the United States.

Nader, I learned, had gone to visit Elman in the hope that he might persuade the FTC to use its broad authority to initiate proceedings against the auto industry for its chronic neglect of the safety of its deceptively advertised vehicles. Elman could offer him no encouragement; the FTC chairman was too timid to try anything of the sort without a congressional mandate. So Elman told Nader to see me.

Nader wryly recalls our meeting: "You were exuberantly self-confident about what you could do, what Senator Magnuson could do, and what the Senate could not do. You just told me, 'Forget it. Do you know how powerful these auto companies are?' I remember saying to myself, 'If Mike Pertschuk is this pessimistic, what am I going to see elsewhere?'"

I thought I had seen the last of this unrealistic visionary, but he proceeded undaunted. He had already begun pounding on more promising Capitol Hill doors than mine. In doing so, he found the ambitious junior senator from Connecticut, Abraham Ribicoff.

As governor of the state, Ribicoff had already demonstrated concern about automobile safety by cracking down on drunk drivers. Though he was not a member of the Commerce Committee, which would have jurisdiction over any automobile safety bill, he seized a low rung on the

Senate power ladder: the obscure Government Operations Committee's Subcommittee on Executive Reorganization, to which he had been assigned as chairman. That least sought-after subcommittee had no legislative jurisdiction; all it could do was hold oversight hearings on the performance of government programs and recommend improvements. For the ambitious Ribicoff, that was enough.

As he was preparing for a hearing on auto safety, Ribicoff's subcommittee staff director, Jerome Sonosky, called and told him they had "struck gold." A friend had urged Sonosky to meet Nader, and during their first meeting, Nader spent three hours explaining why the auto industry had no right to produce unsafe cars.

"I just met somebody," Sonosky told his boss, "who knows more about auto safety than anybody I've ever come across. I don't have to run around town gathering up various experts. I just found him."[1] Ribicoff listened, as I hadn't, and Nader began meeting frequently with Sonosky to feed him documents and help map strategy.

With Sonosky's support, Ribicoff summoned the CEOs of the "Big Four" of Detroit—General Motors, Ford, Chrysler, and American Motors—to testify before his subcommittee in July on their neglect of automobile safety. Unaccustomed to probing from Congress, the executives were not prepared for the questions Nader fed through Sonosky to the senators on the subcommittee. The effect of these questions was explosive.

Robert Kennedy, the junior senator from New York, pressed the General Motors president, James M. Roche, and the board chairman, Frederic G. Donner: "What was the profit of General Motors last year?"

With magisterial indignation, Donner tried to avoid answering the question. "The one aspect we are talking about," he said, "is safety. . . . I don't think that has anything to do—"

Kennedy cut him off: "I would like to have that answer if I may. I think I am entitled to know that figure."

Donner tried to duck again, "I will have to ask one of my associates."

Kennedy continued to press him. He finally got an answer. Then he swung his ax. "You made $1 billion last year."

Donner responded, "That is correct."

Kennedy said, "And you spent $1 million on this [safety]?"

There was no challenge. This damning exchange dominated the widespread media coverage of the testimony.[2]

Although General Motors and the other automobile companies subsequently struggled to inflate these numbers with all activities remotely related to automobile safety, the damage was done. The only thing the phalanx of television cameras and eager journalists heard—drawn by the novelty of automobile executives on the hot seat and the celebrity of President John F. Kennedy's brother, the former attorney general—was a million dollars for safety compared with a billion dollars of profits.

"[This] segment of the new hearings, which electrified the audience," Elizabeth Brenner Drew later wrote in the *Atlantic Monthly*, "receive[d] the most newspaper and TV coverage, and helped put the auto industry on a one-way street to federal regulation."[3]

### Muckrakers' Power—with Nader at the Helm

The title of Doris Kearns Goodwin's political history of President Theodore Roosevelt and his successor, William Howard Taft, *The Bully Pulpit*, alludes to the critical potential power of presidential communicators.[4] In illuminating the source of Roosevelt's success, Goodwin focuses on his cultivation of a team of deep investigative journalists who were able to shift public opinion from opposition to governmental control over the abuses of the great corporate trusts to broad support for the president's enactment of his landmark antitrust laws. Though Roosevelt mocked them as "muckrakers," Goodwin documents his determined courting of them, encouraging them to launch comprehensive investigations of the reigning oligopolies, which would ultimately bring him the political support he needed.

Nader, who hounded influential journalists and columnists in an effort to cultivate their trust in him and in the information he supplied as a counterweight to corporate lobbying, did not enjoy the inherent power of the presidential bully pulpit. But he exhibited extraordinary skill in fueling what he called the 1960s version of Roosevelt's muckrakers: "We live in an age of muckraking on corporate abuse. You need to get a consistent brace of reporters eager to devote continual coverage well beyond a one-day story. There are documentaries on these abuses. There are muckraking stories on these abuses."

Largely through Nader's priming of his "brace" of responsive journalists, the media-driven impetus for action soon expanded to a three-lane, one-way highway to strong automobile safety legislation. The first lane was the unprecedented media coverage of the Bobby Kennedy–General Motors clash. The second lane was opened by the November 30, 1965, publication of Nader's book, *Unsafe at Any Speed*, a fact-based polemic about the auto industry's chronic malfeasance in failing to ensure the safe design of its automobiles.[5] The third lane was a fortuitous blunder by General Motors.

The most inflammatory revelation of *Unsafe at Any Speed* was that test driving by General Motors had uncovered the tendency of its sporty new model, the Chevrolet Corvair, to roll over while turning corners at normal speed. These dangers had been suppressed rather than fixed. By then, political Washington had begun to know Ralph Nader. The publication of his book made him a public figure and an authoritative voice. A review of the book by the magazine *Science* became front-page news in the *New York Times*, and the *Wall Street Journal* reviewed it on the editorial page. Then television picked up the story, and Nader was soon seen on *Meet the Press* and *Face the Nation*.

Nader's publisher, Richard Grossman, who arranged a press conference for Nader in Detroit when the book was published, was mesmerized by Nader's skill with the media: "Ralph was so skillful that I suddenly realized his genius for handling the media. There was nothing in his background that indicated he was going to have this kind of skill. Number one, he was unflappable. Number two, he was a couple of questions ahead of the reporters the whole time. He knew exactly how their minds worked."[6]

Nader's access to the media, through the hearings and the publication of his book, allowed him to accomplish what today would be called "reframing" the issue. The auto industry had long been strategic in supporting driver education, policy focus on drunk driving, and other educational efforts to reduce car crashes by eliminating what one automobile executive labeled "the nut behind the wheel." When Americans thought about the cause of injury and death in what they invariably called automobile "accidents," they were encouraged by all these programs to focus solely on the driver.

Nader, however, drew on the research he had studied to inject a new concept into the automobile safety dialogue. Though car crashes, he acknowledged, could be caused by driver negligence or drunkenness, many were not. More important, the severity of the injuries to the driver or passengers after the collision most often depended on the design of the vehicle. Shattering windshields, the lack of safety belts, sharp edges on dashboards, steering columns that pierced the chests of the driver on impact, and flimsily fastened doors that allowed a collision to catapult the driver and passengers to their deaths were not the result of driver negligence. They were the result of the manufacturers' irresponsibility. The primary framing of Nader's campaign for automobile safety design was what he called the "second collision"—entirely within the control of the car manufacturer. This frame was designed to counteract the industry's subtle effort to shift attention from manufacturing safety flaws to reckless drivers. The industry had long funded national campaigns to shame drivers into safe driving.

The third lane to strong automobile safety legislation was more damning of Detroit than any action Nader had taken, yet it was a self-inflicted wound that resulted from a panicked attempt by General Motors to discredit him. Late in 1965, Nader began to sense that he was being followed wherever he went. Several journalists noticed suspect figures lurking in the hallways where Nader was visiting Senate offices. They cautioned him. From other cities around the country calls came from Nader's friends and relatives that private investigators had been seeking interviews, claiming that they were acting on behalf of a prospective employer of Nader's for an important job, doing a routine background check. Yet the investigators probed far more deeply into his personal life than warranted. They investigated his sexual orientation and his Christian Lebanese immigrant parentage. They unsuccessfully sought evidence that he was anti-Semitic or that he was a Communist or that he was on the payroll of the lawyers who they claimed were exploiting automobile accidents to fatten their own profits, not to help crash victims.

At first, Nader took no responsive action, but the cascading evidence finally led him to brief James Ridgeway, an investigative reporter at the *New Republic*. The facts checked out, and Ridgeway's report, "The Dick," appeared in the *New Republic* on March 12, 1966. The article, Justin Martin reports, caused a "media firestorm, [and] . . . within hours major metropolitan dailies were all over the story one after another, the big auto companies—Ford, Chrysler, American Motors—issued official denials, saying that they had not been involved in any way."[7]

Ribicoff announced another hearing, for March 22. Again he summoned General Motors' president, Roche, to testify, along with the private detective the company had hired to organize the investigation, Vincent Gillen. The hearing room was packed with television news cameras and representatives of radio and print press. Roche was smooth but evasive, despite sharp questioning by several subcommittee members on the extent and ethics of the General Motors–ordered investigation. Then Gillen was summoned. He proved self-incriminating, providing accounts of his mission that demolished General Motors' characterization of the investigation as "routine."

As Drew concludes, these hearings eviscerated any remaining auto industry lobbying clout in forestalling strong automobile safety legislation. One anonymous senator she interviewed said, "It was that Nader thing. . . .

Everybody was so outraged the great corporation was out to clobber a guy because he wrote critically about them. At that point, everybody said the hell with them."[8] The "Nader thing" provided the final momentum for the enactment of an automobile safety law. Everything came together.

In the meantime, Magnuson had become increasingly annoyed that Ribicoff had trespassed on Commerce Committee jurisdictional turf. That gave Jerry and me an opening. Recognizing that automobile safety legislation was exactly the right initiative for Magnuson to take to burnish his identity as the leading consumer advocate in the Senate, we lobbied the Senate parliamentarian, whose friendship we had cultivated, to refer any automobile safety bill to our committee. He did.

### Enter the Still Green Bumblebee

Without hesitation, Jerry assigned primary responsibility for automobile safety to me as the staff member responsible for consumer protection, though he would always have my back.

I understood now that I needed to engage Nader as an ally and erase the stain of my blunt dismissal of him when we first met. I knew little about automobile safety regulation. He, on the other hand, was steeped in knowledge about the legislation required to force the manufacturers into placing safety over profit, and he had proven unequaled in his ability to stimulate media support. Not least on my mind was the lurking realization that Magnuson himself could become a target of Nader's wrath if he failed to live up to Nader's vision of adequate legislation.

I had no difficulty connecting with Nader. He needed me as much as I needed him; I would play a central role in shepherding any safety bill through the committee. More than that, I convinced him that I shared his goals. Nonetheless, he never relaxed his pressure on me to ensure that the bill that emerged was not weakened by auto industry lobbying. Throughout the rest of my time as a Magnuson Bumblebee, and to this day, we would be close allies in working toward the enactment and enforcement of a wide range of urgently needed consumer protection laws.

We also became friends. We never argued; we worked out differences with mutual respect. When Magnuson failed to achieve legislative provisions that Nader advocated, he would acknowledge that we had tried our best. Apart from my wife and children, I spent more time talking with him than with anyone else. From early morning to late at night, he would call me at home, alerting me to auto lobbyists' schemes and pressing me, always civilly, to work harder. He became so constant a presence in my life that when he joined my family in celebrating my birthday, my wife extracted as his birthday gift the promise of never calling me after 10 p.m. again.

Most who remember Nader recall him as a humorless scold. I was later to characterize his role as that of our contemporary Old Testament prophet. But Nader can be whimsical. I remember his calling early one evening and launching into his issue of the day, whose content I have long since forgotten. He was all business, until I tried to escape by telling him that we were almost out the door for dinner.

"Where are you going?" he asked.

"The AV Ristorante," I answered.

He disarmingly digressed. "Some people, "he said, "have a weakness for nobility. Some people display a fondness for Polish counts, others an affection for Hungarian counts. You seem to have an affinity for bacterial counts." Unbeknownst to me, our favorite Italian trattoria had recently received a failing grade in its city health inspection.

### An Unanticipated Obstacle from On High

The media-driven ascendancy of automobile safety as a politically popular cause did not escape the attention of President Lyndon Johnson. In late 1965, Johnson and his key policy staff were hunting for appealing issues with which to distract public attention from budget deficits and the unpopular Vietnam War. Consumer protection regulation, besides being popular with the public, would cost the government little, since the regulated companies would bear the costs.

Although Magnuson was an old friend and colleague, Johnson decided to develop an automobile safety bill bearing his own name. The White House, however, made the mistake of assigning the development of the bill to the Commerce Department, which held responsibility for transportation issues. Unhappily, Commerce Secretary John T. Connor, a former pharmaceutical company executive, viewed his role as protecting corporations, not burdening them. He was easy prey for the automobile industry lobbyists. They knew they could not stop the Nader-charged public pressure for an automobile safety bill, so they concentrated on developing a bill for Johnson that appeared on the surface to respond to Nader's call but contained weak regulations and loophole escapes from serious responsibility for safety deficiencies.

The Johnson White House staff members were not alert to the bill's flaws. They prepared for the president to submit the bill to Congress as

Connor had delivered it to the White House. In his January State of the Union address to the new Congress convening in 1966, Johnson signaled his intention to propose national highway safety legislation. The bill was submitted to Congress on March 2. Nader promptly scorned it as the perfect model of a "no-law law." That same day, Ribicoff rose on the Senate floor to fault its weaknesses and demand that it be strengthened.

Under Senate practice, legislation sent to Congress by the president is formally introduced by the chairman of the committee under whose jurisdiction it would fall. Therefore Magnuson introduced the president's bill under his own name and opened hearings on March 16 with a statement that, with Jerry's backing, I had persuaded him to deliver. He announced that he too believed the Congress should add strengthening amendments to what was now his bill.

### Enter the Invisible Force

Since I was to shepherd the bill through the committee, I needed to work on ensuring that the essential "strengthening amendments" were developed and accepted. I turned to Nader to guide me, and he in turn consulted with the automobile safety experts who had guided him. No one he reached out to proved more effective in developing those amendments—and seeing to it that they were included in the final bill voted on by the committee—than Joan Claybrook.

Claybrook was not a lawyer. She had never before drafted amendments. She had never lobbied. She began with no influence. What she brought to the task was her own passion for justice, ingrained early in life through her closeness with her progressive, politically unintimidated father.

Claybrook grew up in Baltimore. Her father, Warren Buckler, as a young lawyer practicing shortly after the end of World War II, was drawn to public interest advocacy by the sacrifice of so many men for what he believed was the preservation of social justice and freedom. By the late 1940s, as a member of the city council, he was advocating for public housing and legal services for the poor. In 1954 he began fighting for civil rights reforms following the Supreme Court's striking down of segregated schools. He played a singular role in leading the city to peaceful integration—despite its history of racial oppression.

As a teenager, Claybrook had been at her father's side when he crusaded. Her passion for social justice and unbending determination bore his imprimatur. In her early twenties, Claybrook entered public service in Baltimore to work on legislation for the Social Security Administration. She excelled, and in consequence was awarded a fellowship to come to Washington for a year beginning in January 1966, working six months for a House member and six months for a senator, each of her choosing.

She chose to begin with a newly elected liberal member of Congress from a newly created district in suburban Atlanta, James A. Mackay, because, she explains, "he was just fantastic. I could tell the minute I met him he was just a really solid, fantastic, interesting guy. And he asked me to read *Unsafe at Any Speed*." Mackay wanted to introduce legislation on automobile safety, she recalls, "because all the kids in his neighborhood were being killed." But first he wanted to speak with Nader.

Mackay asked Claybrook to arrange a meeting. This was not an easy task. She had not yet met Nader, but she had read a story about him in an article in the *Washington Post* by Morton Mintz. She called up Mintz, who gave her Nader's unlisted phone number. Then she called Nader every day for a week, but could not reach him. Pressured by Mackay, who was anxious to introduce the legislation but not until he met Nader, Claybrook called Nader at midnight and got him. Talking fast, she succeeded in scheduling forty-five minutes for Mackay to interview him.

The eager Mackay, however, determined to impress Nader, spent forty of those forty-five minutes talking about his own condemnation of the automobile industry's callousness, leaving little time to learn anything. So Mackay assigned Claybrook to develop the substance and detail of the bill. Because Nader, until meeting Mackay, had not found a more prominent champion of automobile safety willing to introduce fully effective auto safety legislation, he agreed to meet with Claybrook and tutor her on what he was convinced were the essential ingredients of an effective automobile safety law. She began by sitting down with Nader to listen and take notes. Then she set about getting the Mackay bill drafted. That would normally be the job of a member of the House Legislative Counsel's Office, but, Claybrook says, the counsel assigned to this junior member "was a dud."

Then good fortune stepped in. A call to Mackay's office from a staff member for Senator Vance Hartke inquiring about Mackay's automobile safety legislation was casually referred to Claybrook. Hartke, a member of the Senate Commerce Committee, wanted to introduce the Senate counterpart to Mackay's House bill. We had seen Hartke at his worst when he sold out to the tobacco lobby, but a family tragedy—the death of his sister in an automobile crash—had moved him to seek strong automobile safety regulation. Claybrook assured Hartke's staff member that the bill had no Senate sponsor yet. Nor did Mackay and his staff "have a decent draftsman here." When she asked, "Do you have anyone in the Senate who could draft this damn bill?" the immediate answer was Blair Crownover.

House and Senate legislative counsels generally take pride in serving as scrupulously nonpartisan professional servants of their bodies. They are not Bumblebees. They vary in their skills and in their commitment to the substance of the bills they are called to draft. Crownover, however, a classmate of Nader's at Princeton, was a rare legislative counsel: a superb draftsman but liberally entrepreneurial. He became committed to the drafting of a strong bill containing the strengthening amendments that Claybrook had summarized in her interview with Nader.

The bill Crownover drew up, Claybrook recalls, was "beautiful: simple, clear, straightforward." Both Mackay and Hartke introduced the bill at the end of January 1966, exactly as Crownover had crafted it. It would serve as a prod to the members of both House and Senate committees to produce a strong bill.

Claybrook, however, was not finished doing good through Mackay. Before the House segment of her internship was up, she volunteered to helped Mackay influence the House Commerce Committee's hearings. Unaware that the committee's members had little interest in consumer issues, or that its staff had little entrepreneurial skill, Claybrook decided that she could help advance Mackay's bill by recruiting supportive witnesses for the eventual House Commerce Committee hearings. For help, she decided to approach Sonosky and me.

When she came over to the Senate from the House, I gave her "such a brushoff, it was unbelievable."

I greeted her with, "What do you want?" Then, Claybrook recalls,

I said, "Well, I just want to know how you organize the hearings, because we're going to have them in the House, and Mr. Mackey wants to know who you're having as witnesses, and how we should do this." I had never organized a hearing, of course. You just said, "Why don't you just pay attention to what we're doing." That was the end of our meeting. . . .

Then, I went to meet Jerry Sonosky. He kept me waiting for four hours while he was drinking lunch. . . . I forced him to see me. I then saw him and he was as arrogant as usual: "What does a pipsqueak like you know about anything?"

Undaunted, Claybrook sought Mackay's help when the Senate Commerce Committee began its hearings in March. Magnuson was chairing. Mackay agreed that Claybrook should attend those hearings, and after each one she spoke to the witnesses and asked whether they would be willing to testify in the House. To those who consented, she typed a letter of invitation to the House hearings for Mackay to send them. Neither she nor Mackay appreciated that her actions on behalf of a junior member of Congress were unprecedented until, she recalls, she received a call from a House Commerce Committee staffer who said, "Who the hell do you think you are, inviting people to testify at our hearings?" Mackay received a similar call. He went right to the House committee chair, Harley Staggers of West Virginia, and, pointing out the importance of the witnesses, received permission to invite them.

The House committee hearings were held just after ours. One of the most convincing witnesses for automobile safety, whom Claybrook had secured, was Jimmy Hoffa, president of the Teamsters Union. According to Claybrook, "He had the senators wrapped around his little finger, all the senators and then the House members. He was such a great witness. He knew everything and they knew nothing about safety."

### My Turn

After the Senate hearings on the automobile safety bill ended in late March, I began to prepare Magnuson and myself for the next step in the legislative process: committee markups. We would have to be ready to support strengthening amendments. Until then, I had relied solely on Nader's counsel. I soon realized that (just as I had had to apologize for my arrogant first meeting with Nader) I had better apologize to Claybrook for my early dismissal of her if I wanted to ensure that we had well-crafted amendments.

In April, Claybrook had completed her internship with Mackay and moved to the Senate office of Walter Mondale of Minnesota. Mondale proved very supportive of strong automobile safety regulation but was not a member of the Commerce Committee. Hartke, however, was, and Claybrook had continued to strengthen her bonds with him and his key legislative assistants.

Realizing that the Senate committee markup of the Magnuson bill was imminent, Nader called Claybrook. They agreed to meet covertly one Saturday in the DuPont Plaza Hotel lobby in Washington. Nader would bring Roy A. Schotland, a law professor from the University of Virginia, to draft the critical amendments.

"We were supposed to meet in the lobby," Claybrook recalls, "but he wasn't sitting there; no one was sitting there. I went up to the desk and I asked if Mr. Nader was registered. No. Of course he wasn't using his own name, and he forgot to tell me what he was registered under."

Eventually, Nader wandered down and took Claybrook up to the room where he and Schotland were already at work. They went through all the amendment ideas: Ribicoff's bill on funding an experimental safety vehicle and Wisconsin senator Gaylord Nelson's bill on tire safety, as well as new ideas Nader proposed that included criminal penalties and defect recall. After about three hours, Nader left for meetings in Chicago. Claybrook and Schotland, with a few short breaks, spent until midnight Sunday in Mackay's office revising and writing up about two dozen amendments, plus several paragraphs for each one describing its importance.

On Monday morning, after a few hours' sleep, Claybrook delivered the amendments to Hartke and Mackay. Hartke "loved them" and introduced them on the Senate floor the next day as amendments he intended to offer. Mackay, frustrated that Hartke had moved so fast that he was not able to send the same proposed amendments to the House Commerce Committee staff simultaneously, scolded Claybrook and immediately issued a press release on the Mackay-Hartke amendments—or, as they were called in press releases from Hartke's office, the Hartke-Mackay amendments.

Meanwhile, Mondale was delighted with Claybrook's ability to promote his idea for yet another amendment, one that would make it mandatory that automobile companies disclose defects they had discovered directly to the consumers who had bought their cars. Mondale readily authorized Claybrook to continue helping Hartke.

Claybrook had emerged as a primary force behind the essential amendments. She came to see me to make sure I would work with her as the amendments were developed and to make sure Magnuson would accept them. This time I welcomed her with earned respect and apologized for my initial rudeness. She forgave me, dismissing it as of no importance. I acknowledged that her amendments, following Nader's ideas, made good sense and began collaborating with her to persuade Magnuson and other committee members to accept them. She was as persistent as Nader himself. Claybrook recalls that I was "a little irritated" because, she confesses, she and Nader began "overloading" me with amendments. But she never slowed down.

The committee markup sessions took place that summer. We were ready, but so, too, were several committee senators who had fallen under the influence of a new, potent auto industry lawyer, Lloyd Cutler. By this time, the auto industry, conceding that a safety standards law was certain to pass, had brushed aside its ineffective lobbyists and hired Cutler, a lawyer who was well known as one of the shrewdest lobbyists in Washington (though he grandiosely disdained the label of "lobbyist," preferring simply "lawyer"). Cutler's strategy was to propose small-print, escape-hatch amendments that would have the effect of undermining what would otherwise masquerade as a strong standards bill. "Graying, dapper, and low-keyed," Cutler was close to the major Washington power brokers.[9] He approached his work with disarming reasonableness and the precision of a practiced legislative obfuscator.

Several of the committee members began to offer amendments with Cutler's weakening imprint. As Magnuson resisted, the markup sessions threatened to come to a standstill.

### Learning the Black Art of Leaking from the Master Himself

A few hours after a stalled markup session, I received a call in my tiny office from Magnuson's secretary, summoning me to Magnuson's office. The summons was unsettling because it was unprecedented; I had yet to develop a comfortable working relationship with the chairman, and I had never before been invited to his office. As I entered, Magnuson was at his desk with a distinguished-looking elderly man with a trim mustache sitting in an easy chair at his side.

"Mike," Magnuson said, "tell Drew what exactly happened in today's executive session." Knowing that Magnuson's intent was to expose the subterranean committee foes, I dutifully described in detail the effort to derail the automobile safety bill, and the names of the committee members who had sold out to the auto industry lobby.

I certainly knew who "Drew" was: Drew Pearson. Pearson had long cultivated access to a continual stream of leaks. He was a latter-day unsavory match to the early muckrakers who had inspired Nader. His column, the Washington Merry-Go-Round, appeared seven days a week. Spiced with gossip, it exposed the secret underbelly of the legislative process. So flamboyant was Pearson's muckraking that the sober *Washington Post* editors consigned his column to the comic pages. Still, few in Washington failed to read it, and he was syndicated and published in as many as a thousand newspapers across the country. Pearson, and later his assistant-turned-successor, Jack Anderson, lapped up every investigative story Nader fed them.

"I would go over at night," Nader recalls, "and slip something through his door in Georgetown. And a day and a half or so later, I'd see it in the *Washington Post.* You can't come close to that now."

Once Pearson had his teeth into an issue that appealed to him, he would not let go—especially if he had an exclusive leak from an anonymous source about hitherto secret goings-on. Several of his leakers were motivated as much by fear as by the desire to expose wrongdoing, aware that Pearson thrived on extolling the leakers at the expense of their targets.

In his June 13 column, the day before the next scheduled markup of the bill by our committee, Pearson narrated a first-hand account of the weakening amendments pressed in the previous markup session. He named names, exposing the closed-door duplicity of turncoat Commerce Committee members who had publicly heralded their support for strong automobile safety legislation. He wrote it as authoritatively as if he had been sitting in the room taking notes.

The targeted Republicans he had exposed were not going to welcome the publicity.

### A Sacrificial Lamb

When the committee reconvened the day after Pearson's column ran, the targeted members of the committee were blustering with rage. Hugh Scott, the Republican senator from Pennsylvania—exposed by name—demanded to know who leaked the story to Pearson. One customary method for identifying a Pearson leaker was to look at whom he praised in the column. Pearson—though not for the first time—had singled out Senator Magnuson as the hero for "vigorously" opposing weakening amendments. The offended members knew perfectly well that Magnuson was the likely source of the leak, but none of them had the temerity to charge him directly. Magnuson sternly surveyed the edges of the room where the members' staff sat or stood and righteously demanded, "Have any of you been talking to Drew Pearson?" I could do nothing but sit in terrified silence, expressionless.

What followed was even more devious. Claybrook had not attended the meeting that had given birth to the leak. But that didn't stop Magnuson from a shameful ploy to obscure our guilt. Claybrook recalls:

I wore a bright yellow dress; never occurred to me that I should
wear anything else. It was in the summertime, it was a cotton dress.
Magnuson was sitting all the way at one end and I came in and I was
standing at the other end. I didn't really notice that there were all men

there. There were no women, except me. I had a little pad, and Hartke wasn't there yet—his staff guy was coming with him. So I just stood there and took little notes. That was when there were those blow-ups. The Republican senator from Pennsylvania, Scott, and all the others Pearson named were complaining about this article. No one confessed. Then Magnuson looked right at me, because I was so bright in yellow. He didn't know who the hell I was, so it didn't matter to him what he did to me. He said accusingly, "What are you writing? You in the yellow dress, what are you writing?" I said, "I'm just taking some notes for Senator Hartke. He's not here yet. He's on his way." He said, "Stop writing!" So I said, "Okay." I stopped writing. Then they started the markup.

Magnuson's stratagem worked: the presumed guilt had been shifted to Claybrook, and the scheming senators Pearson had targeted had been unhinged. They retreated from sabotaging the bill. But the aftermath was shameful. Despite the chicanery of Magnuson's calling attention to Claybrook and her note taking, the chairman charged me with the task of telling her she was barred from any further committee executive sessions.

"I was so depressed," she recalls. "I just couldn't believe it. I'd done nothing." As with Nader, Claybrook and I soon became both colleagues and friends and have continued our friendship to this day. I waited several years after the events to get up the nerve to confess to her my nefarious role in the leak. She still likes to tell the story and shame me for it, but with the good humor of distance.

What she doesn't trumpet is that among the strengthening amendments adopted by the committee was the one she had developed that allowed Mondale to achieve a goal close to his heart: making it mandatory for automobile companies to disclose defects. She gave weight to her demand by reminding Mondale to remind Hartke that Mondale had agreed to lend her to him to work for his own amendments, and that Hartke owed Mondale that obligation.

### Balancing the Gap between Lobbying Legerdemain and the Public Will

Strengthening amendments would now dominate the committee markup sessions. Jerry and I had convinced Magnuson that it was in his interest to support the amendments, despite his undiminished dislike of Hartke.

The strong bill was finally ready to be reported to the Senate, but first I had forty-eight hours to draft the committee's report that would accompany the bill to the Senate floor to clarify any ambiguities in the language of the bill itself. To ensure that I captured the meaning and intent of each section of the bill, I invited Nader and Cutler to park in separate rooms adjoining my office for the duration of my drafting session. Nader was grateful—and ready. Cutler was offended. He resented being lowered to the same status as Nader, but he had no choice.

Each time I finished a draft section of the report, I showed it to them simultaneously, seeking their comments and suggestions. Cutler hovered over each sentence with his sharp eye, offering objection first and then subtle changes. Sensitive to his deviousness, I took his suggestions across the hall to Nader, who guided me to reject any poison pills. Every time I redrafted a section, I took it back again to both men. This tortuous process stretched through a long day and into the evening. Neither Nader nor Cutler was fully satisfied, but in the end, the report raised no cries of outrage from Cutler and received sober approval from Nader.

We sent the bill to the Senate floor, where it was quickly taken up and passed by a large margin, averting efforts to eliminate the strengthening amendments that had survived through the committee's markup. It was a moment for celebration. Claybrook remembers that the revelry was initiated by Sonosky, his scorn for her evaporated: "It was a gorgeous day. It was just a beautiful day. I'll never forget."

### The House Commerce Committee Follows Magnuson's Lead

The hammering away at the automobile industry's malfeasance by Pearson and other equally outraged journalists had also intimidated the otherwise chronically inert House Commerce Committee, prodded by its handful of strong consumer protection advocates. These advocates included Mackay and several other members rising in seniority and influence, led by John Moss, a Democrat from California. The House committee accepted the essential elements of the Senate bill and added several strengthening amendments to it.[10]

When the House and Senate bills met in conference, Magnuson was elected chairman of the conference process and willingly accepted the House improvements. The conference report was readily accepted by both houses, and the National Traffic and Motor Vehicle Safety Act was signed into law by President Johnson on September 9, 1966. In her *Atlantic Monthly* analysis of the political trajectory of the bill into law, Elizabeth Drew describes it as one that "Nader could pronounce 'a significant step forward.'"[11]

Credit for this outcome belongs to Nader, Claybrook, Pearson, and, in the end, Magnuson, who, having made his commitment to strengthen President Johnson's bill, fought for the strongest bill every inch of the way. That bill passed because of the trust Magnuson inspired in his peers and the forcefulness of his stand.

### New Twists in the Bumblebee's Quiver of Lobby-Piercing Arrows

By the close of this automobile safety venture, I had learned much more of my trade as a Magnuson Bumblebee from Claybrook, Nader, and Magnuson. I also learned much from Cutler's wiles and General Motors' stumbles. As for the latter, I was put in mind of what I was learning in studying tai chi: the secret of success is to absorb the vulnerability of the adversary and transform it into his fall.

Claybrook taught me the power of perseverance, but Nader had the deepest impact on the Bumblebees' corporate-restraining strategies throughout the late sixties and seventies. His greatest gift to me as I pursued my work with the Commerce Committee was not a strategy, however, but a vision: he expanded my horizon of the possible. Nader also taught me how what we later called "media advocacy" could be a potent counterweight to special interest campaign money and lobbying. Magnuson taught me how to complement Nader's "outside" advocacy by opening the closed doors of the Senate through the disciplined leaking of secrets to which even Nader didn't have access. Together, nonprofit advocates and Bumblebees could effectively fuel awaiting muckrakers.

As we applied these lessons, Magnuson continued to teach us the potential pitfalls in the art of leaking. After the automobile safety battles, Magnuson knew perfectly well that we would be leaking throughout the rest of his tenure as Commerce Committee chairman, and he approved unless we got ourselves—or especially him—"into trouble."

One of our most ardent Bumblebees, Lynn Sutcliffe, recalls a story about getting into trouble that shamed him at first, but which he later came to cherish. A year or so after passage of the National Traffic and Motor Vehicle Safety Act, Sutcliffe was summoned to Magnuson's office. When he walked in, Magnuson wordlessly produced a copy of a memo Sutcliffe had written in confidence to our trusted contact, Morton Mintz, at the *Washington Post*, revealing a conspiracy between a lobbyist and a member of the Senate Commerce Committee to sink an important Magnuson consumer protection bill. Some unknown weasel at the *Post* had seen Sutcliffe's memo, probably in the process of editing Mintz's story, made a copy of it, and sent it to the lobbyist named therein. That lobbyist turned out to be a friend of Magnuson's. Without a word, Sutcliffe told me, Magnuson handed him the pilfered copy of the memo:

> He said, "Let me tell you a story. When I was a young man practicing law out in Everett, I had a partner, and one day this beautiful blonde comes charging into the office, demands to see me. I was not there; demands to see my partner. So my partner invites her into the office, and she says, 'Warren Magnuson made mad, passionate love to me. Warren Magnusson promised to marry me. And I've got it right here in writing.' My law partner looked at her and he said, 'I don't doubt that he made mad, passionate love to you. And he may have promised to marry you. But I'll guarantee you one thing, it's not in writing.'"
>
> Then Magnuson said, "That's all."

# 5

# High Spirits and High Gear

By mid-1966, we had blocked the unbeatable tobacco lobby. We had beaten the unbeatable Detroit. We were high on our triumphs. By we, I mean Senator Magnuson, Jerry Grinstein, and me. Magnuson had rediscovered himself in a new light and gained enough confidence to overcome much of his resistance to conflict. With patient persuasion from Jerry and me, he began to introduce more consumer protection laws, especially public health laws. Our prodding still took subtle forms: "Don't you think it would be a good idea to set up a consumer subcommittee?" "Don't you think you should introduce this bill to strengthen the Flammable Fabrics Act?" He would usually resist the first time we asked him, but on the second or third try we could persuade him—especially if we showed him some favorable consumer press clippings.

Magnuson's growing trust and willingness to introduce—or steal—one consumer protection bill after another unleashed Jerry and me and our gradually expanding team of young, committed committee staff members—churned out by the University of Washington School of Law Magnuson Fellowship program, an inspiration of Jerry's that offered one competitive internship to each graduating class.

Learning from and working with Ralph Nader had been transformative. Nader and other nonprofit advocates continued to confront us with a barrage of consumer injustices. Other committee staffers had begun to catch the consumer protection bug and to develop the nerve to challenge lobbies that had once seemed impregnable.

Magnuson's political campaigns for reelection had hitherto been grounded in his delivery of federal funds to build dams, which produced low-cost electric power systems, and to develop Washington State's ports, which spurred massive increases in job-creating exports. His campaigns had focused on little else. But his near defeat in 1962 had signaled a warning cry. By now, the flood of new voters to Washington from around the country, drawn to the natural appeals of the state, were not impressed by Magnuson's role as the deliverer of "pork." Neither were many older voters, who, inspired by John F. Kennedy, wanted something more from their representatives.

Jerry understood, however, even if Magnuson did not, that it would take more than a handful of media tributes to transform Magnuson's image among the Washington State electorate. We needed to produce a cascade of eye-catching, praiseworthy public health and consumer protection laws to embed Magnuson's new identity in the minds of the voters.

The simplest way to achieve passage of these bills into law was to harness Magnuson's power as Commerce Committee chairman. As chairman, he could appropriate under his own name any bill by any Senate member that was referred to the Commerce Committee. When it came time for committee action, he was free to introduce and propose to the committee a substitute bill—even a barely modified version of the original bill—bearing his own name. We had already seen how the cigarette labeling bill introduced by Maurine Neuberger, the tire safety bill initiated by Gaylord Nelson, and the auto safety regulation propelled into the public spotlight by Abraham Ribicoff's hearings had morphed into Magnuson bills. Though Senator Nelson had been outraged over Magnuson's usurping his bill, Neuberger was more forgiving, acknowledging that though the Magnuson bill was far from what she had wanted, it was the most that could be achieved. And though Ribicoff could go on endlessly calling investigative hearings, corrective legislation belonged to the Commerce Committee and Magnuson.

### The Purloined Magnuson Fair Packaging and Labeling Bill

That was just the beginning of our stealing bills in Magnuson's name. Perhaps the most media-worthy was a bill long sponsored by Michigan senator Philip A. Hart—the fair packaging and labeling bill. Food labels until that time had been virtually meaningless to consumers. When they were not overtly deceptive, they were confusing and full of data that was of no practical use. The food industry was strategically marketing competing foods in differently sized packages and weights to thwart price comparison. The bill was designed to abolish misleading labels (such as "Giant Quart"), label illustrations that exaggerated the size of the product inside, and "slack-filled" boxes, which were filled with three-quarters of product and one-quarter of air. Hart had introduced the bill in June 1961, but because he was then a member of the Judiciary Committee and not of the Commerce Committee, he had structured the bill as a form of antitrust legislation, over which the Judiciary Committee had jurisdiction.

Although the bill had the modest goal of enabling shoppers to make accurate price and quality comparisons, the food industry saw it as a threat to their marketing freedom. Once again, a modest consumer protection initiative faced the massed lobbying power of giant corporate enterprises with a phalanx of influential lobbyists building on years of largess and camaraderie with congressional members and their staffs.

The bill faced the hostile chairman of the Judiciary Committee, James Eastland of Mississippi, and the equally hostile minority leader of the House Republicans, Everett Dirksen, who was also a member of the Judiciary Committee. The bill was buried for four years in the Judiciary Committee. By the opening of the 89th Congress in 1965, Hart realized that his bill would never emerge. His only chance would be to redraft the bill so it would fall within the jurisdiction of the Commerce Committee, on which he had become a member. Again, Jerry and I helped Hart's office staff work with the Senate legislative counsel's sympathetic draftsman, Blair Crownover, to ensure that the bill would come to us.

Dirksen put up a determined fight on the Senate floor to keep the bill within the Judiciary Committee, arguing that substantially the same bill had been referred to the Judiciary Committee earlier and that the committee had held extensive hearings and thereby gained expertise in the subject matter. He also argued that it would be a subversion of Senate protocol to manipulate the language of a bill simply to steer it to a more favorable committee. This argument was disingenuous; shopping for friendly committees was a time-honored practice. Magnuson, more affronted by the Judiciary Committee's encroachment on the Commerce Committee's—his—rightful jurisdiction than moved by a passion for fair packaging and labeling, argued on the Senate floor that the bill belonged to the Commerce Committee.

"At the time it was referred to the Judiciary Committee," Magnuson explained, "I made a mild protest, but it went unheeded. The bill is now 'home,' in the Commerce Committee, where it belonged in the first place."[1] Since Magnuson was a leader of the majority party and Dirksen the minority leader, it was no battle. The bill was referred to Commerce.

Magnuson was not yet convinced, however, that he should take the lead. He opened the committee hearings on the bill with a statement that I had drafted but that he had watered down to be less committed. He then left Hart and Neuberger to run the hearings. But Hart and Neuberger still lacked weight with committee members, and Magnuson was not yet moved to bring the bill before the committee for a vote. He had heard too many complaints of overregulation from his lobbyist cronies as they played poker and drank together at the Burning Tree Country Club. These lobbyists fed his disdain for Hart, whom he referred to as "the Boy Scout." He also remained relatively averse to conflict.

My task was to develop a disguised version of the bill the food lobby had demonized as "Hart's bill" so Magnuson could introduce it as his own, different from and more moderate than Hart's. But I had to retain the most essential elements of Hart's bill. To produce such a two-faced document, I needed expert help. I soon developed an undercover working relationship with two senior Commerce Department staff members, Assistant Secretary J. Herbert Holloman and his general counsel, Gordon Christiansen. They were both knowledgeable about and critical of the industry's deceptive packaging and labeling practices. They had been fighting hard within the department for a stronger bill, but had run up against Commerce Secretary John T. Connor, whose Texas heart belonged to industry.

Christiansen helped me refine the bill. With respect to labeling, the new bill was as strong as the Hart bill and technically less vulnerable to unintended loopholes. We were, however, forced to concede to the industry on the packaging regulations. The weight and packaging size standards would not be mandated directly by the law. The industry was free to develop its own regulatory standards. But, as a safeguard, the bill would also provide that if the Commerce Department determined that voluntary standards were not sufficient, it would be empowered and required to set mandatory standards.

While Magnuson dawdled, President Johnson pursued his diversionary effort to promote consumer protection laws. One day, at a White House meeting on another matter, he took Magnuson aside and urged him to back the fair packaging and labeling bill. Magnuson erupted. He told Jerry and me that he had told the president, "I'll work on the damn bill, if you keep Esther Peterson off my back." Peterson, the passionate head of the President's Committee on Consumer Interests, had been calling Magnuson and sending him letters—hounding him, he felt—urging him to move the bill along. Magnuson grew crotchety when subjected to pressure, but his resistance was not simply pique. He had been taking the pulse of committee members, including several Democrats chronically weak-kneed in the face of industry opposition, and calculated that if he moved the bill along now, it would lose.

By April, Peterson had ceased her siege, and Magnuson, faithful in his pledge to Johnson, brought the revised bill under his name before the committee for markup. Behind the closed doors of the committee markup sessions, the debate was, for Magnuson's committee, uncommonly contentious. Magnuson later described these sessions as "long and painful."[2] Senator Vance Hartke, who had been a hero on the automobile safety bill but an industry pawn on the tobacco bills, was once again an industry pawn. He offered the food industry's amendment to wipe out even the modified size-and-weight packaging standards provision. Magnuson was undaunted. I have a vivid memory of his pounding the table and declaring, "This bill is not the Hart bill!" His passion probably proved more intimidating than persuasive with the committee members. In either case, it reaped him a bipartisan vote of 14 to 4, enough to report his bill favorably, without weakening it, to the Senate floor on May 13, 1966.

Still, the industry lobby wouldn't quit. Senator Norris Cotton tried again to remove all semblance of packaging regulation in the bill. Magnuson defeated this amendment too, by a vote of 53 to 32. In a last gesture of industry obeisance, Senator Dirksen again moved to re-refer the bill to the Judiciary Committee, but to no avail. The bill that passed the Senate on June 9, 1966, was essentially the same as the bill we had designed for Magnuson. The vote was 72 to 9—a measure of the Senate's recognition of the public popularity of consumer protection legislation.

On the floor of the Senate, the normally laconic Senate majority leader Mike Mansfield described passage of the bill as "another triumph for Warren Magnuson," who had won "the well-deserved allegiance of the American housewife, indeed of all Americans, for whom he has worked so hard."[3] Plaudits from consumer advocates followed. Hart, unlike the piqued Nelson, acknowledged that Magnuson "entered the picture at the right moment and in the right way to get the thing passed.

"We lost some things," he admitted, "but by and large it was a good bill and much the same as mine. You know how Maggie can pull that sort of thing off, with his broad sweeping statements which everybody somehow accepts: 'This is a new bill.'"[4]

For me, the process that led to the passage of this bill was also a lesson in the need to expand our informal network of sympathetic experts who resided in relative obscurity within the many agencies whose bosses' political and ideological sympathies were aligned with big business. For Jerry, our passing cigarette labeling, automobile safety, and food labeling reforms had worked and had begun to imbed Magnuson's identity in both the Washington, DC, and the Washington State media as the consumer's champion. But producing these bills was not enough. We needed to accelerate the juggernaut of consumer bills and enacted Magnuson laws well before Washington State's popular Republican governor, Daniel Evans, decided whether to challenge Magnuson for his Senate seat in 1968.

I remember sitting around with Jerry and the eager young staff he had recruited, basking in the reflected glory of Magnuson's automobile safety romp, when one of us mused, "There must be other unsafe products that are either unregulated or ineffectively regulated. Let's see if we can find them and create new Magnuson laws."

### Beyond Legislative Kleptography

While we were working on the automobile safety and fair packaging bills, two senior domestic advisers to President Johnson, Joseph Califano and Larry Levinson, were also at work in the White House. On March 21, 1966, Johnson delivered to Congress a consumer message damning the needless, preventable sickness and loss of life attributable to "gaps in the law dealing with hazardous substances and materials."[5] The president followed up by promising and then sending a child protection bill to the Congress.

Magnuson introduced the president's bill, assuming his procedural role as chair of the committee with jurisdiction. In keeping with Senate routine, it therefore bore Magnuson's name as its principal author. What was not routine was Magnuson's floor statement, which praised the bill profusely as his own, barely acknowledging at the end of the statement that it was the president who had sent it to Congress.

The next stage in Jerry's Magnuson renovation strategy was the scheduling of hearings on the bill as the first hearings of the new Consumer Protection Subcommittee of the Commerce Committee, chaired formally by Magnuson and staffed by me. The president's role had receded; Magnuson was at the helm.

Meantime, my working relationship with Magnuson had emerged from the basement. No longer an insecure novice, I invented a new committee title for myself: Consumer Protection Counsel. A little too puffed up—and still insecure—I ordered an ample supply of gold-embossed business cards from the Senate stationery shop that bore my invented title over the gold Senate seal.

The Hazardous Substances Control Act had been passed in 1960, but its purpose and reach were so narrow that one critic suggested it should have been called the Federal Household Chemical Products Cautionary Labeling Act. Passage of the law had been triggered by lurid media attention to poisonings by household cleaners containing substances such as cyanide and carbon tetrachloride. Left unregulated was a universe of other hazardous products, including children's toys. Even poisonous chemicals could not be banned. Their manufacturers were required only to warn of their risks on the labels. After passage of the bill, the skull-and-crossbones symbol began to appear on containers. But that offered no resistance to curious children.

The bill proposed by Johnson, by now referred to as Magnuson's bill, would be a small improvement by expanding federal control over hazardous substances. The Food and Drug Administration (FDA), which would administer the law, would be empowered to ban substances, including those with a warning label, if "the degree or nature of the hazard involved in the presence or use of such substance in households is such that the objective of the protection of the public health and safety can be adequately served" only by such a ban.[6]

I took advantage of my new free hand in organizing committee hearings and sought out nonprofit advocacy groups and cloistered academics for the hearings on the child protection bill. My efforts meant that the hearings would be heavily weighted with expert witnesses free of corporate-funded thumbs. Their testimony and submission of well-documented reports into the hearing records revealed major gaps in the capacity and focus of FDA enforcement and in the laws governing product safety. None of these gaps would be covered by the new law Johnson was proposing.

We opened the hearings to communications we had received on hazardous products that would fall far beyond the categories covered by the Johnson bill. Among them was an article by a Seattle pediatrician, Abraham Bergman, about unsafe lawnmowers. Bergman had contacted Magnuson, urging him to broaden the scope of the child protection bill well beyond the narrow categories that Johnson had asked for. Bergman then began to harass me to move on it. Our correspondence with Bergman opened a new area of concern: flammable children's sleepwear. He wrote that he and his fellow pediatricians at burn centers were continually responding to hideous burn injuries on small children whose sleepwear had burst into flame.

Warnings about this hazard had appeared in some media years before, but the committee, the Congress, and the president, with textile-state legislators ever alert to overregulation, had responded with what was then the standard regulatory measure. The (1953) Flammable Fabrics Act essentially handed over flammable fabrics standards setting to the textile industry and the sympathetic Commerce Department. The law delegated the task of strengthening flammable fabrics standards to a standing committee made up solely of industry representatives.

Bergman's letter was an effective prod to Magnuson, not least because it came from a Washington State constituent. Bergman had mobilized almost three thousand letters to Magnuson from Washingtonians demanding legislation to ban flammable children's wear. I promised Bergman that we would take a hard look at the inadequacies of the law and its enforcement. We did. What we discovered was that the "standing committee" had never met to oversee or modify the regulations. Of course this discovery was shocking, but we were delighted. Here was an opportunity to create yet another consumer protection bill for Magnuson to initiate.

Soon we had unmasked gaps in coverage of all categories of hazardous products, as well as gaps in the effective regulatory powers and enforcement of those products. We heard testimony about unpackaged hazardous toys that would be free of inspection; flavored pills, such as children's aspirin, that offered no more protection for curious children than written warnings; cuddly imported toy ducks covered with real duckling skins that had been treated with insecticides; dried beans that were sold as jewelry; a water-proofing solution for household use that was more explosive than gasoline; and small fireworks resembling candy that were designed to explode on impact—and would do so if bitten.

What we learned from our hearings on the child protection bill and from consulting with our growing network of public health advocates would turn out to be enough fodder for at least five separate Magnuson bills. The Consumer Protection Subcommittee and Magnuson's direct engagement were progressively expanding into bread-and-butter consumer protection and a broad engagement in public health law.

### *What Could Be More Appealing to Parents Who Vote?*
On August 16, 1966, Magnuson cosponsored a bill that had earlier been introduced by Senator Neuberger and the Republican committee member Thruston Morton to strengthen the Flammable Fabrics Act. It was too late in the Congress to act on the bill, but it set us up for a Magnuson bill in the next, 90th, Congress, deftly co-opting the Neuberger-Morton bill.

Strengthening the Flammable Fabrics Act meant creating something new. We would pursue it, but we were not yet ready to prepare more public safety initiatives. We had explored only episodic illustrations of the wide range of other product safety defects and lax enforcement. We could find no systematic assessment of how broad the problems were, what categories of product regulation needed to be extended, how much regulatory authority was needed to effectively eliminate these preventable hazards, and where in the federal government the new responsibilities should be lodged. Furthermore, we had learned that the Commerce Department was hostile to the firm regulation of business and that the FDA, already overloaded with food and drug regulation, had neither time nor resources to exercise even what little authority it had over hazardous substances.

Despite the pressing need for reform, Jerry and I judged that the time was not yet ripe for broader product safety regulation. We decided to have Magnuson introduce an interim measure, legislation creating a national investigative commission, with two years or so within which it could hold public (and publicized) hearings around the country, reaching out for and taking public testimony from physicians like Bergman as well as independent researchers and victims of faulty, hazardous products. We knew that such hearings would attract already engaged reporters, such as Morton Mintz of the *Washington Post*. We were confident that the sensational testimony would awaken the public to the need for broad corrective legislation, such as a new, permanent, independent regulatory agency that would concentrate on the wide range of consumer product hazards not covered by any existing laws. But first, we had to get the study commission authorized by Congress. The congressional action creating it would add to Magnuson's achievements, and if it did its work well and delivered a broad, fact-based assessment of widespread unregulated product hazards (and in doing so gained significant media attention), it could lay the political groundwork for new regulatory legislation.

Our strategy was to tack language creating the study commission onto the original child protection bill as Title II when Magnuson brought the bill before the committee for markup. No one on the committee objected or even called for additional hearings to consider this new proposal. So the child protection bill with its new Title II, the creation of the study commission intact, passed out of the committee unanimously. On September 1, 1966, it unanimously passed the Senate on a voice vote. Predictably, however, the lobby-indentured majority of the House Commerce Committee responded to the collective fears of a vast array of product manufacturers by dropping Title II from the bill they reported to the House floor. That too was passed unanimously.

The House members on the conference committee held out immovably against Magnuson and his Senate conferees. Since it was only a few days before the end of the 89th Congress, Magnuson relented, knowing that the whole child protection bill would die if he did not give in to the House conferees. The Senate voted to accept the House version of the child protection bill, and President Johnson signed it into law on November 3, 1966. Magnuson vowed to introduce a separate bill creating the national investigative commission early in the next Congress.

By December 1966, Jerry was encouraged but not satisfied with the impressive roster of Magnuson consumer protection laws that had been enacted and the flattering media coverage and praise for Magnuson's role in the 89th Congress, especially in Washington State. Nothing Magnuson had achieved in consumer protection so far had deterred Governor Evans from challenging him in the 1968 race. Jerry's strategy required more—and more media-appealing—Magnuson laws that resonated with voters, especially women. And they had to come before the close of the 1967 session; if Evans was going to run, he had to decide by the end of 1967 to give himself time to develop a 1968 campaign organization and strategy.

We were eager to churn out those suspended Magnuson consumer protection bills whose seeds had been planted in the last session of the 89th Congress. Now, with Jerry's support and Commerce Committee budget legerdemain, I had acquired help in building a consumer protection development team. The team included Edward Merlis, a young staff member employed by a small office deep in the heart of the Department of Health, Education, and Welfare (HEW), an office blandly titled the National Clearinghouse on Smoking and Health but staffed by eager warriors against the tobacco companies' advertising abuses. Merlis had the disciplined mind of a lawyer (without the baggage of a formal legal education), a near-photographic memory, and a taste for mischief-making. He joined the staff later, in 1971. In the meantime, he was moonlighting for me from the clearinghouse, with his superior's unhesitating support. (He would later file a copy of the clearinghouse's mailing list of citizens who had expressed support for action against tobacco advertising. This list was mildly illicit but provided an efficient resource for campaign fund-raising for committee members such as Senator Frank Moss of smoking-averse Utah.)

Another blooming Bumblebee was William Meserve. Meserve came to see me in 1969 because he had heard that there might be openings on the committee staff. "At that first meeting," he recalls, "you, as normal, were in a rush, but you quickly looked at my résumé, and you said you'd like to keep in touch." I did. He had a stellar academic record and an elite law firm associateship. I kept him in mind and was soon able to offer him a job working with us for the Consumer Protection Subcommittee.

At about the same time, I created a committee internship for Edward Cohen, the son of Stanley Cohen, whom I had persuaded Senator Neuberger to hail as a "crusading reporter." I could hardly deny that Stan's public loathing of cigarette advertising in the pages of *Ad Age* (and our friendship) had anything to do with the hire. But Cohen *fils* would prove so competent that by 1971, he would earn a permanent position on the committee staff, working closely with Merlis and other staff on consumer issues. (I remember a wise friend predicting that the adventures Ed was about to encounter as a twenty-one-year-old would forever dwarf the rewards of any future job.)

### Another Hill to Climb

The Republicans had made a strong comeback in the 1966 congressional elections. Though the Democrats still held governing majorities in both houses, those majorities survived only because of the Democratic Party's conservative southern arm, which would later find its ideological home in the conservative wing of the Republican Party. These changes posed yet another potential roadblock to our aspirations.

Despite this shift in the political environment, Magnuson's enthusiasm for consumer protection had blossomed. On December 2, 1966, Magnuson delivered his first comprehensive consumer protection speech at the Seattle Rotary Club. In the speech, which we had prepared, he proudly reviewed his consumer protection victories in the 89th Congress and announced that he intended to initiate a full roster of new consumer protection laws in the 90th. These new laws included those that had failed to pass in the last Congress and others that had been authored by junior senators with Magnuson as only one of many secondary cosponsors. His promises included strengthening the Flammable Fabrics Act, establishing a consumer product investigative commission, and introducing a truth in lending bill.

### Virtuous Competition

At about the same time, Califano and President Johnson were ready to put forward a more aggressive consumer protection agenda for the president to demand from the new Congress. Johnson's embrace of consumer protection meant that the president would twist arms in pressing Congress to enact his bills. Worried that success would be cast as a Johnson achievement and that all the media attention would focus on the president with Magnuson reduced to a shadow, Jerry and I determined that Magnuson would preempt him. On January 16, 1967, before Johnson could announce his consumer protection initiative, with the new Congress barely opened, Magnuson delivered his second annual manifesto on the state of consumer protection on the Senate floor. It encompassed every new bill he had promised in Seattle—and more.

The president's message to Congress on February 16 included verbal support for a stronger Flammable Fabrics Act. Magnuson did not wait for the president's bill. The very same day, Magnuson introduced his Flammable Fabrics Act amendments, which would provide stronger enforcement standards and expand their reach to other household fabrics, such as rugs, bedding, and draperies. The bill would also mandate that HEW conduct research on fire-resistant fabrics that would pressure the Commerce Department to meet the new standards. Magnuson's floor statement did not mention the president.

Magnuson's introduction of his own flammable fabrics bill was not simply a competitive checkmate. Magnuson was more deeply engaged in the pursuit of flammable fabric safety than he had been in much of the earlier consumer protection activity. Magnuson and his wife, Jermaine, at Bergman's invitation, had visited burn victims and their families at Job's Orthopedic Hospital in Seattle, and the experience had "moved him deeply."[7]

We still faced a formidable challenge in getting this bill through. Unlike the bumbling General Motors executives and auto industry lobbyists, the textile lobbyists were savvy. With the backing of powerful senators from the southern cotton-growing and textile-manufacturing states, they were determined and confident that they could stop the bill—confident enough that one of their lobbyists threatened me that blood would run in the halls of Congress before such a bill would pass. I didn't argue, but I silently vowed to prove him wrong.

Our opening gambit was to exercise our control over the recruitment and order of witnesses at committee hearings. First, we needed an opening witness who could draw a surge of television cameras and journalists sufficient to bring nationwide attention to the hearings and elevate the need for strong legislation to the national list of urgent legislative priorities. I chose Betty Furness, Johnson's newly appointed consumer adviser.

Furness was a middling actress, best known to the public as the decora-

tive opener and closer of refrigerator doors in vacuous television adver-
tisements for Westinghouse. To the best of anybody's knowledge, she had
never been a consumer advocate or otherwise engaged in public policy. I
had learned better. Earlier, at a White House reception for Furness, I had
cornered her and praised her on the first issue she had taken on publicly,
the practice of injecting water into supermarket hams with no function
other than to jack up the price. Challenging the meat processors was fine,
I pointed out, but not politically risky. What about taking on the tobacco
companies?

"Fuck the tobacco companies," she responded.

I knew she was tough and ready to fight, so I offered her the opportunity to make a prime-time impression on the skeptics by leading off the
hearings on flammable fabrics. That worked. The hearing room was packed
with media. Her statement was fierce in support of action. All we needed
next was the added power of authentic voices representative of the victims
of burn injuries.

The first of these was Peter Hackes, a nationally prominent NBC news
correspondent who had privately approached us with a personal story: his
daughter Carole had been severely burned when her pajamas caught on
fire. When he took the charred remains of the pajamas to the FTC, which
had no specific jurisdiction over flammable fabrics but broad power to investigate and mandate sanctions on abusive marketing practices, he was
told, he testified, "that the cotton fabric from which it was made lies within
the burning-time standards." He added, "Nothing, in other words, could
be done under the existing law to prevent another Carole . . . from having
to undergo the same torture from a burn caused by the same or similar
fabric."[8] His testimony was deeply moving.

Hackes was succeeded at the witness table by Bergman, who described
the horror of seeing burn injuries to small children. One infant he had
treated was so badly burned, he told the committee, he had "prayed for
her to die."[9]

Magnuson's outrage erupted during the hearing in his examination of
William M. Segall, representing the National Cotton Council. Under the
original Flammable Fabrics Act, the responsibility of developing inflam-
mable sleepwear was delegated to an industry committee. Segall was chairman of that committee, the Committee on Clothing Flammability of the
American Association of Textile Chemists and Colorists.

Segall entered into a technical discussion of why the industry committee had made no progress after seven years in developing a flammability standard. When it turned into an obfuscating technical explanation, Magnuson intervened:

> The CHAIRMAN. . . . It is hard to understand that it would take that
>     long to be able to find something that would burn the fabric to
>     determine whether or not it was flammable.
> Mr. SEGALL. The problem is—
> The CHAIRMAN. We had some tests here the other day that took
>     us about 5 minutes and we could find out whether they were
>     flammable.
> Mr. SEGALL. The problem is, Mister Chairmen, not in
>     determining . . .
> The CHAIRMAN. Isn't it a problem of everybody dragging their heels
>     in this whole field?
> Mr. SEGALL. No sir. No sir, it was not.
> The CHAIRMAN. Well, I think it is.[10]

That did it. By July 25, the Senate Commerce Committee voted to report the bill to the floor with the unanimous recommendation that it "do pass." The Senate did so by voice vote. The House Commerce Committee—acutely aware of the public outrage generated by our hearings—reported the bill out with a set of weakening amendments, and the full House went along. But Magnuson again chaired the Senate-House conference committee and the conferees agreed on a bill that was essentially the Senate's version.

On December 14, 1967, at a White House ceremony, President Johnson signed the Flammable Fabrics Act Amendments of 1967, praising Magnuson but also, stretching the truth, praising Congress for passing another of his own consumer protection bills. Though the credits were shared, Washington State voters would hear mostly about another Magnuson triumph.

### A Product Safety Commission
In his January 16 statement on the Senate floor, Magnuson, as promised in the closing days of 1966, had announced that he would again introduce the bill to create a national investigative commission on product safety. By the time Johnson proposed the creation of a similar study commission in his consumer protection message, Magnuson had already, on February 8, introduced Senate Joint Resolution 33 (the equivalent of a law-making

bill), this time with the co-sponsorship of Senator Cotton, the committee's ranking Republican member. The joint resolution easily passed the Senate on June 6, 1967. In the previous session of Congress, the House Commerce Committee had blocked creation of the study commission, but that committee had begun to show a sprouting of consumer protection sensitivity.

In no small part, this sprouting was due to the ascendancy of a relatively moderate Democratic chairman of the House Commerce Committee, Harley Staggers of West Virginia. Simultaneously rising in seniority through the lobby-enchanted membership of the House committee was the forceful public interest advocate John Moss of liberal Sacramento. Later, as Moss's seniority and his impact on the reformation of the House Commerce Committee took hold, he and his intrepid lone Bumblebee, Michael Lemov, would become our partners in moving strong legislation through the House. For now it was enough that Moss had persuaded the otherwise cautious Staggers to sponsor in the House the counterpart to the Magnuson bill authorizing the creation of the Consumer Product Safety Commission.

At least equally important, the ranking Republican member of the House committee, Jim Broyhill of North Carolina, though conservative, had an open mind on safety regulation. He did not oppose the resolution. The less scrupulous Republican and Democratic members of the committee, however, did oppose its enactment with the lobbyists' contention that it was unnecessary government involvement in the marketplace. After considerable internal committee jousting, the joint resolution was reported out of the committee undamaged and passed in the House—but only when the Democratic House Speaker, John McCormick, outraged at the lobbyist-generated opposition, signified his displeasure with his renegade Democratic members by leaving the Speaker's chair to vote for the resolution. It was rapidly agreed on in conference, and Johnson signed it on November 20, 1967.

The national media were beginning to notice the new Magnuson. Respectful profiles appeared in publications as polar as the *Wall Street Journal* and the *Washington [State] Teamster*. Some went further, portraying a near saintly Magnuson. Though Jerry and I were gratified, we could not help feeling a little guilty about such exaggerated idolization. Jerry told me that *Public Affairs Profile*, now extinct, the employee publication for the Pacific Northwest Bell telephone monopoly, had noted that Magnuson had stood up to the larger industries in the country, "not because he dislikes big business but because he feels a strong need to protect the citizenry when he feels business is not doing it."

Jerry also reported that the state's leading newspaper, Hearst's *Seattle Post-Intelligencer*, which had not always been kind to Magnuson, had written: "He cares about people; just people. When something like 'truth-in-packaging' comes along, Magnuson sits in his office, and way back, somewhere in his mind, he pictures a housewife out in the sticks in some supermarket. And he thinks to himself, 'Why the hell shouldn't she know just how much is really in that package?' That's what really turns him on."

The next day, I received a brief note from Califano, which I savored: "The President, incidentally, . . . asked whether the January 16 speech of the Senator resulted from leaks by us to you, or, conversely, whether we here on the staff were so unimaginative that we had to crib from Maggie's programs to put together the Consumer Message."[11]

### *Paving the Road to Comprehensive Product Safety Regulation*

Passage of the joint resolution had served its political purpose by contributing to Jerry's goal of remaking Magnuson into the consumer's advocate in time to enhance his reelection appeal. Though the formation and work of the National Commission on Product Safety would stretch on for several years beyond the election, the resolution seeded the soil on which would grow national pressure for comprehensive product safety control legislation.

That a mere study commission would achieve this goal was not at all certain. Study commissions were notorious. They tended to be the refuge of legislators beset by constituent complaints they would rather not deal with, and too often the studies and reports they generated many years later were shelved unread and unheeded while public attention had long since turned to other issues.

To avoid these pitfalls, we had structured the joint resolution to give Congress a major role in nominating the commissioners so we could ensure that its members exhibited inquisitorial determination (and a flair for shocking publicity). As members of a temporary commission, nominees would not be required to relinquish their private roles. The president held the ultimate power to name the commissioners, so we worked closely with Califano and Levinson. Despite our not-always-friendly competition, Califano and Levinson cared about the effectiveness of the commission, as they did about the other consumer bills they had persuaded the president to campaign for. They encouraged me to interview the proposed commission chairman, a leading New York City Democratic trial lawyer named Arnold Elkin. A stereotypical New York lawyer, Elkin had a track record of aggressively challenging corporate malpractice and a flair for the dramatic. I met with Elkin and was at once impressed by the strength of his commitment to achieve exactly what we sought. We soon formed a trusting relationship.

The other members proposed by the administration included three majority Democrats (in addition to Elkin) and three minority Republicans. One of the three Democrats represented organized labor; the second, consumer advocates. I was the third. Two of the Republicans were product safety research laboratory directors, faithful to the public interest. The third was a senior executive with the largest retailer in the United States, Sears Roebuck. His primary interest was to ensure that the manifold assortments of products produced by the company's industrial suppliers would be safe. I found nothing in that to trouble us. The appointment of a working congressional staff member was unorthodox, but I felt we still needed an inside monitor to ensure that the commission did its job. I had made this argument to Magnuson and he approved. The White House was not inclined to ruffle Magnuson.

The embarrassing truth, however, is that after the commission members had been safely appointed and throughout their service, I had little to contribute other than to support Elkin's leadership. But I did have an indirect impact on the strength of the commission by helping Elkin recruit a large team of entrepreneurial staff to do the investigative work and develop hearings that would be substantive and newsworthy in order to set the stage for comprehensive hazardous product regulation. Most critical would be the recruitment of the commission's general counsel.

For that job, I turned to Michael Lemov, a neighbor whom I had come to respect. Lemov had been a trial lawyer in New York City and had spent the past two years in routine, uninspiring litigation as a trial lawyer in the civil division of the Department of Justice. Though he would team up with us later, as staff for Representative Moss in the House, at the time he was restless in his ambition to achieve something of broad service to the public interest. I invited him—though that was not my prerogative—to serve as general counsel of the new commission. Dubious about his qualifications for so demanding a position and worried about his preparedness for his initial interview with Elkin, Lemov plunged into a study of the public health concerns behind the formation of the commission.

He needn't have worried. Elkin asked no questions. He simply welcomed him saying, "I understand Senator Magnuson wants you to be the general counsel." Elkin was impressed with Lemov, though the quickness of his decision suggested that he believed my request was made on behalf of the chairman. I did not disabuse him.

Lemov proceeded to recruit an aggressive commission staff team, who, like him, read the commission's mandate broadly. With the support of Lemov and his team, Elkin organized dramatic hearings throughout the country. Each hearing opened with the testimony of a victim of an unsafe product or a member of his or her family. Whenever possible, the witness would be a local citizen or a national celebrity, drawing maximum media coverage and the consequent attention of members of Congress in that district.

As Lemov recalls, the commission heard testimony in Los Angeles from a permanently paralyzed man in a wheelchair who had struck his head on the bottom of an unmarked, sloped swimming pool. "The press cameras clicked." Elsewhere the commission heard from a couple who had bought a vaporizer advertised as tip proof, foolproof, and safe. It bore the Good Housekeeping Seal of Approval and Underwriters Laboratories seal. When it was plugged into a wall outlet and steaming, their three-year-old daughter caught her leg in the electric cord. The vaporizer tipped over, spilling scalding water over the child. She spent five months in the hospital, where she endured a series of painful skin grafts and bore scars for the rest of her life.

In Peoria, Illinois, the commission learned about a toddler who had swallowed about three tablespoons of Old English furniture polish during a few moments when the bottle was left unguarded. The polish had a pleasant odor and the bottle had no safety cap or warning of the fatal risk of ingestion. The petroleum distillates from the polish collected in the child's lungs, and he died forty hours later from chemical poisoning.

After hearing testimony in Chicago from a fourteen-year-old girl who had been blinded in one eye because of a glass soda bottle that exploded, the consumer commission recommended that the government mandate improved quality control and design standards. The FTC had already studied the question of exploding glass bottles for three years before deciding to refer the matter to the Interstate Commerce Commission, which concluded that the voluntary efforts of the bottling industry "were adequate," despite reports of five to seven thousand injuries a year. The commission also heard testimony about a poorly designed football helmet that had resulted in a severe concussion during a tackle, and about injuries in the home from glass doors, lead paint, and unvented gas heaters.

The commission hearings gained extraordinary local and national media coverage. The *Washington Post* dispatched Morton Mintz to cover all the hearings, ensuring that Congress and the White House were confronted morning after morning with the commission's chilling testimony. The hearings would continue for two years. The commission's report to Congress was delivered in 1970. As we had hoped, and as we shall see in a later chapter, the temporary investigative commission had laid the groundwork for the later enactment of a law creating a permanent product safety commission.

# 6

# *Jerry's Juggernaut*

Despite Magnuson's consumer successes in the 89th Congress and our jump-start on consumer protection bills in the 90th Congress, and despite the favorable publicity Magnuson's consumer efforts had garnered in Washington State, Jerry still worried that we had not yet done enough. In August 1967 he ordered a poll in Washington State to measure prospective voters' awareness of Magnuson's consumer protection initiatives.

As Jerry feared, the poll showed no increase in voter support for Magnuson. Worse, his support among women, whom Jerry had considered a promising target for the consumer protection message, had dropped to 43 percent compared with Governor Daniel Evans's 57 percent. For Jerry, the poll results meant ramping up Magnuson's consumer protection output, so he urged Magnuson to make more speeches himself and to encourage his wife, Jermaine, to take her popular presentations to more women's groups. He also recommended that we commission a ghostwritten consumer protection manifesto that would be published under Magnuson's name.

We were nearly blocked, however, by Magnuson himself. Fearing he would not agree, Jerry had never told Magnuson about his grand strategy for a broad reelection campaign based primarily on consumer protection. Instead, we had continued to approach him for approval bill by bill. Though sometimes grudgingly, he eventually went along with every consumer bill we proposed. As early as June 1965, however, after dutifully introducing six consumer bills, he had asked, "Aren't we beating the consumer issue to death?" Then, just as his image was beginning to shift into what Jerry believed was essential to his reelection, Magnuson told Jerry and me to "cool off for a while" on consumer protection bills. No doubt, he was hearing complaints from his corporate friends and advisers.

Drastic measures were called for, and Jerry and I agreed on an aggressive strategy. Drawing on Jerry's insights into Magnuson's psyche, a month earlier I had written a memo to Jerry and Magnuson's old and trusted former administrative assistant, Irv Hoff, who was still in our corner. I had pointed out that whereas two or three years earlier Magnuson's name rarely appeared in the *Washington Post*, the recent increased activity "in the consumer field" had led to "the gradual growth of strong credibility among the knowledgeable Washington press corps." It had also produced "a strong sense of excitement and loyalty to Magnuson" among the committee staff, allowing it "to attract and keep able, young lawyers." Furthermore, Magnuson "has been identified as a leader, an innovator, and an initiator in the public interest. With Senators Hubert Humphrey and Estes Kefauver gone, to some extent Magnuson has become the man to whom 'the little man' looks for championing fair play against big business and big government."

With all the hyperbole I could summon in citing Magnuson's leadership on the issue of cigarette package labeling, my memo warned that because public memory is "notoriously short, even a brief period of silence and inaction will allow the fizz to escape the champagne. . . . Very soon Magnuson's obvious lack of follow-through on current public interest legislation will be apparent. Watch for articles headlined 'Magnuson's Ardor for Consumer Cooled?' and 'HEW and FTC Back Magnuson Bill He No Longer Wants.'" To ensure that I would capture Magnuson's attention, I added, "The office and Committee staffs will lose both their enthusiasm and their sense of identity with their leader."

Hoff took the memo to Magnuson and urged him to take it seriously. From that time on through the 1968 election, Magnuson's far more frequent Washington State speeches cited consumer abuses that needed regulatory prevention, including glass doors, flammable fabrics, televisions (radiation hazards), dolls (attachable and indigestible legs and arms), "accordion" telephone cords (by which children could be hanged), drug bottles (easily opened by children), detergents (highly caustic), hairspray cans (highly explosive), and home appliances (which caused a thousand electrocutions a year and in some instances trapped children inside).[1]

Jermaine Magnuson took to the road, meeting and talking with women's groups in the smaller towns in which Magnuson faired least well in the polling and where women voters were least aware of his consumer advocacy. She proved very effective among her audiences and gained priceless coverage in the local papers and on popular local radio stations. She became a popular speaker, especially among women in parts of Washington State that historically had not been in Magnuson's camp. They saw her advocacy of Magnuson's consumer protection efforts as the housewives' salvation, and along with her popularity, Magnuson's political stock rose.

With Ralph Nader's help, I found a writer sympathetic and knowledge-able about consumer issues and willing to write a book for Magnuson, Jean Carper. Prentice-Hall published *The Dark Side of the Marketplace: The Plight of the American Consumer* in 1968. It was an unalloyed exposé of a wide range of consumer abuses yet to be brought under control. Magnu-son skimmed its pages and gave his tepid approval. To avoid engaging in consumer deception himself, we added Carper's name as co-author, though Magnuson's name came first. The book rang tough enough that Consum-ers Union requested and was readily granted permission to publish forty thousand copies of its own paperback edition. Jerry recalls that the book and Washington State media coverage of the book significantly boosted Magnuson's identity as the consumer's champion.

In an earlier chapter, I quote Jerry as citing Magnuson's "guile." Jerry, himself, was hardly lacking in guile. In that same interview, he confessed to me something that he had never told anyone, including Irv Hoff: Jerry had known for certain as far back as 1966 that Governor Evans would not run for Senate. One of Evans's two closest political advisers, who had also become a trusted friend of Jerry's, had told him. He kept this information to himself he told me, because he was convinced that Magnuson was still in trouble with Washington voters, whether Evans ran or not. Keeping Magnuson and the rest of us wired up to continue to campaign remained essential. Thus I tell the preceding story as the rest of us experienced it.

### It's All Over, but It Isn't

Like most corporate interests today, in the 1960s the Boeing Company—Washington State's premier employer—leaned heavily toward the Repub-licans and secretly financed polling for the state's Republican Party. But Magnuson and Jerry had developed civil personal relationships with key people in the Boeing hierarchy. Thus, in the fall of 1967, after reviewing a new poll they had funded that matched Evans's chances against Magnuson, a Boeing friend leaked a copy to Magnuson's office. It came only a month after the release of the Magnuson campaign poll that had discouraged Jerry, but it painted an entirely different picture of the chances of an Evans campaign. It showed Magnuson defeating Evans for the Senate by more than a 2-to-1 margin, with only 9 percent of the voters undecided. The poll was also leaked to the Seattle papers, whereupon Magnuson's crushing lead became front-page news across the state. Whether or not the poll was accurate, its effect was to undermine any potential Republican Party leader's cries for an Evans run. On November 6, 1967, the *Seattle Post-Intelligencer* reported that Governor Evans "today announced that he will not be a candidate for the United States Senate in 1968."

Jerry did not believe the Boeing poll—his own pollster found that it was deeply flawed and grossly underestimated Evans's strength. Our political work was not done; Magnuson could still be vulnerable to a lesser candidate, as he had been vulnerable to a political novice in 1962. We didn't stop or even slow down, and Magnuson continued to introduce one consumer protection bill after another right up to the 1968 election. In all, Magnuson introduced fifteen consumer protection bills in the 90th Congress, all of which were enacted in one form or another in that Congress or later. Most received attention in the Washington State media when they were introduced.

The titles of the acts (mostly dreamed up by the Bumblebees) and the issues they covered highlight an energized Magnuson defending the public against corporate preying on consumers.

> Flammable Fabrics Act Amendments of 1967
> Auto Insurance Study (1968)
> Deceptive Sales Act (1968)
> Electric Power Reliability Act (1968)
> Fire Research and Safety Act (1968)
> Natural Gas Pipeline Safety Act (1968)
> Recreational Boat Safety Act (1968)
> Unfair Practices in the Home Improvement
>     Industry Report (1968)
> Complement to Deceptive Sales Act (1969)
> Public Health Cigarette Smoking Act of 1969
> Wholesome Fish and Fishery Products Act (1969)
> Fair Credit Reporting Act (1970)
> Federal Railroad Safety Act (1970)
> Consumer Product Safety Act (1972)
> Magnuson-Moss Warranty–Federal Trade
>     Commission Improvement Act (1975)

## The Last Imaginary Commnist Plot
## to Conquer Capitalism

Many but not all of the consumer protection bills Magnuson had introduced were passed during the 1968 legislative session. One bill was squashed by a lobbying tactic I could not have foreseen. It was a bill that Magnuson had taken to heart: the proposed Door-to-Door Sales Act. This bill sought to protect consumers against high-pressure, artful persuasion by door-to-door salespeople trained to pitch fabricated, heartbreaking stories. They would prey on the soft hearts of unwary householders, who responded to the insistent door knocks and came away with their signature on a contract for something they neither needed nor wanted.

Particularly notorious were aggressive sales managers for magazine subscriptions, who would organize and train teams of young people, then travel with them in small groups from town to town. The young people were encouraged to pose as penniless but eager students desperately work-ing their way up the economic ladder through school. Because they were dependent on these managers, the young people were effectively held cap-tive. Their desperation was genuine; their tales most often were not. The bill would provide a twenty-four-hour "cooling off" period, during which the subscriber could reflect and reconsider, read the small print, and cancel the contract.

This time, President Johnson's consumer watchdogs seized the lead and sent their own door-to-door sales bill to Congress. Dispensing with his instinctive resistance to any new idea, Magnuson relished introducing this bill under his own name as the chairman of the committee with jurisdic-tion. He never mentioned the president in his introductory statement, but swallowed it up rhetorically as his own and boasted about it during the monthly talks he now gave (at Jerry's insistence) in Washington State.

One day, shortly thereafter, a very unhappy Magnuson called me into his office, pushed the editorial page of the *Washington Star* under my nose, and pointed to an editorial warmly endorsing Betty Furness's door-to-door sales bill. Furness continued to serve as Johnson's consumer adviser.

"Call Betty Furness," he growled, "and tell her to stop stealing credit for my bills!"

When the second session of the 90th Congress set to work in January 1968, we opened the door-to-door sales bill hearings, convinced the bill would slide through Congress unopposed. Our confidence was strength-ened when the first government witness, Paul Rand Dixon, chairman of the FTC, said to Magnuson, "[The FTC is] heartily endorsing and warmly supporting your bill, Mr. Chairman."

Magnuson interrupted him. "It's not my bill," he said. "It's the administration's bill."

I was stunned. Why would Magnuson disavow authorship of his favorite bill? My confusion only deepened a few days later when I popped into his office to discuss the day's business and he greeted me by asking, "Mike, have you ever been a Communist?"

"No," I said. "Why?"

Magnuson shifted around in his chair uncomfortably and began to explain, haltingly. "A couple of people from the Hearst organization came to see me. And they claim that our consumer protection work is Communist inspired—and they are not too sure that you aren't a Communist agent."

My smartass response was to suggest that surely the notorious international Communist strategic engine, the Comintern, had been meeting in Moscow to plot the downfall of capitalism and had seized on the Door-to-Door Sales Act as the engine of capitalist destruction. Magnuson was not amused.

"Well," he said, "they tell me that Consumers Union was identified by the House Un-American Activities Committee as a Communist front and that you work closely with them."

"If I'm in trouble for being involved with Consumers Union," I replied, refusing to take him seriously, "so are you. Next month, Consumers Union is going to print forty thousand copies of their own edition of your book."

Magnuson was not happy, so I soberly added what I thought would be proof positive that I was no Communist: I told him I had worked with two FBI agents over the past several years to report on contacts I had in the Soviet embassy.

My claim was technically true. The full story, however, was less dramatic. A few years earlier, while working for Senator Neuberger, I had attended a cultural event at the Soviet embassy to which Neuberger had been invited. She detested such meaningless ceremonial events, and I was intrigued to take her place and intrigued too by the exotic prospect of getting to know a Communist apparatchik. One of the Communists I met there was the Romanian assistant secretary, with whom I had lunch a couple of times during the next few weeks. He was smitten with Americans, and we always talked about American and Romanian culture.

A few weeks later, a close friend working in the State Department called me and, in hushed tones, told me that the FBI had taken photos of me entering the Soviet embassy. He advised me that it would be prudent for me to give a call to the local FBI office and offer any help I could give them in monitoring the Communist operatives.

I thought this idea was ridiculous. I had gone to that embassy for another diplomatic event Neuberger had shunned. Furthermore, by 1968, red-baiting McCarthyism, and Senator Joseph McCarthy himself, were dead. Still, my friend's call intimidated me. Though I was ashamed to collaborate in a process I despised, I made the call. Two FBI agents were assigned to visit my office periodically to glean from me any worthwhile intelligence I had gathered. Whenever they visited me, I faithfully reported to them that I had not heard from or recently visited my Romanian friend and that the one or two times that I actually had lunch with him again, he neither gave me any information nor asked me for any information that would interest them. Yet the agents, with whom I became quite friendly talking about sports and other trivia, continued to visit every couple of months. I finally concluded that they were bored hanging around the FBI office and enjoyed the visits to Capitol Hill. Nothing came of nothing.

I told Magnuson no details, only that I had worked closely with the FBI for several years. My admission seemed to satisfy him. He never brought up the question again, and our working relationship remained serene. He was evidently confident that I was not a Communist spy.

He was less sanguine, however, about the Hearst threats. Hearings had been completed on the door-to-door sales bill, and it was ready for action by the full committee. But Magnuson never got around to scheduling it for action. Only recently, forty years after the fact, when I asked Jerry about these events, did I learn why Magnuson lost interest in the bill.

Jerry told me that as soon as I had left Magnuson's office, content that I had quieted his concerns, he had called Jerry into his office and asked him anxiously, "Has Mike gone too far?"

Jerry reacted with the same skepticism I had. He responded, "Look, I can understand about the election, and we don't want to piss off the paper. On the other hand, all that Communism stuff is bullshit. We haven't got any Communists here."

Jerry had been weighted down, however, with a more serious threat. Shortly before the Hearst team had asked for the meeting with Magnuson, Jerry had had an uglier confrontation with their determination to force Magnuson to kill the door-to-door sales bill. The senior editor of the *Seattle Post-Intelligencer* had visited Jerry and charged that the bill was inconsistent with the First Amendment and that it was a Communist plot to suppress the press. Furthermore, he asserted without evidence that Magnuson had been having an affair during his vacation in Reno, Nevada, with a woman who either was or was to become Hearst's wife. The editor threatened to tell Hearst to poison his mind against Magnuson.

"This guy," Jerry remembers thinking, "is really a bully, a brutal bully."

William Randolph Hearst was the owner and publisher of the *Seattle Post-Intelligencer*, one of only two papers that circulated statewide, and the only morning paper in Washington State. Though notoriously conservative, Hearst had made exceptions in the past to support Magnuson. Magnuson's campaign needed that support.

Meanwhile, we had structured committee hearings on the door-to-door sales bill to bring out the most glaring examples of deception and intimidation unscrupulous salespeople used against often poor and unsophisticated consumers. We succeeded. The bill was ready to be considered by the full committee. But Magnuson wasn't. The bill died.

### Sweet (though Unintended) Revenge

One day in the next session of Congress, the 91st, Magnuson summoned me by telephone with an urgent request. He had just left the floor of the Senate on a brief break. A major postal reform bill was under final consideration.

"Bring me an amendment to stop this practice of billing for unordered stuff!" he growled.

I knew Magnuson had become increasingly annoyed by the magazines that arrived in his mail that he had not subscribed to and did not want. He threw them out. Yet every month he received bills demanding payment. He threw those out too. By the time he called me in, he was outraged.

I happened to have sitting on my desk for leisurely review a draft regulatory rule the FTC was contemplating to ban just this practice. I took a quick look at it, crossed out the word "Rule" in the title and replaced it with "Amendment," then ran it over to Magnuson, who was waiting on the Senate floor.

The Senate and House had each passed their versions of the postal reform bill. They had met in conference and agreed on all its details. As I arrived, the Senate floor leaders were concluding a desultory debate, with no opposition in sight. They were ready for the final vote. Magnuson stood up and mumbled something about a simple amendment, handed the paper to the Senate clerk, and asked for unanimous consent that the reading of the amendment be waived and the amendment be adopted by voice vote. The floor leaders for the bill that day, probably tired and ready to go home, must have trusted Magnuson not to do anything crazy. There was no opposition. The amendment was incorporated in the final bill. No objections were raised in the House—most likely because no one knew what was lurking within the final bill. Off it went for the president's signature.

Since that time, anyone who receives anything in the mail that he or she hasn't ordered has three options under the postal laws: (1) send it back unopened, sticking the offending merchant with double postage, (2) throw it out, accruing no financial obligation, or (3) enjoy it as a "gift." For Magnuson, there were no flashy press releases and no media coverage, just the satisfaction of a wrong righted. Jerry insists that Magnuson, in pursuing this amendment, had given no thought to the fact that Hearst, whose door-to-door marketing of its magazines was among the most aggressive and deceptive, would be straitjacketed by this law.

### It Ain't Over till It's Over—Except When It's Already Over

To a political novice like me, the campaign was effectively over: the most serious threat to Magnuson had been Governor Evans's potential challenge. The Republican establishment, convinced by Boeing's poll results, believed that Magnuson was unbeatable. Furthermore, Magnuson had a huge financial cushion. In November 1967, Jerry had organized a hundred-dollar-a-plate "appreciation" dinner designed to build the campaign treasury high enough to fund the massive advertising and communication strategies he planned to ensure Magnuson's reelection.

The dinner yielded an avalanche of contributions. At the time it was almost certainly among the largest recorded hundred-dollar-a-plate fundraising dinners in the history of US politics. Twenty-three hundred paying guests showed up, overflowing the grand Olympic Hotel ballroom and packing the lobby. More impressive—and reassuring to Jerry—were the contributions of twenty-five hundred ticket holders who never even showed up. Heavily represented among them was Magnuson's long-term base of corporate executives and other well-heeled friends. Jerry was relieved that his consumer protection crusade had not alienated them, but he saw to it that the breadth of Magnuson's contributions among business interests was not public knowledge. He disingenuously spread to the media the message, "Magnuson knows his consumer activity will cost him campaign contributions."

The flood of campaign funding was heartening, but Jerry had his own polls, and they were far grimmer than the ones that had driven Evans out of the race. His pollster had concluded that the voters were increasingly "anti-Democratic, anti-incumbent, and anti-age." The pollster's data were reinforced by a troubling pattern of defeat among Democratic incumbents in early 1968 Senate primaries in other states. Most frustrating of all, this polling consistently revealed that Magnuson's image—aging, irrelevant—had barely budged since the 1962 election, when Magnuson had almost lost to the sacrificial Republican candidate. Unless his image was changed to that of consumer champion in the minds of a far greater proportion of voters, Magnuson was at risk against even a weak Republican opponent.

Meanwhile, the Republican establishment had settled on a just such a candidate: Jack Metcalf, a little-known novice Republican state senator from a small Washington town. Metcalf had been greatly encouraged by tête-à-têtes with Magnuson's previous foe, the Reverend Richard G. Christensen, who assured him that the aging Magnuson was even more beatable than he had been when Christensen nearly beat him 1962. Metcalf was also cheered by the knowledge that Magnuson was closely identified with the increasingly unpopular President Johnson and that polls now showed 1968 was sure to be a strong Republican election across the board. For these reasons, Jerry set about constructing an overpowering advertising campaign. He began by hiring the Madison Avenue agency Lois Holland Calloway.

In April 1968, two of the partners, George Lois and Ron Holland, met Jerry and me in Washington. We laid out Magnuson's consumer protection record over the past six years and gave them a pile of glowing newspaper articles, editorials, and columns. Jerry also showed them his own polls. Lois and Holland were intrigued and returned to New York to come up with a campaign advertising strategy proposal.

By early June they were ready. I joined Jerry in the Magnusons' apartment home in the Shoreham Hotel's elegant annex one Sunday morning for the unveiling of what Lois and his partners had developed. Magnuson greeted us at the door clad in his usual Sunday morning attire, a bathrobe barely covering his protruding belly.

Lois Holland Calloway's challenge was to gain Magnuson's buy-in to a most unconventional campaign for a most conventional politician. Using a folding easel they called their "dummy board," Lois flipped through a series of posters, each filled with a brief, hand-written sentence highlighting one of Magnuson's consumer protection laws: "There's a law that forces tire manufacturers to prove their tires are safe. Senator Magnuson's Law!"; "There's a law that protects kids from poisonous paint on toys. Senator Magnuson's Law!" Four others with similar wording followed. At the bottom of each poster was their proposed campaign tagline: "Keep the big boys honest. Let's keep Maggie in the Senate."

Their plan was to launch dozens of billboards throughout the state. Every day one of six different Magnuson laws would appear. It was exactly what we needed. Jerry and I loved it. Magnuson was troubled. As noted earlier, Jerry had never briefed Magnuson directly that his plan as campaign manager was to build and then exploit Magnuson's record as the consumer's champion. He had relied on our persuading him, step-by-step, that each bill we came up with was good and popular. When Lois finished his presentation, Maggie said, "I like it. But how come it's all on consumers? This is not what people are concerned with. That's not what they're thinking about. How about something like education and civil rights and 'Veetnam'?"

The irrepressible Lois looked straight at Magnuson and said, "You've done something big about Vietnam? I'll do something about it." Magnuson was silent. Then Lois challenged Magnuson with the same question about education and civil rights. No answer. Finally, Magnuson, one of the most conventional of political campaigners, grudgingly endorsed a campaign proposal that was revolutionary in political advertising. The Lois campaign was on.

Holland had scrawled the proposed texts by hand on the dummy board just to show what themes they were using. He and Lois explained that they would print the ads in orderly block letters. Jerry intervened. "Oh, no," he said. "You want to go with that script."

"I knew it would work," he later told me. And it did.

By the time the campaign was in full swing, three hundred billboards had been set up throughout the state. Lois Holland Calloway next designed full-page newspaper ads that scrolled through the torrent of Magnuson laws, always ending with the scrawled "Keep the big boys honest. Let's keep Maggie in the Senate."

They also wrote TV script that violated every rule of conventional political advertising. Each was to be filmed in the agency's New York City studio. Jerry and I would accompany him to keep the ad guys honest. So, on a Sunday morning in late summer, I took the train from Washington to New York with my nine-year-old daughter, Amy, who came with me as a lark. Jerry and I were enthralled by the unconventional concept and scripts. Magnuson, horrified at first, reluctantly agreed to participate in the filming.

The setting was simple. Magnuson, made-up, dressed, and coiffed as elegantly as possible, considering his age and physical deterioration, sits in front of the camera, responding with simple gestures while the voice-over challenges, "Senator Magnuson, there comes a time when every young senator shows that he's putting on years." (Maggie turns his hands palms up as if to say, "What can I do about it?") "Senator Magnuson, there comes a time—sure as fate—when once slim senators assume a less 'trim' figure." (Maggie glances ruefully at his belly.) "So, Senator, once youth is gone, once dash has gone, what can you possibly offer the voters of Washington?" (Magnuson hesitates for a moment; then taps his forehead with a sly expression— once, twice, three times.) The voice-over then intones, "In his rumpled suit, carrying twenty extra pounds, and showing some signs of wear, Warren Magnuson remains a giant in the United States Senate. Let's keep him there." The filming required many takes, but Magnuson seemed to enjoy acting his part, especially the triumphal tapping of his head with a knowing smile.

On the third day, we were scheduled to view the rough cuts and judge the final, edited version. Early that morning, when we gathered in Magnuson's hotel room to plan the day, Magnuson announced that he did not want to see the cuts, that the rest of us were to decide. Instead, to my utter surprise, he turned to me and said he'd like to take Amy on a little outing. Amy, who had barely met Magnuson, agreed to go. She even took the initiative: she said she needed a nice coat, despite it being a beautiful day in June.

Magnuson readily agreed, and the two of them set off for Bergdorf Goodman, then the temple of New York fashion, next door on Fifth Avenue. By midday, when our viewing was over and the ad approved, we returned to the hotel. I found Amy reading in her room. Hanging in the closet was an elegant white fake-fur coat with a matching muff.

With good humor, Magnuson told me that when they arrived at the young girls section at Bergdorf's, a saleswoman had asked Amy, "Is he your grandfather?" Without hesitation, she had answered yes and began looking at outrageously expensive coats. Then she spied the white coat and muff on display. She yearned for that coat. Magnuson, she told me, was "wonderfully kind and gentle." The coat and muff were hers.

As Jerry watched Magnuson's unimaginative opponent, Metcalf, exhaust his energy and financial resources rehashing tired themes from Magnuson's 1962 campaign, he kept the Lois campaign secret until Labor Day, just two months before the November election, in an effort to leave Metcalf too little time to retool his response. Meanwhile, the Bumblebees, who had taken unpaid leaves of absence to work on the campaign under Jerry's direction, gained access to what marketing people call "free media" or "unpaid media" (news stories) by continually churning out press releases highlighting the speeches Magnuson and Jermaine were making, targeted to the media in the cities and towns where they were speaking.

After the election, Metcalf admitted to Jerry, "Those first billboards hit us like a ton of bricks." He had never considered that Magnuson's consumer protection activities over the past six years would even be a part of his campaign. After they appeared, he had flailed out with weak responses, including the assertion that "true consumer protection" would occur only with his ability to create new jobs in Washington State. His mention of consumer protection, however, allowed Jerry's campaign team to disclose on Magnuson's behalf that Metcalf had voted against every consumer protection bill presented to the Washington State Senate throughout his service there.

As soon as the ads had begun to make their impression, bright green buttons and bumper stickers were distributed in the same bold hand-written strokes, truncated to resonate with the basic information about Magnuson's achievements implanted in voters' minds by the ads: "I'm a housewife. I'm for Maggie." And "I've got kids. I'm for Maggie." Later, they were even shorter, "Keep the big boys honest!" And, finally, simply, "Maggie."

A year earlier, in August 1967, Jerry's pollster had presented prospective voters with the statement, "I tend to admire Senator Magnuson because of the work he is doing to protect consumers." Among those polled, only 40 percent agreed with the statement, 20 percent disagreed, and 40 percent said they were "not sure." Just before Election Day, a follow-up poll was run, using the same statement. By then, Jerry had activated all the elements of his campaign to bring Magnuson's consumer protection achievements to public attention, but he withheld Lois's striking—but potentially risky— ads playing on Magnuson's aging and physical deterioration. When he saw the results of the new poll, he knew that they weren't necessary.

### Price Is Right

Lois's campaign reinforced Magnuson's extraordinary consumer protection achievements in the minds of voters. But Magnuson's transformation had been launched by Jerry three years before the reelection campaign. He had pursued it relentlessly, despite Magnuson's reluctance. It is unlikely that any of the multitude of consumer protection laws Magnuson authored would have been enacted without Jerry's driving force and strategic direction. Or that, in the face of the potent opposition from the affected industries and the most influential lobbyists of that time, they would have retained their strength unimpaired. Without Jerry's vision, the popular governor, Evans, would have challenged a politically weakened Magnuson and most likely defeated him.

Jerry's method was to transform the staff of the Senate Commerce Committee from inert time servers into a team of entrepreneurial staff, driven by their commitment to the substance of their legislative goals and their commitment to Magnuson. Jerry's success offers strong support for David Price's thesis that the public interest is best served in the Senate by entrepreneurial staff fully attuned to the political needs of the senators they serve.

This was Jerry's gift to Magnuson and to the country. But credit too goes to Magnuson. Three times he tapped his head in Lois's commercial. The first tap signified his legislative power, the second his legislative skills and legerdemain, and the third his legislative prowess, which he exercised to finish the job on almost every bill bearing his name.

# PART II

OVERLEAF: This photograph, unique in many ways, was taken by a congressional photographer on December 17, 1974. It is a portrait of the Senate Commerce Committee in "closed session," meaning secret, including no photographs. The Senate historian told us that no other such photographs still exist in the library. This picture was taken in violation of the rule in order to honor a special occasion: the last committee session before the close of that Congress—the last committee meeting that Senator Norris Cotton, the ranking Republican committee member, would attend before his retirement. Following tradition, Chairman Magnuson and Senator Cotton are sitting at the head of the table. For this occasion, however, Magnuson, at Cotton's right, is relinquishing his authority as majority committee chairman to Cotton.

The scheduled business of the committee was the markup of a minor, noncontroversial bill. But Magnuson and almost all the other committee members were in attendance for the planned celebration of the shared comity and respect for Senator Cotton. Six committee staff members were also in attendance. Two of them were Bumblebees whose stories appear in the book. Tom Allison, standing behind Magnuson, was the staff member in charge of managing the bill. Ed Merlis, sitting at Allison's right, was assisting him. Fred Lordan, a senior staff member whose story also appears in the book, is sitting at Allison's left. The Republican and Democratic staff directors, Arthur Pankopf and I (wearing glasses), are standing together to the side, smiling most likely in appreciation of our bosses' mutual affection. Photo courtesy of the US Senate Historical Office.

# 7

# Colonizing the Bumblebees

As early as 1966, Jerry was already planning for his successor. He had laid the foundation by transforming the Commerce Committee into a consumer protection juggernaut. His first priority, however, was to lead Magnuson's campaign for reelection in November 1968. To take formal control of the campaign, in compliance with Senate rules, Jerry would have to relinquish his direction of the committee. Since he was free to campaign as a member of a senator's personal office staff, he moved to Magnuson's office as his top staffer, his administrative assistant. There he was able to manage the campaign openly and still informally oversee the committee staff in ways that, while not overtly political, would advance Magnuson's campaign—as long as he could trust his replacement as committee staff director.

Jerry was a resolute planner but he was inclined to keep some of his plans to himself. One of those plans was to test whether I was capable of succeeding him as staff director of the committee in 1967 when he took charge of the campaign. Assuming his role on the committee was the furthest thing from my mind. Thus, only now do I understand why Jerry arranged for me to join him and Magnuson on a diplomatic trip to Russia in 1966. Even though I had no useful role to play in supporting Magnuson in the tasks he was to perform there, Jerry needed to see how Magnuson and I would get along in close contact, so he seized on the opportunity to allow Magnuson and me to spend informal, concentrated time together away from Congress and Washington, DC.

In late 1966, Magnuson had been invited by the Johnson White House and the Commerce Department to play a modest diplomatic role in the warming of relations with the Soviet Union: the brief "détente." As a senator representing a state with a large economic stake in ocean shipping, and as chairman of the Senate committee with jurisdiction over shipping and related industries, Magnuson seemed a natural candidate to engage in these politically neutral discussions. The announced purpose of the trip to the Soviet Union was to engage in talks with that country about ways and means to protect salmon from high-seas overfishing. The principal villain was Japan, so part of the talks were to focus on what the United States and the Soviet Union could do together to reduce predation of a valuable resource. Magnuson was then to proceed to Bulgaria to participate in one of the first US trade shows in a communist country. Since I knew nothing about either ocean shipping or trade, I assumed Jerry had chosen me to come along as congenial company. I was puzzled by the invitation but delighted by the prospect of an adventure.

When we got to Moscow, members of the US embassy quickly took Magnuson and Jerry to a secure room attached to the main building but surrounded by a sound barrier designed to eliminate anyone's overhearing the briefing. There they told Magnuson and Jerry that the Russians were quite disturbed about US testing of high-level underwater explosives near that country's claimed territory. The Russians suspected the tests were done to prepare for an attack, though their objection focused on damage to fishery resources. The US position was that these were low-level tests that would not affect underwater life. As Jerry recalls, the briefer said, "Under no circumstance should this issue be discussed. If the Russians raise it, do not engage in a discussion. At most, say you will look into the allegation when you return to your country." The briefer also explained that a speaker should say two or three sentences, at most a paragraph, then wait for the translator to finish before going on. Magnuson nodded understanding of that guideline.

The official meeting the next morning with the Soviet minister of fisheries began with a cordial and warm introduction. Then it was Magnuson's turn to make an opening statement. He started by talking about the purpose of the meeting, then, completely forgetting the advice about speaking briefly to facilitate translation, he moved on to the interests of Washington State before laying out a case for the vulnerability of anadromous fish. The Russians appeared to be attentive while he rambled on. Then, to Jerry's horror, after about fifteen minutes, Magnuson turned to the explosive testing, explaining that he had been assured the tests would have no effect on Soviet fishery resources. After another five minutes, he suddenly realized that the process had gone off course and waved to the translator, who had been furiously taking notes, to go ahead and tell the other side what he had just finished saying. The lengthy retelling elicited alternate grimaces and smiles from the Russians. When the translator finished, the fisheries minister made a brief response, assuring the senator that he shared the concern about high-seas interception of US and Russian salmon but that the senator was misinformed about the explosive testing. Mercifully, the meeting concluded with the same cordiality that had marked its beginning.

"I've always wondered," Jerry told me recently, "what the US Department of State report on that meeting said. Probably something to the effect that a wild card had been played with manageable damage."

Manageable or not, this episode was a lesson for me about Magnuson. During the years I had worked for him, I had known Magnuson only as a formidable power in the Senate, comfortably authoritative with his colleagues. But I learned from this anxious performance that Magnuson felt insecure in unfamiliar environments, and I understood that I needed to be sensitive to this insecurity if I were ever to develop a close working relationship with him.

The required social events were stiffly routine. Beluga caviar had no allure for Magnuson, but the innumerable varieties of vodka did—especially the one flavored with a yellow herb that translated as "lemongrass" but that we called "lemon piss." With every mandatory toast to peace, we grew more at ease with each other. By the time we headed for the city of Plovdiv in Bulgaria, where Magnuson was to deliver a speech opening the trade show, Jerry and I, cherishing Magnuson's propensity for malaprops, began cautioning him not to confuse the name of one of his friends in Seattle, a dentist named Plotnick, with Plovdiv. We were certain that our surreptitious effort to plant the name "Plotnick" in his head would result in his garnishing his speech with "Plotnick." He knew exactly what we were up to and in delivering his blandly appropriate speech, he never slipped. By the time we returned to Washington, I had developed a genuine fondness for Magnuson that was to ripen into a comfortable intimacy that lasted for the nine years I served him and beyond.

By early 1968, Jerry had almost ensured that I would succeed him as Commerce Committee staff director. But there was an impediment in the path to this felicitous arrangement: the job of Magnuson's office administrative assistant was still occupied by Fred Lordan. Clinging to that seat and fueled by envy of Jerry's influence over Magnuson, Lordan missed no opportunity to pass along to Magnuson a stream of complaints from old Magnuson hands about everything Jerry and I were doing. Worse, Lordan would repeat fears from Magnuson's early political advisers that the direction Jerry was taking in the 1968 campaign was unnatural for Magnuson and doomed to lead to defeat. Though Magnuson's confidence in Jerry had gradually neutralized Lordan's influence, his loyalty to his old friends reinforced his chronic aversion to confrontation and stood in the way of his firing Lordan to make way for Jerry.

For support, Jerry turned again to Magnuson's most trustworthy friend and adviser, Irv Hoff, who, like many of Magnuson's old friends, had become a profitable lobbyist. Hoff was the chief lobbyist for the US domestic cane sugar refiners, who relied on government-imposed quotas to keep out cheap sugar from abroad. Unlike the others, however, Hoff put Magnuson's interest ahead of his employer's, and he fully supported Jerry's leadership. Agreeing that Magnuson would listen to straight talk from Hoff, he and Jerry hatched a plot. Hoff sat down alone with Magnuson and warned him that if he did not replace Lordan with Jerry, he would lose Jerry and throw his reelection into doubt. Though, he pointed out, Magnuson could be spared the pain of firing Lordan by offering him a face-saving exchange of titles that named Jerry administrative assistant and Lordan Commerce Committee staff director. Jerry had persuaded Magnuson to grant me the previously nonexistent Commerce Committee title "general counsel."

Lordan was placated; I was perplexed. Rhetorically impressive, this inventive title offered no clue about which of us, Lordan or me, would actually manage the committee's professional staff. Jerry had figured that out too. In a move that was a lesson in strategic staff geography for me, Jerry physically isolated Lordan from Magnuson. He arranged to burnish Lordan's long service to Magnuson by giving him a new and grand committee office to go with his new position. It was spacious, but it exiled him to a separate building that housed committee administrative staff. Jerry then placed me in the office he was vacating. It was modest, but right across the hall from Magnuson. Jerry had a new office adjoining Magnuson's, while Lordan's was a ten-minute walk away. To ensure Lordan's further inaccessibility to Magnuson, Jerry arranged with Magnuson's secretaries (no admirers of Lordan) to require that he make an appointment when he wanted to visit Magnuson. Jerry was then alerted to sit in on any such meeting or to drop in and disabuse Magnuson of any Lordan propaganda.

With Jerry available to join me whenever I needed support, I gradually assumed power over the Magnuson committee staff. Lordan never stopped complaining, but with no easy access to Magnuson, he gradually lost his influence over the chairman. He retired in 1973, and I became (in name as well as function) committee staff director and chief counsel.

Jerry came back to Washington after the election and continued to serve Magnuson as his administrative assistant until spring 1969, when he left to practice law in Seattle. He remained close to Magnuson and other Washington State political leaders and soon emerged as the informal Democratic political boss of the state.

Of course I was grateful to succeed Jerry, but could I do as well as Jerry without Jerry standing by? I could not imagine having the influence on Magnuson that Jerry had had. Nor could I see how the committee could produce as many new laws in the public interest as it had under Jerry.

The most formidable obstacle in our effort to challenge corporate lobbying power would be the new president, Richard Nixon. The consumer protection adviser Nixon had appointed, Virginia Knauer, was an active Republican campaigner and no consumer advocate. Her advocacy would be limited to calls for voluntary corporate self-regulation.

In his domestic policy, Nixon occupied a place slightly to the right of center—and the right at that time was considerably to the left of where it is today. What the books lauding Nixon's domestic policy fail to make clear, however, is the context in which he was operating and his role in the legislation for which he is so highly praised in hindsight. At the time, no one, including Nixon, thought of him as a liberal. Nixon was a pragmatist. He spoke of himself as a conservative who wanted smaller government, but he faced an activist Democratic Congress. If he wanted to avoid being a veto machine, he had to compromise with the Democrats, sometimes after a fight that he lost. He is therefore given credit for signing into law several bills to improve the environment, including one establishing the Environmental Protection Agency.

At Jerry's urging, I recently interviewed William Ruckelshaus, Nixon's appointment as the first head of the Environmental Protection Agency and a close friend of Jerry's. Ruckelshaus, a pained lapsed Republican, confirms our suspicion that Nixon was as determined a foe of aggressive regulatory legislation as he could get away with being. To illustrate, Ruckelshaus told me about a conversation he had had with John Whitaker when they were on a panel together talking about Nixon and the environment at a program in the Nixon Library commemorating the fortieth anniversary of Earth Day.

Whitaker, who was Nixon's deputy assistant for domestic affairs and, later, undersecretary of the interior, was always a big proponent of environmental policies in the White House. But he ran into a lot of resistance from the president. Whitaker told Ruckelshaus that one day about a year before Nixon died, Whitaker was in his office in New York and Nixon was with him, standing at a window looking out at the street below.

Nixon turned to Whitaker and said, "Well, John, you'll have to acknowledge that—we all have to acknowledge we did a lot of great things during our administration."

Seeing an opening, Whitaker had replied, "Yes, Mr. President, you'll go down as one of the greatest presidents in the history of the environment."

Nixon turned around, looked at Whitaker, and said, "God, I hope not, John."

Ruckelshaus elaborated:

Nixon really didn't care about the environment. He didn't know much about it. He'd never have campaigned on it. Nobody had ever asked him much about it when he ran for office. And all of a sudden this explosion of concern in the country about the environment took place. Nixon had no choice. He felt he had to respond to that. Otherwise, he would get into real trouble. That's the way democracy is supposed to work. He'd get back a bill he didn't really like very much, because it was so much—in his eyes—more extreme than what he had sent up there. But he then was faced with a dilemma of either vetoing something that looked like what he had introduced or signing something he didn't like. That increasingly bothered him. I think that what Nixon was doing was responding to public opinion.

A couple of years ago, I gave a talk to the Teddy Roosevelt Society. They asked me to [compare] Roosevelt with Nixon on the environment. I said, "The difference is that Roosevelt was way out in front of public opinion and Nixon was being dragged along by public opinion—even though they both had a remarkable record on the environment."

Nixon did have the good sense, however, to appoint the warm and witty Tom Korologos as the primary White House Senate lobbyist. I remember confronting Korologos in the corridor of what was then known as the Old Senate Office Building to express my outrage over some malfeasance from the Nixon administration. Korologos disarmed me. Lifting his hands in mock humility, he replied, "Republicans are just not fit to govern."

Lyndon Johnson had governed powerfully, with the support of Democratic majorities numbering more than two-thirds in both houses of Congress. In the 1968 elections, these majorities had narrowed. Worse, on regulatory issues Republicans were the natural allies of conservative southern Democrats. The confidence the liberals needed to pursue aggressive regulatory legislation was shaken, while the corporate lobbyists savored the new opportunities to derail all such efforts.

With a shrunken majority in the Senate, the Democratic majority in the committee had also shrunk. I was worried that after Magnuson's overwhelming reelection victory in 1968, without the fear generated by his shocking near defeat in 1962, the Magnuson of the 1950s and early 1960s would reemerge—the man more at home playing poker with his lobbyist friends than frustrating them. Would he again bury his New Deal brotherhood with workers? Would he abandon the cloak of consumer champion he had wrapped himself in, at Jerry's prodding, for reelection? Would the pre-1964 Magnuson reemerge, whose taste for wealth had led him to accept a little help from business titans?

An orphan who had grown up with financially stressed adoptive parents, Magnuson was not averse to easy money and readily accepted friendly offers of discounted investments from his corporate insider friends, including a substantial interest in a major television station in the Northwest. He had a close relationship with Frank Stanton, president of CBS, then the dominant television network, and, through the Commerce Committee's Communications Subcommittee, chaired by the like-minded Senator John O. Pastore of Rhode Island, he was attentive to broadcasters' wishes. We Bumblebees enjoyed the hospitality of lobbyists but kept our distance from their pleas, unlike Nicholas Zapple, the staff member in charge of communications matters, who demanded their largess. He even invited them to his daughter's wedding—a prime opportunity for lavish gifts.

Magnuson liked the feeling of having money in his pocket. During the 1968 campaign, when Magnuson resided in the Olympic Hotel in Seattle, Jerry had to race him to the front desk as soon as the day's mail arrived. If Magnuson got to the mail before Jerry did, he held the incoming letters to the light to see whether they contained small cash contributions. If they did, he pocketed them.

Harley Staggers, chairman of the House Commerce Committee since 1966, though a Democrat, was another obstacle to our efforts to pass laws in the public interest. Staggers shunned controversial bills with even more vigor than Magnuson, especially those opposed by lobbyists for the industries in question. He didn't fight the bills openly; he just saw to it that the committee did nothing to advance them, or he loaded them down with lobby-appeasing amendments that Magnuson could never accept. Staggers's strategy had derailed or weakened many of the aggressive regulatory bills Magnuson had passed through the Senate.

Unlike Jerry, who made sure that staff hires would be entrepreneurial, Staggers insisted on controlling all his committee's professional staff members to ensure that they would do nothing on their own to stimulate committee action. As Michael Lemov recalls: "This meant that if anyone was going to tangle with big business over safety regulation of consumer products . . . or any of the other consumer bills Magnuson was pumping out of the Senate Commerce, they would have to first get the permission of the resistant Staggers. Yet, if any staff member worked on such touchy issues without [Staggers's] permission, they risked being fired." Under Staggers, a former high school football star and college football coach, the committee was "like a high school football team under the control of the head coach."[1] In 1969, Staggers began the new Congress with only four staff members to serve the thirty-three-member committee.

Staggers's resistance to the flow of Magnuson's bills was also abetted by the institutional disdain of House members for the senators who sat across the table from them when Senate-House conference committees haggled over divergent versions of bills. House members usually served on only one or two committees, while the senators served on three or four. Therefore the House members commonly paid more attention to the details of bills passing through committee and often had more expertise in their subject matter than their counterparts from the Senate. Magnuson and other committee senators rarely bothered with the fine details of any but the most controversial bills. What really affronted the House Commerce Committee conferees was Magnuson's habit of turning to a young committee staff member and delivering a brief lecture on the virtues of the Senate-passed bill and the flaws in the House-passed bill. The House conferees were inclined to reject Senate differences out of spite.

### It Could Have Been Worse

Happily, the bleak landscape I had envisioned proved delusory. Most cheering was the unexpected postelection enthusiasm of our leader. Magnuson was elated by his reelection as the consumer's champion. He enjoyed his role in "keeping the big boys honest." It had transported him back to his earliest days as a passionate New Deal foe of electric utilities and other corporate fleecers of consumers and small business. After his early-November reelection, he lingered in Washington State for a few weeks, continuing to serve up vigorous consumer protection speeches. He vowed to fight for passage of the consumer protection laws that had been stalled in Congress and promised to introduce even more.

As for Nixon, if left to his own predilections, the new president would have turned his energy to peeling back the consumer protection regulations that troubled his corporate patrons. But his election against Democratic candidate Hubert Humphrey had been very close and thus did not signal the end of the "liberal hour" of the 1960s. Magnuson's efforts to promote consumer protection still resonated with the Washington State public and the media. Mainstream journalists, as conservatives had been charging, did indeed lean liberal, aggressively reporting on price-fixing, unsafe products, corporate deceptions, legalized bribery masquerading as legal campaign contributions, and other forms of corporate greed.

Despite having lost the presidency and seats in both the Senate and the House, Democrats still controlled both houses of Congress. Furthermore, organized labor, which had not yet lost its political power, continued, through its lobbying, to provide a boost to strong consumer protection laws. It also remained a primary source of campaign financing for Democratic legislators' campaigns. As a result, most Democratic legislators, including Magnuson, did not have to indenture themselves to corporate lobbies (as they would after Ronald Reagan's election in 1980 and the progressive shrinking of labor and its financial clout).

The center of labor lobbying in Washington, DC, was the AFL-CIO, the national coalition of most US labor unions. The coalition included the International Ladies' Garment Workers' Union, for which Evelyn Dubrow was the Washington lobbyist. In an obituary published after her death in 2006, the *New York Times* describes Dubrow as "one of the most colorful and respected lobbyists in Washington, and one of the first powerful women among them."[2]

"Evy," as we came to know and cherish her, was also chair of the AFL-CIO consumer protection lobbying group. This "tenacious and effective union activist," the *Times* writes, had been "a force for social justice and improved labor conditions by working for increases in the minimum wage, health care reform, family and medical leave, and pay equity for women." But her lobbying did not stop there. She and her team members lobbied vigorously for many of the consumer protection bills Magnuson and other Commerce Committee members sponsored. I have a vivid memory of her standing—all four feet, eleven inches of her—in the waiting room adjacent to the Senate floor, where, through a Senate page, she had summoned a senator who was wobbling on one of our consumer protection bills. He readily appeared, tall and imposing. Undeterred, Evy stood as close to his face as she could reach, as if to grab him metaphorically by the tie around his neck, demanding his vote for our bill. I can't remember the bill or the name of the wayward senator. What I remember is that he didn't say a word but went back to the Senate floor and voted for the bill.

Nixon shifted his public posture in response to the media attention, pledging his support for the consumer protection bills Magnuson was promoting. He even felt pressed to follow Johnson's precedent by delivering to Congress a consumer protection message promising a similar array of such bills. The catch was that these bills offered only the weak provisions that corporate lobbyists sought, and thus threatened our efforts to promote effective new legislation. But Nixon's rhetorical support kept the media's attention on the need for such laws and hence high on the public's agenda. A chagrined Nixon felt too politically vulnerable to threaten to veto bills that he nominally supported, even if they came to his desk far stronger than what he had proposed.

Thanks to Jerry's nurturing and our trip to the Soviet Union, my lingering insecurity about the solidity of my relationship with Magnuson evaporated. I found him warm, even playful, and soon I felt free to pinch the boxes of fine cigars that continued to flow in from lobbyists who knew Magnuson was an avid cigar smoker. What they did not know was that he had no taste for good cigars. He was partial to the cheap—two for a quarter—El Productos.

Magnuson knew very well about my pilfering but never complained. One day, however, I walked into his outer office and confronted a handwritten sign posted on his door. It read, "Warning: trespassers will be prosecuted to the full extent of the law!" I got the message. Magnuson's birthday was coming up, and I bought him a gift: a cigar humidor with a key. He accepted it graciously, adding, "I know you have a duplicate key." (I didn't, but it was never locked.)

To give myself daily one-on-one time with Magnuson, I followed Jerry's practice of joining Magnuson's driver to pick up the senator at his apartment house. During the trip to his office, I would go over the committee issues he needed to consider that day—bills, strategies, and personnel decisions—and extract his approval or not. In the spare fifteen minutes the drive took, I kept my presentations short. Magnuson didn't need details and he rarely asked questions or resisted. As he delegated more and more of the committee's consumer protection and other activities to me and the other Bumblebees, his standard response became, "Do what you think is right—so long as you don't get me into trouble."

Since his marriage to Jermaine in 1964, Magnuson, the once-renowned Lothario, had become prudish. On one of our morning drives up Constitution Avenue, he looked out the window at the cluster of Senate office buildings and said, "Mike, behind those doors, bad things are happening. These young staff members are having sex with the young secretaries. That's just not right." Then he added, "When I was a young congressman, we used to get our women from the Agriculture Department." Images of a virtual harem nestled somewhere in the bowels of the stony-faced Department of Agriculture building during the Roosevelt era erupted in my startled brain.

I heard the same echo of the bygone ladies' man one day when we were in New York driving down Park Avenue to a Cancer Society fund-raising event at which Magnuson was to receive an award for his initiatives in creating and funding the National Cancer Institute. "You know, Mike," he said, "it takes a lot of money to keep a woman in New York."

During the late mornings, before the daily flow of vodka had begun and Magnuson's head was clearest, I would sometimes visit him to discuss a new proposal, bringing with me the staffer who had developed the idea. He didn't like to say no to us. A few times he even reluctantly agreed to introduce a bill that we pressed him on, despite harboring serious doubts about it. In 1973, we proposed one such bill during the gasoline shortage that plagued Washington and much of the rest of the country, raising suspicions that the big oil companies were conspiring to withhold supplies so that they could create an artificial shortage to justify their escalating prices. The bill would have established a federal oil and gas corporation (inelegantly nicknamed FOGCO) that, theoretically, would operate fairly and in the public interest and provide a yardstick against which the prices and practices of the private oil companies could be measured. After hearing us out, Magnuson muttered, "You guys ought to go back to [communist] Cuba." Nevertheless, he did introduce the bill. We even persuaded a junior committee member, Senator Adlai Stevenson III, to hold hearings on it. But Magnuson's heart was not in it, and he never brought it before the committee.

Sometimes we got too cocky. In early 1969, while Nixon was still forming his cabinet, Jerry and I learned that under consideration for secretary of health, education, and welfare was a moderate and respected progressive California Republican named Robert Finch. Nixon's decision was imminent and Jerry and I urged the chairman to support the nomination. Magnuson was grouchy.

"How do I know he's so great?" he demanded.

"Because," I said, "we read your letter to the president supporting his nomination." A week earlier, before Magnuson had returned to Washington, we had sent a letter to President Nixon bearing the senator's name. Magnuson was quiet for a moment. Then, without a flicker of acknowledgment, he proceeded to the next item on our agenda and never mentioned the incident.

The independence Magnuson allowed us did have limits. When Manny Rouvelas was hired as counsel for the Merchant Marine Subcommittee, Stan Barer, Magnuson's administrative assistant at the time, cautioned him: "The unwritten rule for a Bumblebee," Manny recalls, "was that I got to stand on the bridge. I got to wear the uniform. I got to have the captain's cap on and hear the horn go, 'Toot! Toot!' But if I reached for the wheel, my arms would be cut off."

### Blessed by the Best of Senators

My greatest fear had been the effect Magnuson's withdrawing from active committee leadership would have on the agenda of bills he had promised to propel out of the committee. But when the Senate committees were partly reformed after the 1968 elections, the roll call of Democrats willing to assume consumer protection leadership roles had expanded.

Magnuson withdrew as chairman of the Consumer Protection Subcommittee, which Jerry had created with the 1968 reelection campaign in mind. He was still chairman of the full committee, but less active as a consumer advocate. Senator Frank Moss of Utah, who replaced Magnuson as subcommittee chairman, readily embraced consumer advocacy and warmly welcomed our support. Equally fortunate for us was that Senator Philip A. Hart, who had been among the earliest Senate consumer advocates, shifted his efforts from Judiciary to Commerce. Year after year, his attempts to advance his consumer protection agenda through the Judiciary Committee had been blocked by the committee chairman, James Eastland of Mississippi. Giving up on the Judiciary Committee, Senator Hart now turned to the Commerce Committee to pursue his consumer protection goals. Other committee members, moderate and even conservative, also willingly stepped forward—or were persuaded by us—to take leadership on bills on our agenda that had a particular appeal to them.

Even the staunchly conservative ranking Republican on the committee, Senator Norris Cotton, and his conscientious minority staff director, Jeremiah Kenney (and later Arthur Pankopf), were prepared to work with us and to join with Magnuson and the other Democrats on some consumer protection bills.

We had lost no ground, but we had much more work to do. There were many nascent bills awaiting action from past years and important new issues threatening to come before the committee. Without Magnuson's hands-on leadership, we would need to develop strong confidence, and then trust, with each of the diverse committee members who would be taking on consumer protection leadership roles. I would now have the primary responsibility for building and managing a larger staff.

### Building a Team of Bumblebees for a Heavier Load

Although Congress convened in January 1969, Magnuson largely stayed away—in his vacation home in Palm Springs—until April. Because he would not delegate the recruiting and managing of the committee's majority staff to the other committee members, that task fell to Jerry and me. This was heady authority. We would need greatly to expand the roster of Magnuson staff members, especially those who would have the entrepreneurial spirit and skills to help advance the ambitious agenda we had laid out for Magnuson in his campaign speeches. Once Jerry left in May, I would be on my own.

To move our expansion through the Rules Committee smoothly would require bipartisan support from Senator Cotton. The requested budget covered both majority and minority allocations. Senator Cotton had never complained about the budgets Magnuson had submitted before, but just in case he might be inclined to balk at the sharp increase, I followed a strategy I had learned from Jerry: generously seducing Cotton and other Republican committee members with the promise of funding more staff members of their own, a strong currency within the Senate.

I would draft an annual heart-tugging statement for Magnuson to deliver before the Rules Committee, outlining the formidable new workload imposed by that year's unique committee agenda (much of which we imposed on ourselves in our unquenchable pursuit of good works). Magnuson would present the statement, stoking his most ingratiating warmth toward his good colleagues, then excuse himself from having to answer questions, citing another urgent, nonexistent meeting. The clincher was that the Rules Committee chairman much of this time was Senator Howard Cannon of Nevada, who also chaired our Aviation Subcommittee. He greatly appreciated the staff Jerry had assigned to support him. The budgets were routinely approved as proposed, until we had enough.

### A Bumblebee Team Worthy of Challenge

I had by now internalized the lessons from my rocky introduction and understood better the qualities required of an effective Bumblebee. A Bumblebee needed an agile brain, resourcefulness, and technical competence. Resourcefulness was needed to remove any obstacles that impeded the forward progress of a bill. It might involve the strategic structuring of a hearing to ensure that the most appealing, friendly witnesses would appear early, while the journalists were present and the TV cameras were turned on. Those hostile to the bill would be shuffled off until late in the afternoon, when all but the most intrepid reporters had fled to file their stories. Legal training was useful, but a Bumblebee needed to set aside the law school–prescribed personal neutrality of the lawyer and embrace the political philosophy of his boss. A Bumblebee's corporate-averse advocacy could not be muffled by a preoccupation with laying the foundation for a future corporate legal or lobbying practice.

In my catalogue of essential Bumblebee qualities, I included a talent for indirection. Ralph Nader, for all his brilliance and passion, would not have made a good Bumblebee. Successful Bumblebees had to be comfortable with ambivalence; none of the senators they would work with would prove all good or all bad. I had learned that contradictory beliefs and impulses resided in senators' brains, and that some of those beliefs and impulses would be abhorrent to the staff members who were assigned to work with them. They would nonetheless need to be comfortable with this congeries of conflicting feelings and learn how to work around it, as well as how to evoke their bosses' public interest impulses while bypassing their fundraising hunger and political timidity. They would also need to be comfortable with blurred ethical lines in order to undertake such tasks as leaking or spinning the presentation of a bill before the committee to highlight its most appealing qualities while glossing over its political risks. A Nader would never tolerate such ethical ambiguities.

Yes, our delegated power and authority from Magnuson was heady: High-ranking bureaucrats and eminent lobbyists answered our calls and even feigned interest in our confident words of wisdom. Journalists covering a bill we were assigned were eager for us to brief them, on and off the record. (On the record was especially tempting to the egotist.) We faced the lures of seeing ourselves celebrated as a "101st senator." The near-irresistible temptation of fame called for humility.

We had always to be reminded that we were not elected members of the Senate. Without the commitment and trust of the senators we served, we would have had less personal power than the lowliest bureaucrat. At our most successful, we could do no more than guide or accelerate the legislative activity of the senators. Persuasion was our only real power, tempered to ensure that we maintained the more resistant senators' support. Nonetheless, staff members imbued with the disciplined zeal of the Bumblebee were able to place their stamp on the bills working their way through the committee, though their pride in doing so had to be kept silent.

Unlike the one hundred or so corporate lobbyists hired in 2010 to staff the Republicans' newly achieved committee and subcommittee chairmanships and their offices, the Bumblebees we sought were part of the generation of young people, Democrats and Republicans, who were drawn to Washington by the 1960 election of the young and glamorous John F. Kennedy, inspired by his words, "Ask not what your country can do for you, ask what you can do for your country." Those restless young lawyers and others sought adventure and the opportunity to advance public interest objectives while, when necessary, thwarting the special interest lobbyists. This is not to say that we Bumblebees did not also seek our own interests. We all had career ambitions that would be burnished by service on the committee. A few would graduate to private interest lobbying at two or three times the salaries they had earned at the committee. I would never have been appointed by President Jimmy Carter in 1978 as chairman of the FTC had I not served on the very committee that oversaw it.

None of us Bumblebees, however, had been nurtured from within the world of Washington's special interest lobbies, and almost none of us harbored such ambitions during our service to the committee. Those who saw service as a staff member on a congressional committee primarily as a career stepladder to richly remunerative lobbying generally avoided progressive entrepreneurial senators or members of Congress campaigning for public interest regulation. The very association with such entrepreneurial legislators would tarnish their résumés with corporate lobbyists. Once, a friendly corporate adversary who had hired a young Bumblebee I knew complained to me after a few months, "Can't get the government out of that boy!"

The longer we stayed, the more useful to the committee we became. In the days before Jerry took charge, the normal career course for staff ascension was (as it is now): build on-the-job expertise and, more important, build relationships with powerful senators for a term only long enough to establish these credentials, then cash in as a lobbyist in the same field. So established was this career path that Magnuson was truly puzzled by why so many of us hung on. We stayed, we told him, because we loved our work for him.

### Imagine Bipartisan Comity

Magnuson was committed to building trust among committee members by treating members of both parties fairly. Doing so was in his nature; it was also politic. We Bumblebees were expected to follow Magnuson's example. Our relationships with most of our Republican committee members and staff—not all—were civil and sometimes affectionate. Under the umbrella of Magnuson's benign rule, we earned their confidence and their goodwill. They knew that if they asked our advice about how to vote on a bill, we would be unbiased in our response. But we were also candid with liberal senators, disclosing the weaknesses in our case and the force of the opposition.

The staff members' professional courtesy also extended to special interest lobbyists. Knowing that rigidly principled staff members might avoid all such people and that lazy staff members might meet only with the ones knocking at their doors, I told them: "When you are assigned to manage a bill, you need to meet with the paid lobbyists who knock on your door, no matter how repellent they may be to you and how villainous you view their employers. Your obligation is to listen. By listening, you can learn a lot. You can learn about the workings of the industry that will be regulated by the proposed legislation and investigate the lobby's invariably exaggerated claims of the costs and technical hardships it could cause. You can deflect complaints to Magnuson by a lobbyist's committee friends that committee staff members are arrogant, biased, and unprofessional. You can also test your assumptions about the objections the lobbyist's client might have to the bill and be alerted to the 'poison pill' that may lurk in any amendments they develop for their committee friends."

I cautioned new staffers to avoid inadvertently disclosing our strategic plans and to avoid being seduced by the charm of power and celebrity. I also told them that they would encounter lobbyists who played it straight, who made their case for their clients while acknowledging where they might be vulnerable.

"In time," I said, "you and lobbyists like these may come to trust each other sufficiently to negotiate mutually acceptable modifications. But," I added, "don't get carried away by your own confidence. It's never enough to hear out only the well-funded lobbyists who come to us. You must test everything those lobbyists assert by reaching out to well-informed public interest advocates and independent experts who support the bill. They may live outside Washington, perhaps cloistered in some corner of academia, without the support or funding to come to you. You go to them. Your obligation to the committee is to make sure that you understand the arguments for and against the bill and any potential amendments."

As we moved into the 1970s, the number of professional committee staff members hovered around forty, the full complement we needed to serve as a counterweight to the regulation-averse Nixon administration and their corporate lobbying allies. Staff members now brought complementary skills. The foot soldiers were the cadre of Magnuson Fellows from the University of Washington School of Law. They had begun as green interns, but we had hired them to the staff when their internships were over if they had proven their Bumblebee craft.

By 1969, they had become seasoned and dedicated Bumblebees assigned to concentrate on our consumer protection agenda. Others had been assigned to the committee's traditional tasks involving bills that fell within different committee jurisdictions, such as the transportation industries.

We had all become at least minimally knowledgeable about the issues we were assigned to work on, but we rarely mastered those that required technical sophistication. When the committee began dealing with the nation's energy crisis, for example, we needed credentialed expertise on staff. In 1974, as I describe in the next chapter, I invited David Freeman to serve as a paid consultant to the committee. Freeman was so competent that President Carter later appointed him head of the Tennessee Valley Authority, where, among his other reforms of this lapsed public agency, he closed unsafe nuclear energy plants. I also hired a brilliant, liberally passionate legislative draftsman named Robert Joost to ensure that we would not be stuck in the hands of the mostly neutral, unimaginative bill drafters randomly supplied to all committees by the Senate Office of Legislative Counsel.

We hired two or three experienced investigators to help strengthen the committee's ability to evaluate the fitness of presidential nominees for the major regulatory agencies and other positions. These investigators were professional and nonpartisan. While not entrepreneurial themselves, they critically supported the Bumblebees' determination to fully vet regulatory nominees. So too did many of the administrative and legislative assistants to the senators we worked with most closely. Like us, they were infected by the progressive activism of the committee and relished the favorable media attention it wrought for their senators, reinforcing their bosses' enthusiasm for our projects. Several had Bumblebee passion and skills comparable to ours. They figure in some of the stories that follow.

### Managing a Widely Dispersed and Aggressively Entrepreneurial Staff

As I took on the full responsibility of staff director, I was able to build on the vision that Jerry and I had developed for our consumer protection agenda. Still, I had learned little about the other broad committee areas of jurisdiction and had never managed anyone other than myself, and that, loosely. Though I could brief new staff members on their responsibilities and would readily counsel those who came to me for guidance, I was not inclined to provide day-to-day supervision of each staff member. Like Magnuson, as I came to trust each staff member's abilities, I was quick to delegate responsibility.

Also like Magnuson, I was conflict averse. I gave praise readily but shied away from negative feedback, even when it could have ameliorated dysfunctional behavior. I rarely fired anyone. When trouble arose for any staffer that called for my intervention, especially when Magnuson was unhappy, I would do what I could to bail out the delinquent staffer.

I soon realized that I needed a disciplined planner and manager, someone comfortable with the advancing technology of the times. I found the right person already on the staff—Lynn Sutcliffe, the 1968 Magnuson Fellow. Sutcliffe had quickly demonstrated the qualities and drive that I lacked. Within six months of his arrival on the committee staff, I brought him into my office. We worked closely together for the next seven years.

Sutcliffe introduced what proved to be an effective system for drawing on the diverse skills of our staff members. Expanding the practice Jerry and I had followed of assigning one staff member to each bill, Sutcliffe began to organize teams of staff members to collaborate with the lead staff member. He then exercised day-to-day monitoring of each team, taking an active role when he determined it was needed.

While Sutcliffe was closely managing, I was able to pursue a very different kind of task. I had already come to know and work comfortably with several of the committee members. Whenever one of them asked me to stop by and brief him on the niceties of the legislation I had been working on for the committee, I had made it a point to be scrupulously honest, regardless of his leanings. These informal conversations, often involving casual exchanges of Senate gossip, helped deepen our mutual trust. But I didn't know the new members at all, and they certainly didn't know me. I set about developing the same kind of easygoing working relationship with them that I had with the other members.

I learned, however, that I had a new advantage—status. Most of the committee members naturally believed that, as staff director, I was more fully informed about the legislative activities of the committee than their own legislative assistants. Some even assumed that I was wise and that my counsel was valuable. I knew just enough to be credible. Sutcliffe would do the same. He, too, was developing working relationships with these members, who recognized his competence.

I had another advantage as committee staff director—I could be an intermediary between committee members and Magnuson. Many members found him intimidating and unapproachable, and he disliked some of them. I was able to develop goodwill among the members by adding their requests to the list of committee matters Magnuson would quickly check off on our morning rides to the Senate. I had only to ask and Magnuson would authorize a member to hold a media-worthy hearing in his own state on a bill that would appeal directly to the state's voters or to a large state employer. Or he would agree to add an important constituent to an otherwise closed list of scheduled committee witnesses or even to allow a member to travel to exotic lands as a committee representative on a mission connected with "commerce," though only 10 percent of it might involve work and 90 percent the notorious pleasures of the "junket."

Meanwhile, sharply focused on our legislative goals, Sutcliffe persuaded me that, to continue to be legislatively productive, we needed structure and organization. He began by developing a consumer protection bill timeline for each year, laying out a tentative schedule with target dates for introducing bills, holding hearings, completing committee markups, and taking action on the Senate floor. With the help of a friend who worked at IBM, he streamlined the process by introducing technology in the Senate: voice recorders and electronic typewriters hooked up to a full dictation system.

"So when we got to the Senate floor and an amendment popped up that was unexpected," Sutcliffe recalls, "we could get on the phone off the Senate floor, call the office, dictate a response to the amendment, and have copies printed and ready to hand out to all the senators within ten minutes."

In all the years I have known Sutcliffe, his drive and ambition has always focused on public service. That drive was manifest in his political campaigning in high school and in representing his school at Washington's Boys State, where he ran for governor and won. He encapsulates his motivation in his college motto: "Princeton in the Nation's Service." "Patriotism" is a much abused concept. But Sutcliffe recounts that he early responded to Princeton's sentiment that one is "expected to serve the nation in some capacity." After he served Magnuson and the committee, Sutcliffe went on to become a founder of a Washington, DC, law firm dedicated to serving the underserved and later, in a fledgling industry, committed to building the private infrastructure for making energy conservation economically viable.

Despite our different natures, Sutcliffe and I developed an untroubled management partnership. David Freeman recalls: "You have round edges. Sut had sharp edges. Sut once said to me that he had sprained his ankle over the weekend. I asked, 'What are you going to do about it?' He said, 'I'm going to walk on it.'" He was, Freeman adds, "indomitable, completely fearless, and determined to achieve what we needed to achieve. He would say, 'If there's an obstacle there, we got to either kick it away or jump over it.'"

Freeman continues, "You struck me as being a bit more thoughtful and encouraging all of us to do our thing, a bit more forgiving if we didn't quite get everything done that we said we were going to. Sutcliffe showed no signs of having any forgiveness in him at all. You had to be sure that everybody got to do what they wanted to do and that they didn't get into trouble with Magnuson, which was a big job, since he still had the conservative cronies around him that you had to keep in check."

Together, Sutcliffe and I developed a committee staff with the full capacity to give Nixon and his corporate allies a swarm of Bumblebee stings. Skilled, ambitious, and appropriately politically disciplined, Magnuson's Bumblebees were increasingly able to fulfill his dictum (and a little more). We had only to do what we thought was right—so long as we didn't get him into trouble.

# 8

# *The Flights of the Bumblebees*

By the fall of 1970, all the Senate Commerce Committee staff members
—not just those working on consumer protection—were itching for
Bumblebeehood. Some would bring their creativity and entrepreneurial
spirit to the newly pressing issue of energy conservation and the wide range
of environmental hazards never before faced by the committee. Others
would tackle the list of Magnuson-led consumer protection bills that had
readily cleared the Senate before 1968 but had been sidetracked for years by
the House committee, which sought what Magnuson mockingly referred to
as "a fair advantage." Those working on transportation issues would upset
the Senate committee's habit of rubber-stamping federal subsidies for the
maritime and surface transportation industries by proposing regulatory
legislation.

### Taking on the State Department
### and Fourteen Other Countries to Save the Oceans

Among the staff members who chafed under the load of uninspiring non-
consumer issues they had been assigned to deal with was Manny Rouvelas.
Nurtured by Jerry for his potential as a Bumblebee from the time he was a
progressive undergraduate activist at the University of Washington, Rouvelas had been hired as counsel for the Merchant Marine Subcommittee. His
assignment amounted to little more than helping Magnuson ensure that
subsidies continually flowed from the federal treasury to help support US
shipyards, US flag shipping companies, and US labor. Magnuson was a
strong supporter of the merchant marine and was one of the most powerful members of the Merchant Marine Subcommittee, whose jurisdiction
embraced legislation vital to one of Washington State's economic engines:
the great ports and thriving merchant shipping throughout the Pacific. But
Magnuson also cared about fisheries and oceanography and was developing

increasing environmental awareness and concern. Rouvelas had plunged into teaching himself what he needed to know to deal with merchant marine matters. Once he became aware of longstanding merchant marine safety and environmental hazards, dating from the early years of ocean shipping, he was convinced that the committee had to take some action to curb these hazards.

Rouvelas's worries about maritime safety were aggravated by the taunts of his officemate, the staff member for the committee's Aviation Subcommittee, who asked, "How is it that airplanes fly at 550 miles an hour in three dimensions and they don't bump into each other very often, whereas ships float around in two dimensions, moving ten kilometers an hour, and they keep colliding?" (The problem was eventually solved by the Bridge to Bridge Radio Telephone Act of 1971, which replaced the customary whistles, toots, and flags.)

Rouvelas was soon ready to test his relationship with Magnuson and to build relationships with the three other powerful members of the Merchant Marine Subcommittee: Senator Russell Long, from Louisiana, which, like Washington, had a thriving port in its merchant marine economy, Senator Daniel Inouye, from Hawaii, which was economically dependent on low-cost ocean shipping, and Senator Ernest Frederick "Fritz" Hollings of South Carolina. Rouvelas would need their support, as well as Magnuson's, to change the committee's focus from pampering the merchant marine industry to regulating it.

Rouvelas had no difficulty developing a close relationship with Magnuson, who sensed what Rouvelas describes as his "unbounded appreciation, affection, and respect" for the senator. Rouvelas had grown up believing what his parents had told him, that Magnuson's intervention had blocked attempts by the Immigration and Naturalization Service to deport his father as an illegal immigrant when Rouvelas was two or three years old. Those acts, Rouvelas says, "had allowed me to grow up in the United States." He adds: "The guy who is responsible for changing your life that way, for allowing you to have the opportunities that none of your first cousins had, like a college education, would get a lot of slack for whatever else he does. So I loved him."

Rouvelas soon also developed deep loyalty to Senator Inouye, whom he describes as a "complex, principled, and courageous man" whose character had been shaped by childhood poverty and service in the army during World War II. Like everyone else, Rouvelas says, Inouye had "personal flaws and philosophical inconsistencies," but "he was committed to fairness and lifting up underdogs."

The key relationship for Rouvelas to cultivate, however, was with Senator Long. Here, too, he had no difficulty. Long was always respectful, never condescending. "Long just accepted me," Rouvelas says. "He never questioned or second-guessed me." After the passage of one maritime act, Rouvelas accompanied Long to the White House for the signing ceremony. There, Long, who well could have stood up and taken credit, instead pointed to Rouvelas and said, "This is the guy that did the work."

"Senators," Rouvelas says, "didn't do that."

Rouvelas recalls going to Long early on and outlining his options on a piece of legislation from another committee that was pending on the Senate floor. Long asked Rouvelas how he should vote. Rouvelas replied, "Well, Senator, frankly, I think this is the better policy side of it, but I do need to tell you that the only constituent that you have that I am aware of that really cares is on the other side of this." Rouvelas bemoans the fact that politicians no longer respond as Long did: "Well, you know, we have six-year terms around here, and that gives us about four and a half years to be statesmen."

Meantime, in his effort to promote ship safety legislation, Rouvelas found two Coast Guard engineers who had developed supporting data for needed construction safety equipment, including "double bottoms" for tankers to help prevent water-polluting oil spills by requiring an extra hull and water chamber before the tank containing oil. Though they were not authorized to communicate directly with anyone in the Congress, Rouvelas says, "they were open and helpful in providing me their expert advice and the language to achieve these goals."

An oil spill from a tanker at an Atlantic Richfield Company refinery in Cherry Point (the largest oil refinery in Washington State) provided the impetus by threatening to pollute Puget Sound. Though Rouvelas readily admits that the cause of the oil spill had nothing to do with vessel construction standards ("Somebody had left a valve on"), the public uproar aroused Magnuson's attention and gave him the means and the energy to get seriously into tanker shipping safety.

"We followed exactly the strategy that the Bumblebees had developed," Rouvelas recalls. "We seized upon an opportunity we knew would engage Maggie: the oil spill at Cherry Point and another notorious oil spill in San Francisco Bay."

President Richard Nixon had recently submitted to Congress a proposal on vessel operating safety developed by the Coast Guard leadership. With the approval of Magnuson and Long, Rouvelas organized a series of hearings. Among the witnesses he made certain to have testify were the independent maritime safety experts, the Coast Guard environmental experts, and lawyers from the Sierra Club, who, though scorned by the oil and maritime industry lobbyists as "crazies," did some of the best and most thorough legal and technical work presented to the committee.

Meanwhile, the House Merchant Marines and Fisheries Committee reported to the House, and the House passed a version of Nixon's bill that totally ignored any requirements to improve vessel construction and engineering requirements, such as double bottoms.

When the hearings concluded, Rouvelas, with the collaboration of the Republican minority staff director, Arthur Pankopf, developed and brought before the Senate Commerce Committee a working draft for the members to consider. They had transformed the Nixon bill passed in the House by adding mandates to improve vessel design and construction.

The next hurdle was the opposition of foreign governments, oil companies, and ship owners in the formidable International Maritime Organization, which operated under the umbrella of the United Nations. Because the bill would require all merchant ships using US ports to comply with new standards, ship owners in every country with substantial shipping interests were aroused. Arguing that the standards were unnecessary, impractical, and excessively expensive, they lobbied foreign governments and the International Maritime Organization to forcefully oppose the amended bill.

Rouvelas attended international negotiation sessions in London in the offices of the International Maritime Organization, accompanied by one of the "covert Coast Guard guys" and others. They challenged the organization's members at the meeting and even the US Navy, which feared retaliation in their international operations. Their primary foreign ally in the meeting, Rouvelas recalls, was the Soviet Union, but ranged against the new standards were the international oil companies; plus Greece, because of its powerful shipping oligarchs; England, because of British Petroleum; and the Netherlands, because of Shell. Rouvelas listened to their complaints but made no commitment to change any of the provisions of the amended bill.

On the night before the Senate Commerce Committee was scheduled to meet for the markup on the bill, Pankopf called Rouvelas with the news that he was going to deliver an urgent letter from the State Department to Magnuson protesting the bill on behalf of fourteen governments. The proposed legislation, these governments declared, violated international treaty rights because the United States had no authority unilaterally to set standards on foreign vessels coming into US waters. The White House had also informed Pankopf that Nixon's advisers were prepared to recommend that the president veto the bill as it was presented to the committee.

At that moment, the fate of the bill rested solely in Pankopf's hands. "I have this letter," he told Rouvelas. "I want to be able to talk with you about it after the markup. I don't think I have time to put it in the briefing book for my Senate members."

If the letter had landed, Rouvelas says, the whole process would have been postponed. "We would have lost momentum."

The next day, while the letter rested on Pankopf's desk, the committee met as scheduled, and with little debate, the staff draft was reported unanimously without change and sent to the Senate floor. Senators Long, Inouye, and Magnuson (and the Republicans) were not aware of every detail of the new bill; they simply trusted Rouvelas and Pankopf. No member of the committee learned about the State Department letter until after the markup and the unanimous vote to report the bill to the Senate floor. Before the bill could be acted on by the Senate, Rouvelas and Pankopf knew that they had to take into account some of the valid arguments against it, but now they had the unanimous committee vote behind them.

"We didn't collapse," Rouvelas says, "but we modified it some. And we did that in between the markup and Senate floor consideration. The key provisions remained intact." The bill passed the Senate without opposition.

The two bills that reached the Senate-House conference bore little resemblance to each other. The big oil companies had enlisted the House conferees to hold out for the elimination of the most revolutionary of the Senate bill's safety provisions. But, Rouvelas recalls, thanks to Long, who made it clear to the House conferees that he backed the Senate bill to the fullest, "we got 90 percent of what we wanted in that conference." Long, in his usual way, had walked into the conference and, speaking to the five House members, had said, "You guys passed a really good bill. We made a few minor changes in it and Rouvelas here can explain what they're about." The conference bill was approved by both houses.

Rouvelas feared, however, that Secretary of State Henry Kissinger, backed by shipping lobbyists close to the White House, would urge Nixon to veto the bill. White House staff had even threatened that Nixon would do just that if Congress challenged him. But Magnuson knew Nixon better. Nixon had sent a ship safety bill to Congress; Congress had approved a ship safety bill. Nixon's ego, Magnuson understood, would lead him not only to sign the bill into law but to sign it with a flourish. Magnuson told Rouvelas not to worry, the president would sign it. A few days later, in a staged press conference in San Clemente, California, with the ocean in the background, Nixon stood before the television cameras and congratulated Congress on passing the first piece of his environmental program, the Ports and Waterways Safety Act of 1972.

"The Nixon bill that we appended everything to—" Rouvelas recalls, shaking his head, "our toughest content had nothing to do with him, and in fact his people had threatened to veto it. But he just took credit for it."

Years later, another staffer, Tom Allison, the 1973 Magnuson Fellow, pulled off a coup similar to Rouvelas's. The embodiment of late-sixties rebellion, Allison had arrived at the committee with a long ponytail, prompting Magnuson to gripe, "Why does he have to wear his hair so long?" The bulging briefcase he always carried became known as his "doctor's kit" for the substances, neither prescription nor over-the-counter, it contained. But Allison had an instinct for the political jugular. By the time I had left the committee, Allison had trimmed his hair, and Magnuson had appointed him chief counsel, working with Ed Merlis, staff director of the committee.

In the late 1970s, because of several leaks from oil refineries close to Puget Sound, the citizens of Seattle and the surrounding communities had grown increasingly sensitive to the global risk of oil spills. Yet the environmentally blind Washington State governor, Dixie Lee Ray, was promoting an increase in oil tanker activity in Puget Sound with the proposed enlargement of an oil tanker port. Allison was paying attention. Before long, he hatched a plot.

In the midst of a frantic effort by the Commerce Committee to churn out as many new bills and reauthorizations as possible to meet the new, tighter deadline of May 15 for the Appropriations Committee to act on the funding required for each of them, Allison turned to Merlis and said, "Let's keep supertankers out of Puget Sound and let's use the Marine Mammal Protection Act to do that." He then wrote an amendment to the noncontroversial reauthorization bill, which was expected to pass the Senate by unanimous consent. The amendment would prohibit an increase in the amount of oil brought into Puget Sound.

Allison and Merlis's recommendation was enough for Magnuson, who did not trouble to keep track of most of the amendments his staff prepared. He gave his approval. Magnuson's approval was enough for the committee Republicans. So Merlis, according to his usual practice, prepared the script for the Democratic majority leader of the Senate, Robert Byrd of West

Virginia, to use when he called up the bill. As Merlis recalls, "Byrd calls the bill up, and in a monotone offers this amendment to the bill, as he had done with many others, and calls for unanimous consent. There's no objection. It passes the Senate in five minutes."

To ensure that the bill was passed by the House and landed on the president's desk before the oil lobby and the Washington governor learned what was happening, Merlis and Allison enlisted the help of Norm Dicks, a former Bumblebee who had leapt from his position as administrative assistant in Magnuson's office to the House, where he represented the Tacoma area. Dicks skillfully smoothed the path in the House, and Allison arranged to have the Senate-approved reauthorization bill carried by hand to the clerk of the House by the next day so that it was included among bills with no opposition from either party that could be passed on a simple voice vote. Again it passed with unanimous, unwitting, consent. Puget Sound would be saved from further oil pollution.

Merlis caps this story of Allison's triumph with a simultaneous scene in Olympia, Washington's state capital.

> Jerry is in Dixie Lee Ray's office that very afternoon, sitting in a waiting room, prepared for a friendly visit having nothing to do with Puget Sound. No friend of Magnuson's, she excoriates the available Jerry. Later, she publicly denounces Magnuson as "the dictator," because he kept the supertankers out of Puget Sound without even consulting her. Jerry could do nothing but plead ignorance.

Though chagrined, Jerry soon forgave Allison. After all, it was he who had created the Bumblebees.

### On Land As Well As by Sea: Foiling the "ASTRO Caper"

George Smathers was elected as a Democratic senator from Florida in 1950. He served until 1968. Though he is not remembered for any particular service he rendered to the public in the eighteen years he served in the Senate, once he retired as senator he flourished as a lobbyist, aided by high-level bipartisan intimacies, including with presidents Johnson and Nixon. Even a columnist as jaded as Drew Pearson was unnerved by Smathers's casual intimacy with Johnson. In his diary, Pearson writes of a visit to Johnson in a hotel room in Orlando, Florida, where the president was resting after attending a fund-raising event in Miami.

"I was a little taken aback by the fact that George Smathers was sitting on the sofa alongside him, his long, spindly legs stretched out on the coffee table."[1] Smathers collected trusting cronies, not least among them Warren Magnuson, who much appreciated how lavishly Smathers entertained.

Early one evening in 1972, Rouvelas recalls, Magnuson was grumbling around his office about unexpected roll-call votes on the Senate floor that were delaying adjournment for the day.

"You'd think we could get our work done on time and get out of here," he said to Rouvelas. "I was supposed to fly up to New York for the premiere of a new movie called *The Godfather*. Now I'm going to miss it." When an innocent young staffer said, "Gee, Senator, you must be really disappointed to miss the movie," Magnuson replied: "Oh, I don't care at all about the movie. But I was supposed to fly up on a small plane with Smathers and could have taken those guys for a month's salary playing cards during the flight."

Daniel O'Neal, the 1966 Magnuson Fellow, quickly earned Jerry's and Magnuson's deep trust. They assigned him to an arena of committee jurisdiction that was important to Washington State's economic interests but offered little opportunity for Bumblebee action. To thrive, the Washington ports and shippers depended on low-cost shipping from the trucking, inland water carriers, and railroad industries. Many of these charges were regulated by the Interstate Commerce Commission, governed by legislation overseen by the Senate and House Commerce Committees.

O'Neal performed his assignment diligently, though his tasks were not inspiring. He had to deal with mostly heavily lobbied competition over costs and profits among the several modes of transport carriers and their industrial and agricultural customers. Magnuson was most invested in keeping the Washington State industries content.

In late 1969 and early 1970, however, O'Neal's responsibilities escalated dramatically when the Penn Central Railroad began to experience severe financial trouble. Penn Central was then the largest railroad in the country, serving the Northeast sector of the United States, which was heavily dependent on the railroad's performance. Numerous efforts were undertaken in the financial world to keep the railroad financially viable, some of which included ill-advised bank loans. None of them worked.

As the threat of the railroad's demise loomed, the Penn Central's stockholders and executives pressed for federal funds to keep it out of bankruptcy. They turned to Maurice Stans, Nixon's secretary of commerce, to develop a scheme to dump the costs of rehabilitating the Penn Central on the taxpayers before it could be restructured. Stans arranged a closed meeting for Saturday, June 20, 1970, with key congressional members of both parties. His objective was to ensure congressional support for bailout legislation to avoid Penn Central bankruptcy. O'Neal was disgusted by the proposed treasury raid and worried that Stans would muscle it through without the Bumblebees' cautionary counsel. Stans, wary of staff meddling, had excluded O'Neal and other staff members from the meeting.

On June 19, with input from supportive Department of Transportation staff, O'Neal developed a one-page memo listing in bullet points the most compelling arguments for not supporting Stans. He handed it to Magnuson as he was leaving for the evening. After only a cursory conversation, Magnuson slipped the note into his pocket and went home. O'Neal was not at all sure that Magnuson would read and pay attention to his warnings.

When Stans's meeting was over, O'Neal learned from the journalists who swarmed outside the Commerce Department that Magnuson had raised his bullet points one by one. His clincher to Stans was pure Magnuson: "This is Alice in Wonderland." It was clear to all that the hostility of the key committee chairman to Stans's scheme doomed it.

With no lifeline coming from the federal government, the Penn Central filed for bankruptcy the next day, Sunday, June 21, 1970. At the time, it was the largest corporate bankruptcy in US history. O'Neal was now faced with a potential national economic catastrophe. Immediately he developed and husbanded emergency legislation, which was readily passed, for federal support to keep the railroad operating.

Still, railroad operations in the Northeast needed a major reordering. Over the next two and a half years, with access to public and private information about the Penn Central and with the aid of new hires, O'Neal and another talented Magnuson Fellow, John Cary, plowed ahead with an analysis of the causes of the Penn Central disaster. O'Neal and Cary spent November and December 1972 editing and finalizing a 750-page report titled *The Penn Central and Other Railroads*. It itemizes the management flaws that led to the railroad's collapse, undermining any argument that the managers and stockholders of the railroad were entitled to a taxpayer bailout. The report also identifies other factors, including inflexibility, accounting manipulation, an arcane revenue divisions regime, intense competition from trucking, outdated and lapsed regulatory requirements, and inappropriate investments in non-railroad businesses. In short, O'Neal says, it explains "how the Penn Central could have reached such a sorry state." He applauds Cary's contribution as "brilliant." Later, that report would provide the foundation for legislation that would truly serve the public interest.

Desperate, the railroads, knowing the Bumblebees were "cooking something," hired Smathers to lobby for them. Now O'Neal had an opponent lobbyist as formidable as any of us had yet faced. Smathers was the right man to resuscitate an unconditional taxpayer bailout of the Penn Central. He recognized that the railroads' primary competitors, the powerful American Trucking Association and the Inland Water Carriers, would mobilize to halt any such largess, so he developed a simple scheme: give all three of the competing industries equivalent federal subsidies and ease their safety and other regulatory requirements. With one stroke he would transform potential spoilers into hungry supporters. From the beginning, O'Neal was appalled by what he came to call Smathers's "ASTRO caper." ASTRO stood for America's Sound Transportation Review Organization. As a lobbyist, Smathers would hide his name behind the soberly named Association of American Railroads, which created the organization. But the colorful acronym *ASTRO* was surely a Smathers invention.

All that Smathers needed now was a rubber-stamp from the Senate Commerce Committee. Securing that should have been quick and easy because of his close friendship with Magnuson and his connections with other key committee members of both parties. But standing in his way were O'Neal, Cary, and a few members of the minority staff who were leery of the Smathers proposal and quietly cultivated doubt about the bill among the committee's Republicans. What would prove critical, however, was the addition of Ernie Franklin to their team. Franklin was a lawyer/lobbyist in Tacoma, Washington, who represented the "Washington parties," a group of transportation-dependent shippers of goods from Washington State that included the port authorities, local shippers, and some public entities who feared that they would be burdened by several aspects of Smathers's plot.

The bill languished while the senators left town to attend the Democratic and Republican conventions in Miami in the summer of 1972. Magnuson spent convention week at Smathers's Miami residence, lavishly catered to—and no doubt prospering at poker. There is no record of the conversations that took place in that palatial setting, but as soon as Magnuson returned from Miami, he summoned O'Neal to his office and said he thought it was time to bring the ASTRO bill to the committee executive session markup. O'Neal was surprised. Magnuson had never mentioned the bill to him. He quickly realized that Smathers had lobbied Magnuson while the senator was enjoying his hospitality, and that Magnuson was agreeable because he had paid little attention to the details of the bill Smathers was hustling.

Desperate to ensure that Magnuson understood the legislation's dangers and the strong interests of his constituents in Washington State, O'Neal urged Franklin to get his message to Magnuson immediately.

"I drafted a telegram to Magnuson from Franklin," he recalls. He "made a few minor adjustments and sent that telegram directly to the chairman's office."

At the executive markup session, Senator Vance Hartke, who chaired the committee's Transportation Subcommittee and had succumbed to Smathers's assurance of campaign support, opened the discussion with a strong pitch for the legislation. Then, O'Neal says, "Magnuson turned to me and asked, 'Where is that telegram?' I just happened to have it with me, of course. Prior to that I'd had very little opportunity to talk to him about the bill, though I had cautioned him that there was strong Washington State opposition to certain provisions." Magnuson used the telegram as his checklist on the bill, dealing with every one of Franklin's objections by adding several amendments. Those amendments, which O'Neal and Cary had drafted earlier, undermined the legislation. The Republicans on the committee had always been concerned about the subsidy provisions; the Democrats, trusting Magnuson, followed his lead, and Hartke only mildly asserted his objections. The committee agreed to report out the amended bill.

A few days later, Smathers came to see O'Neal. As O'Neal told Magnuson, Smathers was dismayed by the reported bill and said the industry could not and would not support it. The legislation never made it to the Senate floor. Magnuson's innocent excuse to Smathers was, "I had to protect my constituents."

### No Small Bumblebee Triumph: Saving the Country from a "Major Economic Catastrophe"

O'Neal's action against Smathers's ASTRO caper had foiled a corrupt scheme in characteristic Bumblebee style. The 92nd Congress ended with no action on the ASTRO bill. It died quietly. With O'Neal's guidance, the committee and Congress went on to approve emergency legislation with a federal subsidy to keep the Penn Central providing essential services, but only through 1974. The absence of further action by Congress would shut down the Penn Central, putting in jeopardy the rest of the nation's financially precarious but essential railroads and all the shipping industries that were dependent on them. In Lynn Sutcliffe's words, the collapse of the Penn Central "threatened a major economic catastrophe in our country." The responsibility for further legislative action lay with the Commerce Committee—and within the Commerce Committee, the burden of developing a solution fell on the staff.

By 1973, O'Neal had moved on. President Nixon had appointed him to the Interstate Commerce Commission. (Under the law, the president can name only a bare majority of commissioners from his own party; Republican committee members, as well as the Democrats, warmly supported O'Neal's appointment.) Later, President Jimmy Carter appointed him chairman of the commission.

When O'Neal left, Sutcliffe formed a team of Bumblebees to come up with and sell to the committee (and Congress as a whole) a solution that did not raid taxpayers' pockets. The team, headed by Sutcliffe, included Tom Allison, who shifted over from consumer protection, and Paul Cunningham, another strong Magnuson Fellow who had completed his internship and joined the staff. At their disposal was the skilled legislative draftsman I had hired earlier, Robert Joost.

The team needed a free hand from our two central bosses in this process: Magnuson and Hartke. Sutcliffe presented the situation to Hartke so compellingly that Hartke transformed again into a responsible legislator. The team of Bumblebees also got a long leash from Magnuson to work out the proposed legislation.

In an effort to ensure support for any plan they developed, the team proposed the creation of an advisory board on which representatives from the major interest groups had a voice. Convening this group, as Sutcliffe recalls, "allowed everybody to negotiate; everybody ended up giving something away." In the end, the Regional Rail Reorganization Act of 1973 (known as the "3R Act") was passed. It was enacted in January 1974, just in time to avoid the still-pending collapse. The 3R Act provided interim funding to run the Northeast railroads, while a new entity created by the act, the United States Railway Association, was given authority by the Interstate Commerce Commission (ICC) to substantially restructure the railroad and in doing so to abandon unprofitable lines. It was also charged with putting together a plan that would enable the railroads to survive once they were reorganized in bankruptcy. The final plan, enacted as one of the titles of the Railroad Revitalization and Regulatory Reform Act of 1976 (the "4R Act"), called for the creation of a government-controlled corporation that became known as Conrail. Thus, the railroad received taxpayer money but in a highly controlled arrangement that involved oversight by the Department of Transportation; the ICC; the United States Railway Association, which had on its board the chairman of the ICC, the secretary of transportation, the secretary of the treasury, a mayor and a governor from the Northeast, and some citizen appointees; and a new, independent, hybrid organization, the Rail Services Planning Office, which provided regulatory expertise to the planning effort. None was controlled by the Penn Central.

In less than ten years, the process produced a slimmed-down, more efficient railroad system valuable enough for the federal government to sell it to two private railroads, the Norfolk Southern and CSX, for close to two billion dollars. Because of the Commerce Committee's rational approach to restructuring, the suffocation of the Smathers effort, and Magnuson's killing of the pre-bankruptcy bailout, the taxpayers got a new railroad at little cost (proving that the federal government can do some things right). The taxpayers were reimbursed and transportation in the Northeast flourished. Success in this instance, Sutcliffe says, involved "sound economics and listening to industries' creative ideas and testing them and massaging them and then working it through the Congress the way we had always done."

That, however, was not the end of Bumblebee rail revitalization. Allison pushed it further. Since he was a child, Allison had been fascinated with speed. As Ed Merlis recalls, "Tom relished moving fast in cars, planes, boats, or on skis, for that matter. One of Tom's favorite allusions was to the 'facial distortion' that occurred at high speeds on the Bonneville Salt Flats. It was a term he often used to describe the thrill of going fast."

When Allison delved into the Penn Central miasma, he learned that passenger rail traffic along the Eastern Corridor was eroding away. What engaged him most was the potential for high-speed rail to entice a new generation of passengers. He saw the potential for Amtrak and developed yet another title to the 4R Act that would authorize the funding of its high-speed trains—today's Acela—traveling from Washington, DC, with only strategic stops all the way to Boston.

As one of a cohort of Bumblebees who joined the Carter administration, Allison was appointed general counsel of the Department of Transportation. Because he had access to the senior levels of the department, he developed yet another proposal, to authorize the rehabilitation of DC's iconic but decaying Union Station. During his tenure with the department, he also initiated efforts to restore other, equally iconic central city railroad stations across the country.

### A Partnership Forged in Bumblebee Heaven

Few of the rewards we Bumblebees encountered in working with the senators on the Commerce Committee could compare with the delights of working with the South Carolina Democrat Fritz Hollings. Each of us who worked with him grew close to him, melding seamlessly into his own staff. Though Magnuson appreciated us, he was often unaware of our work—unless we got him into trouble. Hollings, by contrast, recognized that the staff team we had built was a unique resource that could strengthen his desire to legislate effectively. So he reached out to us professionally and personally. He studied us and learned our strengths and weaknesses. He greatly enjoyed working with us, and we with him. We found his wit irresistible.

Hollings was a politician from the Deep South. More important, he was a moderate Democrat, often more conservative than we, but his social concerns and empathy would be unthinkable today for a southern politician. Even his mandatory defense of South Carolina's entrenched segregation was as minimal as it could be without jeopardizing his political support.

Hollings so respected the Kennedys that after Robert Kennedy's assassination, he was moved to memorialize him with action. One of Kennedy's passions had been to bring to public attention the willfully suppressed prevalence of deep poverty and hunger in many parts of the country. In 1968 and 1969, Hollings toured the impoverished areas of South Carolina, accompanied by leading South Carolina journalists. Establishment South Carolinians were outraged by the negative attention he drew to their state. Hollings characteristically turned aside the criticism with scornful wit, responding, "I don't want [Secretary of Housing and Urban Development George] Romney and [Senator Edward] Kennedy coming here to look at my slums. As a matter of fact when I get caught up with my work, I think I may go look at the slums of Boston."[2] When a critic charged him with "scheming for the Negro vote," Hollings, who had seen both whites and blacks living with hunger and poverty, responded, "You just don't make political points on hunger. The poor aren't registered to vote and they won't vote."[3]

In February 1969, Hollings testified before the Senate Select Committee on Hunger and Human Needs, chaired by South Dakota senator George

McGovern. Hollings called passionately for a federal program that had not previously appeared on the public agenda: food stamps to be distributed free to the most needy in the country. The next day, McGovern announced that a pilot program for such aid would be undertaken in South Carolina— the first step toward implementation of the national food stamp program. This was the kind of senator a Bumblebee longs to work for.

And work with him we did—with pleasure. As we've seen, Magnuson had largely withdrawn from most of the heavy work of the committee and had effectively freed us to recruit willing committee members to lead initiatives on new and continuing legislative ventures. Thus, when we saw the need for a subcommittee to handle the rising set of nationally critical issues involving energy regulation that fell within the committee's jurisdiction, we suggested to Magnuson that Hollings was the right person to take on these challenges. He liked Hollings and readily agreed. We approached Hollings and told him about the staff resources we could provide him, especially David Freeman. He too agreed.

Freeman had served as a senior energy expert in the Johnson White House and, though a liberal Democrat, he was sufficiently respected in his expertise to be carried over to the Nixon White House. He was the author of a report, funded by the Ford Foundation, called *A Time to Choose: America's Energy Future*. According to Freeman, "It really was the first time that the idea of energy efficiency as a major source of power was published by an authoritative agency. Up until then, no one had really thought of the idea that all of the energy we were wasting was the cheapest and quickest form of electricity if we just made the small investment needed to save it."

When McGeorge Bundy, head of the Ford Foundation, asked Freeman whether "this terrific report [was] going to be something else that just sits on the shelves of intelligent people," Freeman replied, "No, I have a friend named Mike Pertschuk, and I'm going to go see him and see if I can't join the Commerce Committee and work to enact the report's major findings in the law." Asked how long it would take, Freeman said, "Mr. Bundy, it's going to take years, but we're going to give it a hard lick."

I managed to leapfrog the slow Senate hiring procedures and avoid clearing Freeman with Magnuson, who had little use for experts who didn't come from Washington State. Freeman came to work with us as a contractor several months before the Ford Foundation report was published in October 1974. He stayed until July 1977, when he was nominated by President Carter to chair the Tennessee Valley Authority.

Freeman recalls my asking him what was most important in the report. He replied that it was the recommendation that a law be passed requiring Detroit to make more fuel-efficient cars.

"Cars were averaging twelve miles to the gallon back then, at most. You didn't argue with me. You said, 'That's it. We have to draft a bill, and we have to get a horse.'" (By "horse" I had meant a senator who would hold hearings on the bill. That senator was Hollings.)

Freeman, who, like Hollings, grew up in the South, soon became a close member of the Hollings family. Freeman describes Hollings as "the funniest guy I've ever met" with a "knack for saying things that were hilarious, just kind of off the cuff." In a televised debate in 1986, for example, Henry McMaster, Hollings's Republican opponent, challenged Hollings to take a drug test and make the results public. "I'll take a drug test," Hollings replied, "if you'll take an IQ test." Freeman recalls, too, that Hollings was quick to push back at any of us who offered untutored advice: "We were on the Senate floor with him one day. I had suggested he offer a certain amendment. He turns to me, and he says 'Son, are you about to make a consultant out of me? This is a cash-and-carry Senate. These people have not been bought, but they have been rented for this issue. And if I offer this amendment, I'd just look like a fool. So just forget it.'"

My own dealings with Hollings were not as intimate as Freeman's, but I was fond of him, despite our philosophical differences, and we worked well together. Long after Freeman had left the committee, he made a social visit to Hollings and recalls his saying, "You know, I spend half my time protecting Pertschuk up here. He's making a lot of work for me. He gets in trouble about once a week, and I have to bail him out."

### Dining on CAFE Standards

Freeman believes that the passage of the Corporate Average Fuel Economy Act, in 1975, soon known informally as the CAFE Standards Act, was "by far the most important goal that we accomplished." The cast responsible for its passage goes well beyond the committee, though Joost was the primary technical draftsmen of the bill, and Freeman and Sutcliffe guided the substance. But passage also depended on the efforts of Senator Hollings, Senator Kennedy, House Speaker Tip O'Neill, and Sutcliffe's secret weapon, Robert Redford, who was then at the peak of his fame as an actor and a national influence as an environmental advocate.

Having been burned by their Nader imbroglio, the still economically and politically dominant US auto companies took a subtle approach to the proposed federal fuel efficiency standards. They embraced the need for transforming fuel efficiency and bloviated in testimony before Hollings that they were deeply committed to improving the fuel efficiency of their cars and were in fact already hard at work trying to achieve this worthy goal. The auto industry executives testified that they had letters from the presidents of the auto companies promising that they were going to make their cars more fuel efficient.

As Freeman recalls, "They assured Senator Hollings that the word of the automobile presidents was plenty good, and they didn't understand why we wanted to waste our time with this legislation." But we had also scheduled simultaneous hearings chaired by Hollings on a companion bill the team had developed to mandate energy-conserving insulation standards and other conservation standards in every home that was bought with a federal mortgage guarantee—a huge component of all home sales. The housing bill was not contested by the construction industry, so Hollings challenged the auto industry witnesses. As Freeman recalls,

> Hollings said to one witness, "Well, we have legislation here for the
> housing industry and the automobile industry, and we're going ahead
> with the housing legislation without any apparent opposition. So why
> is it that you guys think that we should pay any attention to what
> the automobile executives have to say?" When the witness answered,
> "Senator, the auto executives are honorable men," Hollings shot back,
> "Is it your testimony, son, that the housing officials are dishonorable
> men?" Silence. That effectively ended the hearing.

The CAFE bill passed the committee with overwhelming support. When the Senate passed the bill, Hollings commented to Freeman, "You know this is one bill that is going to be enforced, because it makes so much sense." But it stalled in the House. The failure to act reflected the chronic lethargy of the House Commerce Committee, of which a majority of members were pushovers for the auto executives' plea that they were honorable enough to carry out their pledge. Furthermore, President Gerald Ford was threatening to veto.

Hollings, with Magnuson's full support, tried again in the next Congress. Now Freeman assumed an entrepreneurial role that none of us Bumblebees had hazarded before. Armed with an innate boldness and my assurance that he could work with any senator on energy, Freeman connected with Senator Kennedy. Together they developed the strategy of hooking the CAFE Standards onto the Federal Energy Agency (FEA) reauthorization bill. They figured President Ford would not veto a bill that included the CAFE Standards as well as reauthorization of the universally supported FEA.

The bill readily passed the Senate, but Freeman worried about its fate in the House, fearing it would stall again in the House Commerce Committee. He needed reinforcement. As he recalls: "When Ted Kennedy was moving a bill, his staff person had his complete attention. He told me that it didn't matter who was in his office; that if I needed him to do something to get that bill passed, that I should just barge right in. And I did from time to time."

And so, before the crucial House committee meeting, Freeman went to Kennedy's office and there, he reports:

> He [Kennedy] picked up the phone and he called his good friend Tip O'Neill, the Speaker of the House, and he began the conversation like this. He says, "Tip, do you want to be in my Cabinet or not?" I didn't hear the other side of the conversation. But Kennedy says, "Well then, you've got to do A, B, C, D. You gotta get your Commerce Committee chairman to hold a hearing on this bill and pass it, blah, blah, blah"— he listed about six things O'Neill had to do.

As Freeman was leaving, Kennedy called him back and said, "Tip is gonna forget what I said about thirty seconds after I said it. I want you to go out there and dictate a note that includes all the things that I've said and put my initials on it and get it over to his chief of staff and make sure that all this happens."

Speaker O'Neill did his job. To our amazement, he had gained the support of a senior member of the House Commerce Committee, John Dingell, hitherto representing Detroit with unremitting fervor. Dingell had fought every bill he had ever seen that restricted the freedom of the auto industry to do as it pleased. But he was as fiercely independent as he was strong willed. He listened to Speaker O'Neill and was apparently convinced that this time the CAFE bill was in the long-term interest of Detroit.

Prospects for passage through the House Committee had become stronger. Still, one resistant vote needed to be turned around, that of Lud Ashley of Ohio, a junior Democratic member of the House committee who had been swayed by the auto companies' arguments—and, most likely, their campaign generosity. That's when Sutcliffe called in Robert Redford.

Redford's wife, Lola, had formed and chaired a pioneering environmental advocacy group called Consumer Action Now. Sutcliffe had been invited to address the group's meeting to provide them guidance in effective lobbying. Sutcliffe's insights were much appreciated, and he became a professional and personal friend of the Redfords. Redford always readily responded to Sutcliffe's requests for help in persuading wavering legislators to vote with the environmental advocates. This time he agreed to meet with Ashley.

To prepare Redford for the meeting, Sutcliffe met him in his office and laid out the provisions of the bill. "He's a good study, a quick study," Sutcliffe says. Redford then met with Ashley and promised to go into his district and campaign for him if he supported the CAFE bill. Ashley agreed and voted for the bill, though the lobbyist for the Ford White House was sure she had his vote. The bill was then favorably reported out of the House committee. A year later, Redford kept his promise and did a radio ad for Ashley.

"At the heart of it," Sutcliffe says, "was Chairman Magnuson's willingness to let us do damn near anything to get good legislation passed. And President Ford did sign the bill."

Freeman laments that Senator Kennedy never really got credit for his help with O'Neill because it was a Commerce Committee bill. The last time he saw Kennedy was at a fund-raiser in Washington a couple of years before he died.

> He saw me at the other end of a large room and he yelled, "Hey Dave, come over here. I got a guy that you need to talk to," and it was Senator [John] Kerry, who was running for president. Kennedy said, "You know, Kerry, you're a slouch if you can't even get an amendment passed to strengthen this bill that Dave and I got passed in '75. You need to listen to Dave for a while and let him tell you how to get the bill passed."

Alas, even Freeman had limits. In response to his urging Hollings to consider a tax on gasoline to encourage more efficiency, the senator replied: "Sonny boy, let me give you a fundamental lesson in politics. If I pass a tax on gasoline, people are going to be really pissed off at me. If the oil industry raises prices, they're going to be pissed off at them. There is no way on God's green earth that I will ever vote to increase the price of gasoline."

"Unfortunately," Freeman says, "he was right and he spoke for one hundred senators. Because presidents from Nixon through Obama, including Clinton and Carter, and everybody else that tried failed to get any increase in taxes in whatever form."

Freeman worked with Hollings on other important energy conservation laws, however, and with Sutcliffe on major auto safety law improvements. But, as Freeman says, "the CAFE law is at the heart of our energy policy still, because energy efficiency is now considered by Republicans as well as Democrats our best, cheapest, quickest source of energy."

# 9

# Finishing Unfinished Business
# —with Bumblebee Guile

Along with the flights of the Bumblebees into previously unpollinated fields, sampled in the preceding chapter, the Commerce Committee did not slack in its relentless pursuit of consumer protection laws. Though Magnuson, no longer driven by reelection anxiety, largely withdrew from chairing the Consumer Protection Subcommittee, its new chairman, Utah senator Frank Moss, unlike Magnuson, welcomed the Bumblebees' schemes enthusiastically. I made sure that a proven Bumblebee, Ed Merlis, would be always at his side.

Since 1967, Merlis had shown commitment and skill, though he was only on shadowy loan from the Health Department's Clearinghouse on Smoking and Health. By 1971 it was time to formalize his presence on the committee staff. Doing so required a little sleight of hand. As Merlis reminded me: "When you got me onto the committee paid staff, you went to Magnuson and told him that I was Moss's guy and Moss wanted this guy on the committee staff. And you went to Moss and told him that I was Magnuson's guy, and Magnuson wanted this guy on the committee staff. Moss was very willing to accept me in that role, and Magnuson raised no objection." Six years later Merlis took over from me as staff director.

As we have seen, Magnuson had already been delegating the hard work—though not the credit—to other committed senators on the committee, especially Philip A. Hart of Michigan, who, along with Maurine Neuberger, had been an early pioneer in the consumer protection awakening of the 1960s. Now, in the 1970s, several new committee members in addition to Hart were ready to pitch in. Magnuson remained supportive of their efforts—even though he privately dismissed Moss and Hart as "Boy Scouts." Yet after 1968, Magnuson did not entirely relinquish authorial credit—or effort—on ambitious goals that had been largely frustrated by the House Commerce Committee. His goals included strengthening federal regulation of the broad range of hazardous consumer products that remained unregulated, reforming the ubiquitous deceptive practice of diluting nominal "warranties," and strengthening the inadequate legislative powers of the FTC, nominally the national police force for attacking any "unfair or deceptive" business practice.

Magnuson had won passage of legislation that strengthened the earlier ineffective Flammable Fabrics Act, though only after fighting constant lobby-inspired resistance by the House committee. A far larger range of negligent product safety risks remained to be policed.

### Plucking the Fruits of the Investigative National Commission on Product Safety—with a Couple of Lightning Rods

After spending more than two years unearthing product hazards and identifying hundreds of consumers who had been deeply wounded by those hazards, the National Commission on Product Safety delivered its report to Congress on June 30, 1970. The commission members had voted unanimously to stand behind the report. In so doing they set a bipartisan tone. The report documents dozens of unregulated—or inadequately regulated—consumer hazards and concludes that self-regulation by manufacturers is "patently inadequate."[1] It urges Congress to create a new and permanent independent agency that would be called the US Consumer Product Safety Commission, with broad regulatory authority over hitherto unregulated product hazards such as those chillingly enumerated in the report. I assigned Lynn Sutcliffe to transform all the recommendations in the report into a bill promptly introduced by Magnuson, as committee chairman, with the Consumer Protection Subcommittee chairman Frank Moss as cosponsor.

As hearings on the bill progressed, it became clear that the Nixon administration, especially the highly respected secretary of Health, Education, and Welfare (HEW), Elliott Richardson, was dead set against the creation of an independent consumer product safety agency. All existing product safety regulation—however inadequate—had long been the domain of the Health Department's Food and Drug Administration (FDA), under the direct control of the secretary. The full roster of consumer product producers feared an unhinged independent agency less reliably amenable to responsible corporate pleas than the FDA had been. Plus the bill would still have to be approved by the lobby-driven House Commerce Committee.

Sutcliffe was wary of the Nixon administration's hostility to the creation of an independent agency. To ward off the inevitable attacks on the bill, Sutcliffe developed a strategy he called a "lightning rod"—in effect, a sacrificial lamb. A lightning rod must be at once a credible threat and a provision that can be given up in order to preserve the central objective of the bill—in this instance, the creation of the permanent Consumer Product Safety Commission in the form recommended by the study commission. Thus, when the time came for the Commerce Committee to mark up the bill for full Senate consideration, Sutcliffe prepared an alternative proposal, the lightning rod. Taking regulatory powers far beyond the recommendations of the investigative commission, it would have removed the entire food, cosmetics, and drug regulatory authority of the FDA.

Richardson was outraged by the Magnuson bill. He testified in our committee hearings in opposition to the very concept of an independent consumer product safety agency, but he was even more passionate in his opposition to the transfer of the whole FDA from his department. The lightning rod terrified the food and pharmaceutical industries. The creation of an unknown independent agency immune to lobbying interference through the politically approachable White House or the HEW secretary might be far less malleable than the FDA they had grown cozy with.

Nonetheless, the whole Magnuson bill was marketable to the Senate because of growing public disillusionment with the FDA's chronic cave-in to companies' resistance to costly safety standards for their products. So despite the opposition, the post-hearing Magnuson bill sailed through the Senate committee as introduced—along with the audacious transfer of the whole FDA—and passed the full Senate on June 21, 1972, by a final roll-call vote of 69 to 10, brushing aside amendments offered on behalf of the Nixon White House and the affected lobbies to strip the transfer of the FDA to the new commission.

The real hurdle for the bill would be the House Commerce Committee, which had routinely blocked or weakened many other Magnuson-sponsored consumer protection bills that had passed the Senate. But the balance of power on the House committee was changing. A small group of aggressively progressive members who had previously lacked sufficient seniority to exercise power had risen in seniority. Several were now entitled to the chairmanship of subcommittees.

The most determined member of this group was John Moss. As a first step, Moss introduced his own House version of the consumer product safety commission bill, which, like Magnuson's, incorporated all of the study commission's recommendations. Moss's bill did not include the Magnuson transfer of the FDA to the new Consumer Product Safety Commission, but it had another lightning rod: the creation of an independent federal consumer advocate with a mandate to prod any regulatory agency throughout the government to action whenever the advocate determined that the agency had become sluggish or overly influenced by companies resisting effective regulation.

Magnuson's bill and Representative Moss's bill were fought over relentlessly through several months of hearings before Moss's subcommittee. Finally, impatient, Moss brought the subcommittee members into a markup, even though he lacked one vote: a business-indentured conservative, Democrat Williamson Stuckey, who was prepared to vote with the Republican opponents.

Michael Lemov recalls that, during the hearings, the ranking Republican on the committee, Jim Broyhill, had said, "One could not fail to be impressed with the evidence of dangerous consumer products documented by the study commission." By Lemov's account, Broyhill "recognized that there was a basic 'government responsibility' to ensure the safety of products sold to American consumers."[2] These comments placed Broyhill in an uncomfortable position. He still had to avoid openly opposing the White House and undermining the otherwise uniform opposition of his Republican subcommittee members, of whom he served technically as the minority leader. Thus, during the committee's final deliberations, as Broyhill sat next to Moss on the podium, he stealthily signaled to Lemov to come to his side and, in a whisper, asked him to tell Moss that if he would give up the federal consumer advocate section of this bill, Broyhill would vote for the consumer product safety commission. Lemov took a few steps to his right and whispered the message to Moss, who, without looking at Broyhill, replied, "Fine."[3]

It was a silent deal. Moss and Broyhill kept their words. With Broyhill's vote, the subcommittee forwarded the Moss bill to the full committee, which, unhappily, voted for a disabling stew of amendments. The committee substituted the weakened bill for the content of the Senate-passed Magnuson bill before it was sent to the full House. There it was passed and sent back to the Senate.

In the conference committee to resolve differences between the Senate and House versions, Magnuson conceded that not all of the FDA needed to be transferred to the new commission. He conceded nothing else. Sutcliffe's lightning rod had served its purpose. The conference report, agreed on unanimously by both houses, still embodied all of the recommendations of the study commission, most of which Nixon's administration had opposed. Nonetheless, Nixon signed it with a flourish on October 27, 1972, boasting that the new law, the Consumer Product Safety Act, answered what he called a "long felt need" and that he was happy to give his approval. Yet, in my imagination, I can hear Ehrlichman as he drafted Nixon's signing speech, muttering to himself about Bumblebee fingerprints.

We've reached the last consumer protection law bearing Magnuson's name as author. Among its distinctions is that it mobilized a more formidable phalanx of corporate enemies than any bill Magnuson had proposed before. It took from 1967 to 1975 to pass. The tortured legislative path of the law that strengthened the power of the FTC has been well told by Lemov, so I focus here on the critical role innovative Bumblebee tactics played in gaining final passage of this transformative law. It greatly strengthened federal consumer protection against unfair and deceptive business practices.

### Empowering the "Little Old Lady of Pennsylvania Avenue"
In 1970, Sutcliffe took the lead in developing strategies for advancing reform initiatives that culminated in the Magnuson Moss Warranty-Federal Trade Commission Improvement Act. The act took effect in January 1975. Our inspiration was a flamboyant Nader's Raiders investigation of the FTC that was authenticated soon after by a parallel investigation by the American Bar Association.

Weakness at the top, the former federal trade commissioner Philip Elman told me, perpetuated the problems at the FTC. Shortly after his election, President John F. Kennedy had commissioned Abe Fortas (whom we glimpsed earlier wearing his lobbyist's black hat for the tobacco lobby) to prepare a candid evaluation of all the regulatory agencies the president had the power to change through the nomination of new commissioners. At the bottom of Fortas's list of all the regulatory agencies was the FTC, which he labeled "a whorehouse."

That apt label can be traced to a deal struck in the mid-1930s between President Franklin Roosevelt and the Tennessee Democrat Kenneth McKellar, reactionary chairman of a key Senate appropriations subcommittee. McKellar was at once balking at funding the president's high-priority programs and pleading with the president to engineer federal jobs for his unemployed Tennessee cronies. In exchange for McKellar's agreement not to block funding for New Deal legislation, Roosevelt allowed him to install his chosen friends and constituents on the FTC payroll. Almost none of them was competent or committed to the mission of the FTC. When McKellar retired from the Senate, he was succeeded by Senator Estes Kefauver, who successfully lobbied President Kennedy to appoint a Tennessee football hero then on the staff of the FTC, Paul Rand Dixon, to serve as chairman of the FTC. Dixon remained chairman throughout the 1960s. His lassitude affected many other FTC staff members, who became known, scornfully, as "the Tennessee Gang."

### The Art of Piggybacking

The FTC was hardly known or understood by the public. Thus, there was no public outcry for strengthening its powers. Sutcliffe and I figured if we could find a widespread consumer deception that would arouse the ire of the public, then introduce legislation that would engage broad public support by empowering the FTC to take effective action, we might be able to tack on provisions that would reach far beyond warranties to expand FTC powers broadly.

We seized on a vehicle for generating public outrage: the widespread practice of phony warranties. Studies have demonstrated that most consumers do not read manufacturer warranties—until their appliance or their car or other device falls apart. Before the passage of remedial legislation, ignoring that fine print could be disastrous. Now, when you buy a warranted product, if you see the words "full warranty," you have nothing to worry about. Anything that goes wrong with your new car that was not caused by gross negligence will be fixed. If you see "limited warranty" and ask what it means, you will be shown a straightforward, legible description of what will and will not be covered.

In 1968, the FTC—prodded by Commissioner Elman—submitted a report urging Congress to enact legislation that would empower it to (1) make warranty language easier to understand, (2) clearly define classes of "full" and "limited" warranties, (3) provide for safeguards against the disclaimer or modification of implied warranties, and (4) provide consumers with access to practical and effective consumer remedies for violation of warranties. Our strategic initiative was to develop for Magnuson and Frank Moss a bill that included all the popular warranty reform proposals advocated by the pre-reform commission and to tuck within this proposal, with little fanfare, the FTC reform package. The FTC reform package was the more comprehensive, though controversial, objective of the bill because it granted the FTC the authority to adopt industrywide regulatory requirements known as trade regulation rules, which were designed to prevent unfair or deceptive practices. Adding it this way was another Bumblebee strategy—

piggybacking. Piggybacking was the reverse of Sutcliffe's lightning rod strategy, the inclusion of a deeply desired objective, but one lacking in sufficient popular support to be adopted alone.

The rousing media coverage of deceptive warranty practices and the public response carried the full bill through the Commerce Committee to the Senate, where it passed, twice. On its first trip through the House subcommittee on consumer protection, John Moss fought hard for approval, but the lobbyists had done their work with his subcommittee members. He lacked the votes even to report his bill to the full House committee.

John Moss and Lemov, however, were not without their own guile. The strongest argument industry witnesses made to provide cover for House committee members to oppose the bill was a claim that the industry had been actively engaged for the past several years (beginning as soon as the threat of legislation loomed) in a program of highly publicized self-regulation to remedy the flaws in their warranty practices. On the bill's second trip through the House committee, however, Moss, through Lemov, initiated an investigation of two hundred warranties issued by fifty-one major US companies. With appropriate media fanfare, Moss reported to Congress in 1974. The report concludes:

> Today's consumer product warranties are replete with limitations on the manufacturers' and sellers' obligations. Any actions taken on the part of manufacturers and trade associations to clean-up [*sic*] these guarantees during the past five years appear to have had minimal results. These certificates, often marked "Warranty" and printed on good quality paper with a fancy filigree border, in many cases serve primarily to limit obligations otherwise owed to the buyer as a matter of law. This is done by disclaimers and exemptions and by ambiguous phrases and terms.[4]

This report effectively undercut the lobbyists' only credible objection and disconcerted at least one key member of Moss's subcommittee, Representative Broyhill. Once again, the conscientious Broyhill was open to supporting the whole bill, provided Moss would accept a modest compromise: if the FTC were granted broad rule-making powers, industry lobbyists were eager to grant company lawyers the right to cross-examine FTC witnesses who supported trade regulation rules. Broyhill approached Moss to explore adding this right to the rule-making provisions. Moss and Broyhill reached a compromise that allowed unlimited cross-examination, but only on material issues of fact, not policy or distractive technical issues. Nonetheless, the rule-making provisions would remain largely intact. Broyhill again gave Moss the vote he needed to report the bill to the full committee.

The full committee reported the Moss bill to the full House, but only after first passing an amendment eliminating one of the key provisions of the FTC improvement package: the right of consumers injured by violations of the bill's warranty regulations to obtain financial redress for their losses. The weakened bill passed the House.

The House bill went to conference with the Senate conferees defending the Magnuson bill. The differences were hard fought, but all conferees finally agreed to accept the House bill without the redress provisions. As the presiding chairman of the conference committee, Magnuson was responsible for presenting to the conferees a final report reflecting their votes. Sutcliffe, whom Magnuson assigned to interpret the conference committee's actions and draft the conference report, slipped the consumer redress provision back into the bill. The House conferees were then faced with a procedural dilemma: they would have to vote to remove the redress provision from the written report. This time, however, they lacked a majority, and the redress provision survived in the final conference report. When the conference committee report was brought before the full House, the House conferees could have staged a fight to kill the whole bill. But Christmas Eve was near, and House members were more eager to get home than to kill the popular warranty reforms. The House approved the conference report, as did the Senate. Magnuson called the final bill "a Christmas present for the American consumer."

**POSTSCRIPT:** I did not play much of a role in this achievement. But there is one pleasing fillip to the law that I claim. From the time that Magnuson introduced the first warranty reform bill in 1967, Senator Frank Moss was the principal cosponsor of the bill and energetically carried the burden of organizing the hearings and negotiations that carried it through for the next eight years. For this reason, it was referred to informally as the Magnuson-Moss bill.

On the day in 1974 when the Magnuson version of the bill was being debated by the Senate, Magnuson was, as usual, the floor leader for the bill, and Senator Norris Cotton was the leader of the opposition. You will recall the warm personal relationship between Magnuson and Cotton, despite their philosophical differences. So just before the debate was over and the Senate was preparing to vote, I approached Senator Cotton and asked whether he might consider formalizing for posterity Magnuson's leadership on this significant law by offering an amendment to call the law the "Magnuson Moss Warranty-Federal Trade Commission Improvement Act." He readily agreed to do so.

I then went back to Magnuson and told him of Cotton's intention. He was pleased but somewhat discomfited. He didn't much like Frank Moss for what I believed was no good reason other than that Moss tried too hard to ingratiate himself with Magnuson. This troubled me. So I disingenuously assured Magnuson that the "Moss" whom Cotton intended to honor was John Moss, the indisputably forceful House advocate of the bill. Magnuson was satisfied, and the Cotton amendment was accepted by unanimous consent.

The bill passed both houses and was sent to President Nixon, but there was strong resistance among key White House staff members at the strengthening of the bill. The crowning achievement of the Magnuson-Moss saga—and a testament to the comity across party lines—was a phone call Magnuson made to Republican senator Ted Stevens over the Christmas recess, urging him to call Nixon to sign the bill. Demonstrating his commitment to the bill and his affection for Magnuson, Stevens made the call.

After the law had been signed, I disingenuously assured both Senator Frank Moss and, through Lemov, Representative John Moss that the bill was named after them. They both died believing it.

### More, Much More, but Not Here

While I remained on the committee staff and continuing after I left in April 1977, the Bumblebees' public health and consumer protection engine continued to churn out a stream of public health and consumer protection bills, a fair percentage of which were shepherded to passage. Magnuson continued to afford us almost free rein. He generally played a supporting role, but took the lead on the Senate floor when necessary. Several other engaged committee members and their staff members became entrepreneurial advocates themselves, but they were always led by teams of committee Bumblebees, prodded and educated, in turn, by Nader and other independent experts, often cloistered far from Washington in academic centers, who equipped us to counter the ever-present business lobbyists' claims. Sometimes we were able to forge alliances with like-minded Republican committee members or their willingly subversive staff members. We continued to slant hearings to put forward the most effective supportive witnesses while remaining scrupulous, as Magnuson insisted, about allowing opposition witnesses their time before the committee. We also never stopped nurturing our relationships with like-minded journalists—leaking when necessary, but never in writing.

The other consumer protection laws and laws otherwise serving the public interest that originated in the Senate Commerce Committee from the mid-1960s to the late 1970s ranged wide. They too have their stories. To reconstruct all of them would overwhelm this book. Readers who seek the stories of any of these laws in the conventional legislative histories (which focus on their senatorial authors and cosponsors) will not find the names of the Bumblebees—without whom few would have survived the legislative maze or have even been proposed at all.

# 10

# Advise and Dissent

Under the Constitution, the Senate is granted the power to give "advice and consent" to the president on such matters as the appointment of ambassadors and Supreme Court justices. Senate committees have the authority to evaluate the presidential nominees who pass through their committees and to recommend to the Senate that they be acted on. When the Senate committees are led by members of the same party as the president, they tend to rubber-stamp presidential nominees, as they did routinely for presidents John F. Kennedy and Lyndon Johnson. (The rare exceptions were instances in which the unfitness of the nominee had roused public indignation or the nominee had lied in his or her testimony to the committee, causing a greater affront to the Senate's dignity than whatever the nominee was covering up.)

Evaluating President Richard Nixon's regulatory appointees, however, required serious attention. Too often, the regulatory nominees that fell within the Commerce Committee's jurisdiction were regulation averse or, worse, they were chosen by Nixon's corporate supporters to undermine the very regulatory laws they would be entrusted to enforce.

### A Virtual Regulatory Nominee Hearing

In the summer of 1971, one critical Nixon administration regulatory appointment triggered deep concern. Peter Hutt, a lawyer who specialized in defending giant food and drug companies against regulation by the Food and Drug Administration (FDA), had been named general counsel of the FDA. Alerted by Ralph Nader, I talked the appointment over with Ed Merlis, who had become the staff member working closest with Senator Frank Moss, the new chairman of the Consumer Protection Subcommittee. We decided that we should suggest to Moss that he summon Hutt to testify in a nomination hearing for his new role.

We had no justification for doing so. Hutt was not a presidential nominee. He had been appointed by the general counsel of the Health Department, who had the only attorney position in that department that required a presidential nomination. Moreover, he was already serving as the FDA's general counsel by the time we became concerned. We might have used the rationale that this was an "oversight hearing," but even there our Commerce Committee jurisdiction was wobbly. An oversight hearing to explore Hutt's fitness for his role would have appropriately been conducted by the Labor and Public Welfare Committee. But we knew that no such hearing would be undertaken by that committee, because it was chaired by Senator Harrison Williams of New Jersey, whose constituents included the nation's most powerful and politically influential drug companies. Thus we had no formal authority to either advise or consent. As Merlis acknowledged, however, "that never stopped us."

Knowing that his limited familiarity with the FDA's congressional mandate and its current failures to carry out that mandate faithfully was not sufficient to put an FDA expert like Hutt on the defensive, Merlis, at Ralph Nader's suggestion, conferred with James S. Turner. As the leader of a group convened by Ralph Nader to study the FDA, Turner had written a scathing report titled *The Chemical Feast*.[1] Over a weekend at Merlis's home, Turner helped Merlis put together a list of questions for Hutt that probed for potential conflicts of interest and financial issues that might be a barrier to his fulfilling his responsibilities or might raise questions about it. The two men hoped to reveal how Hutt might use his position to benefit his former clients.

While Merlis prepared, I told Senator Moss that Senator Magnuson wanted the hearing and that he wanted Moss to chair it. In truth, I had noted the idea only in passing during my daily briefing of Magnuson. Moss did not need to be coaxed. Merlis had earned his trust by writing several speeches Moss used for Senate floor statements on tobacco control issues and by preparing him for a *60 Minutes* interview and an appearance on the PBS show *The Advocates*. As Merlis recalls, Moss's "instincts were in the right place, and he recognized the accolades that he could receive."

Merlis did not interview Hutt before the hearing, so we had no idea how he would respond. To our surprise, Hutt was unintimidated. He saw the hearing as an opportunity to address accusations that he was a food and drug industry plant by demonstrating his deep commitment to the FDA's mandate. His answers were full and uncompromising. He treated the hearing as though it were an oversight hearing of the agency and used it to affirm his determination to reform the FDA's chronic weakness in challenging the food and drug industries' unsafe products.

We would never know how much our requiring Hutt to face our doubts in a hearing drove him to make commitments in public to which he otherwise could never have been held. Without the hearing, his behavior as the FDA's general counsel would have been virtually anonymous. Merlis, for his part, believes Hutt would have behaved ethically even without our hearing. Throughout his tenure, he drew consistent praise from early critics of his appointment.

### Ratcheting Up

The Hutt hearing turned our expectation of a hostile inquisition on its head. Hutt saw the hearing as an opportunity to force his own reform initiatives. For us it became the starting place for the gradual development of a rigorous, systematic committee nomination process that would make certain that Nixon's regulatory nominees were competent, free of even shadowy conflicts of interest, and committed to carrying out the mandates Congress had given them. Eighteen months later, Nixon nominated Lewis Engman to chair the FTC. This nomination fell squarely within the Commerce Committee's jurisdiction and became the Consumer Protection Subcommittee's assignment.

We studied the curriculum vitae the White House had supplied for Engman and found no whiff of a conflict of interest. Engman had practiced law in western Michigan, and his only political affiliation was with the Kent County Republican Finance Committee, of which he had been a member from 1965 to 1970. In 1970, he had been appointed director of legislative affairs for the President's Committee on Consumer Interests and had gone on to serve as general counsel of that committee (later renamed the Office of Consumer Affairs). If he had served either Kennedy or Johnson in these capacities, his credentials would have been impeccable, but the president he had served was Nixon, a surreptitious opponent of consumer interests.

That gave us pause. The FTC was at the center of federal consumer protection activities, and the appointment of its chairman was of prime concern to consumer advocates. We were close to enacting a law to strengthen the FTC's powers to enforce its consumer protection mandate. If the FTC was not now headed by someone committed to using the act properly and setting the appropriate precedents, our efforts in pushing through the legislation might have been for naught. So Merlis, with my blessing, decided to subject Engman to rigorous scrutiny.

Mindful of gaps in our preparation for the Hutt hearing, despite its favorable outcome, Merlis went to work diligently preparing for Engman's hearing. In addition to its consumer protection authority, the FTC shared antitrust powers and responsibilities with the antitrust division of the Justice Department, about which we knew little. So Merlis invited the staff of the Antitrust Subcommittee of the Senate Judiciary Committee, chaired by the progressive senator Philip A. Hart, to collaborate in developing probative questions.

Merlis was wary of the risk he had taken with the Hutt hearing in not knowing in advance how the nominee would respond to the prepared questions, so he developed a new procedure. First, he submitted the questions to Engman in advance and insisted that he provide his answers at least five days before the hearing. Then, in an unprecedented move, he made Engman's written answers public, sending them to the media and consumer protection and antitrust public interest advocates. He submitted follow-up clarifying questions and asked for Engman's answers to those questions sufficiently in advance of the hearing so that he could alert Senator Moss and prepare additional responsive follow-up questions and comments.

When Engman's hearing finally took place, his answers were generally satisfactory, though not as wholeheartedly assuring as Hutt's. Still, Engman was as likely to be faithful to the FTC's mission as any other potential Nixon nominee. As with Hutt, it was hard to prove that the process had revved up his commitment to vigorous consumer protection. Nonetheless, Engman proved a faithful chairman.

Merlis had added one other innovation, drawing on the skills of the experienced committee investigators we had recruited. The information we had requested from Engman included rigorous financial disclosures. In the past, Senate committees had resisted such requests as invasions of privacy, making them only after serious questions of financial wrongdoing had surfaced. Merlis's tactic was to offer the nominee a choice of supplying three years' worth of tax returns or giving detailed responses to a series of questions about his or her sources of income, assets, and liabilities.

"For simplicity's sake," Merlis recalls, "some nominees would just provide a tax return, because that doesn't require much work; you just pull it out of a drawer." Asking for such financial data from nominees became routine for us on all future nominations.

We built on our experience with Engman's nomination hearing by making sure that the staff member assigned to any nomination had been working on that agency's issues long enough to have developed knowledge of the agency's requirements and to be able to formulate a properly inquisitorial questionnaire and know whom to contact in the consumer advocacy community to fill in any gaps.

## What Do You Do When a Friend Is Nominated?

The next Nixon nomination for the FTC was Elizabeth Hanford in 1973. She was nominated to one of the two commissioner seats that the president was required to fill with someone not of his party. At the time, Hanford was an Independent, with a consumer protection record that was seemingly far more impressive than Engman's. She began her public life as a Democrat, campaigning in her home state of North Carolina for the election of John F. Kennedy as president in 1960. Later she served in the Johnson White House as deputy to Esther Peterson, whom Johnson had named to the newly created post of special assistant for consumer affairs, and then to her successor, Betty Furness, both strong consumer protection advocates. Hanford also became an advocate for women's rights and an ally and friend to several members of our committee staff, including me. We had become close enough that I visited her in the hospital during this period while she was recovering from a severe injury. We knew her as "Liddy."

When Nixon took office in 1969, all but one of the staff members of the White House Consumer Protection Office who had served the previous administrations resigned as a matter of course; not Hanford. She chose to remain in the White House as deputy assistant to Virginia Knauer, whom Nixon had appointed as special assistant for consumer affairs. In that position, Hanford adopted the new administration's opposition to aggressive government regulation and its belief in the virtues of self-regulation. To the consumer advocacy community, Hanford had become a turncoat.

At the time, I chanced to have a conversation with the staff director of a Democratic senator from Hanford's home state, B. Everett Jordan. He and the rest of the staff had helped Hanford fulfill her desire to serve in the Johnson White House as a consumer protection advocate. He had known her as a passionate liberal Democrat. He shook his head ruefully at what had become of her, saying, "She is an engine of ambition."

One afternoon four years later, Hanford called me and told me she was under consideration for nomination by President Nixon as a federal trade commissioner. She asked for my support. I told her I could not give it, adding that the committee would likely bar her appointment. She had become too entwined with Knauer's opposition to consumer protection regulation.

"Is there anything I can do to change your mind?" she asked.

"I don't think so," I said. When she persisted, I conceded, "Well, if your nomination would be supported by consumer advocacy groups, I could hardly stop it." Confident that all the advocacy groups would oppose her, I dismissed her from my mind. I soon learned, however, that her ambition to rise overrode any aversion she might have had to swerving again, back to a promise of aggressive consumer protection regulation through the FTC.

The following Monday she asked to see me again and this time reported that national consumer protection advocacy groups had agreed to support her nomination. That weekend the Consumer Federation of America, the umbrella group for national and local consumer advocacy groups numbering well into the hundreds, had held its annual national conference. Hanford had jumped on a plane and flown to the conference to woo the consumer advocacy leaders. With a heartfelt pledge to serve as a dedicated consumer advocate were she to serve on the FTC, Hanford persuaded several of the leading consumer protection advocacy leaders to support her nomination.

I was cornered. With the support she had gathered, we could not in good faith deny her confirmation. We put her through our full process of the questionnaire and the hearings. Nothing we didn't know about her came up, and the committee and the Senate routinely approved her nomination.

When I was confirmed as FTC chairman in 1977, Hanford was still serving her seven-year term as a commission member. For several years we worked together. She proved to be my most reliable ally on every consumer protection initiative we undertook, some of which broke new ground. Before the end of her term as commissioner, she married Senate Republican leader Bob Dole. Shortly after their marriage, she debated with him on NBC television about the merits of what was then Ralph Nader's highest-priority consumer protection proposal: the creation of an independent federal office of consumer advocacy, charged with prodding other lax federal regulatory agencies into greater action. Senator Dole, like most other Republican senators, was opposed; Hanford—now known as Hanford Dole—argued strongly for Nader's bill, undaunted by her husband's efforts to unnerve her and shake her stand with the same caustic retorts he would have used with any other adversary.

Who knows who the real Elizabeth Hanford Dole really is, other than ambitious? What I do know is that she kept her word as an FTC commissioner. She stood her ground, faithful to her pledge to the consumer advocacy groups and the committee. We have remained friends.

## An Abrupt Exit

We disposed of one FTC nomination without any process at all. It was for Thomas Sowell, whom Gerald Ford nominated in April 1976. Sowell, a nationally prominent economist and an expert in the economic consequences of regulation, was an impressively credentialed candidate for the position. We might well have been intrigued to learn that as a young economist he had published a paper supporting Marxist thought, but he had switched allegiance to the opposite camp and become—as he remains today—a leading advocate of the neoconservative Chicago school of economics. He consistently mocks regulation in his syndicated columns. Sowell was not a prime candidate for a regulatory commission. Ford nominated him for the remainder of a vacant FTC term that ended the following September and for the full seven-year term that followed, though Jimmy Carter, challenging Ford at that time for the presidency, had a good chance of winning.

Ed Merlis and I had a frank discussion with Sowell. I told him that we might confirm his nomination for the term ending in September, but not for the full seven-year term, which would begin only six weeks before the next election. He thanked us coolly, adding, "I'm not interested in a summer job," and headed straight to the White House to withdraw his name from nomination.

This peremptory dismissal may smack of partisan politics. But—in contrast to the process later undertaken by partisan-obsessed Republicans—the robust nomination gauntlet we developed involved examining the nominee's demonstrable competence and his or her commitment to the mandate of the FTC. One mark of our nonpartisanship was that our Republican staff colleagues were unreservedly welcome to join the process. We showed them our proposed questionnaires and kept them informed of all the intelligence we gathered about each candidate. They were free to add questions or to protest any part of the process. They almost never did.

More proof that this was not a partisan charade came after the election of Democratic president Carter and my departure from the committee. My successors, appointed by Magnuson—Merlis as staff director and Tom Allison as general counsel—strengthened the process further and became more sophisticated in analyzing the financial data they demanded. Along with other staff members in different fields, they were able to develop a record that led committee members to reject even some of Carter's nominations. Merlis and Allison also offered their counterpart Republican staff a greater role in investigating nominees, and their senators a greater role in the nomination process. Finally, as the following two stories illustrate, Merlis and

Allison found a way to engage in benevolent conspiracy with investigative journalists, yielding rewards for both the committee's nomination process and the journalists, and reminding us how critical an entrepreneurial press was to our own enterprises.

### A Non–Zero Sum Game with Muckrakers

An exchange of damning evidence between an investigative reporter and the Commerce Committee staff helped shape the committee's handling of a politically sensitive appointment by President Carter in the summer of 1977. The president nominated a high-ranking Florida Democrat, the Speaker of the Florida House of Representatives, Donald Tucker, to the chairmanship of the Civil Aeronautics Board (CAB). The appointment was of great interest to Florida's tourist industry because the chairman of the CAB had the power to ensure ample and inexpensive airline service to Florida's vacation centers. Though Carter's regulatory nominations had been uniquely free of political payoffs, the Tucker nomination was promoted by the president's political advisers, who were eager to provide Florida Democrats with evidence of Carter's help in protecting its tourism businesses.

Early in his evaluation of the Tucker nomination, Merlis became suspicious of "some questionable contacts and how he got to this position." By this time, the Carter administration had agreed to our insistence that they provide committee investigators access to reports prepared by the FBI for the White House in vetting their intended nominees. Previously, Senate committees had not routinely requested such reports.

In the interests of bipartisanship, Merlis sought support from the ranking Republican member of the committee, James Pearson of Kansas. Pearson was the kind of Republican that has virtually disappeared: a political moderate and, even more, a collaborative colleague whom Magnuson trusted. Pearson assigned a young woman on his staff, Mary McAuliffe, to join the staff investigating Tucker's rise to power. Joining them was the investigative staff of Magnuson's fellow Washington Democratic senator, Henry "Scoop" Jackson, chairman of the Permanent Subcommittee on Investigations. Jackson's staff included one investigator who had been in naval intelligence before he joined the subcommittee. This robust group dug into the White House investigative material on Tucker, including his FBI report, and found evidence to justify the concerns about Tucker's integrity that had already been raised.

They did not uncover enough data, however, to establish solidly that

Tucker should not be confirmed. So they turned to an investigative reporter for the *St. Petersburg Times*, Martin Dyckman. Dyckman was a journalist in the tradition of the late-nineteenth-century muckrakers Theodore Roosevelt cherished.

When Tucker was nominated, Dyckman had already uncovered Tucker's wrongdoing in a series of articles scrutinizing his behavior. But, like Merlis and his team, Dyckman had not yet uncovered enough evidence against Tucker to challenge his nomination. That came after Merlis arranged for our committee investigators to collaborate with Dyckman without directly disclosing FBI materials. Our investigators were able to guide Dyckman to public records that would enable him to confirm Tucker's corruption, as detailed in his published articles. Those articles, in turn, were cited by the staff members in their report to the Commerce Committee, thus establishing the basis for rejecting the nomination. The committee was unanimously persuaded by the report and authorized Magnuson to inform the White House that Tucker would not be confirmed. The Carter White House withdrew the nomination.

### Activating "Advice"

By the time Congress finally enacted the law creating the permanent Consumer Product Safety Commission (CPSC) in 1972, Johnson was gone and Nixon was in the White House. This change in administration did not bode well for the rigor of the new commission. Nixon's four initial nominees to the five-member commission were passable, though hardly crusaders. Three were Republicans and one was an Independent. Still, our hearings revealed nothing to justify denying them confirmation. These first four were nominated together, vetted and approved together, and sworn in together on May 14, 1973.

According to the legislation, only three of the five commissioners could be members of the president's party. Thus, one opening remained for a non-Republican. We were hoping for a more committed final nominee. By chance, one day in late summer a young man walked into my office unannounced. His name was David Pittle and he came from Pittsburgh, Pennsylvania. He was an engineering professor at Carnegie Mellon University with a strong interest in consumer product safety. Also, he was a lifelong liberal Democrat who had created and led an aggressive citizen advocacy group fighting for consumer protection. He said to me simply, "I'd like to be a member of the Consumer Product Safety Commission."

"Not a chance in the world," I replied reflexively. I was convinced his liberal advocacy credentials would be anathema to the Republican president Nixon's White House.

Then Pittle added, "I think Senator Scott might support my nomination." Hugh Scott was a moderate Republican senator from Pennsylvania. Still, I doubted he would support so radical a candidate; and even if he did, I was confident that the White House, still to be heard from on this vacancy, would not pick him.

Without much confidence, I activated the "advice" provision of the Constitution and called the White House staff person in charge of such nominations to offer favorable "advice" in support of Pittle. I had developed a civil relationship with the staffer in earlier nomination-related exchanges, and he agreed to meet with Pittle. Meanwhile, Scott did indeed tell the White House that he supported the nomination. The White House staff person I called was impressed with Pittle's expertise and Scott's endorsement, but perhaps even more influential was his assumption that my involvement as Magnuson's committee staff director meant that the senator wanted him appointed. I did not disabuse him of that assumption, though, in truth, I had only briefly noted to Magnuson on one of our daily car rides from his home to his office that there was an appealing candidate for the CPSC. He hadn't reacted. That was enough for me to remain silent with the White House. Nixon nominated Pittle. We did just enough investigation to confirm Pittle's account of himself to me, and he was readily confirmed.

David Pittle proved to be among the most effective commissioners in the history of the CPSC. Among his initiatives was an attempt to curb cigarette manufacture and marketing practices by employing a legislative clause in a way that had never been intended. Ed Cohen, who by now had matured into a veteran Bumblebee, discovered that though the language in the early Hazardous Substances Control Act (now in the jurisdiction of the new CPSC) had been motivated by a rash of poisonings from the fumes of chemical cleaners, by authorizing the regulation of "any substance causing injury to humans through inhalation," the law seemingly embraced cigarette smoke.

Nothing in the entire legislative history of the Hazardous Substances Control Act suggested cigarettes. Without question, lobbyists for the Tobacco Institute would have exercised all of the institute's influence to kill any suggestion that cigarettes fell within the reach of the law. Nonetheless, with our encouragement, Pittle persuaded a majority of his fellow commissioners to assert jurisdiction over cigarette manufacture and marketing.

The tobacco lawyers immediately took the CPSC to court, challenging its reading of the act, but lobbying power proved swifter than the courts: within six weeks, our own committee, led by Kentucky Democrat Wendell Ford, without objection from Magnuson or any of our otherwise allied committee members, voted to amend the Hazardous Substances Control Act expressly to exclude tobacco products from its reach. Still, Pittle had vigorously made the effort, knowing all along that it was a long shot.

So passionate and entrepreneurial was Pittle that when his term ended, President Jimmy Carter, who had taken office the year before, reappointed him, at the urging of Ralph Nader, for another full term.

### One Misstep Short of Our Blocking a Destructive CPSC Chairman

As the CPSC was struggling to fulfill its potential, we came very close to thwarting the nomination of a Ford White House appointee who would paralyze the commission's progress for several years. By this time, Pittle and his colleagues had developed industrywide standards for only three consumer products that had posed risks: swimming pool slides, window-panes, and matchbook covers. But they were close to issuing a mandate to guarantee the safe redesign of a widely marketed, severely hazardous consumer product: chainsaws.

Since 1973, the first commission chairman, Richard Simpson, had worked hard to develop chainsaw rules. When Simpson resigned just before the election of Jimmy Carter, President Ford nominated as his replacement S. John Byington, a conservative who displayed a clear preference for voluntary self-regulation. We knew immediately that he was not fit for the job. Nothing had been clearer from the authoritative 1970 report on the investigative commission's findings than that the sort of voluntary standards Byington supported were inevitably tailored to the manufacturer's profitability rather than to consumer safety.

Ed Cohen ably handled the Byington nomination. He employed the full range of nomination procedures we had developed, and with the strong recommendation of Consumer Protection Subcommittee chairman Moss, who chaired Byington's nomination hearing, and with my encouraging Magnuson's support, the committee voted not to recommend Byington's nomination. (This outcome was the functional equivalent of a no vote.) Moss and Magnuson then led a successful fight on the Senate floor to defeat the nomination. Cohen sat beside Moss, fully occupied with the process of the vote, while I sat in the back of the chamber gleefully taking in our success.

So enchanted was I that I forgot a basic Senate procedural rule: any initial Senate vote can be reconsidered at the behest of any senator who has been on the winning side of the vote. Routinely, following a Senate vote, the sponsoring senator on the winning side would immediately submit a motion to reconsider the vote, and a Senate ally would immediately rise to table that vote. The object was to kill further reconsideration of the vote. After fourteen years of working in the Senate, I should have known to leap forward and remind Moss to move to reconsider. By the time I realized my lapse, it was too late. After the initial vote, which the administration had assumed would confirm Byington, they now had time to pressure every Republican senator who had voted to reject Byington to support him. Two days later, the nomination was again brought before the Senate. In this vote, Byington was confirmed by a narrow margin. We had lost what we had first won. Cohen took responsibility, but I should have been awake.

The determined Byington soon persuaded three other commission members to abandon the chainsaw rule-making proceeding and turn instead to a pledge from a recently formed industry organization, the Outdoor Power Equipment Institute, to voluntarily develop a chainsaw safety standard. Four years later, the industry group had produced nothing, and the commission had to start the chainsaw rule-making procedure all over again.

Eventually, however, the CPSC fulfilled its promise. Presidents Jimmy Carter, Bill Clinton, and Barack Obama made strong appointments to the commission, and Pittle remained a primary moving force. In 1977, he was reappointed as a commissioner by President Carter, and for a while he served as acting chairman. Now, almost forty years later, the commission still follows his inspiration and that of his brilliant protégé, Robert Adler, whom Pittle hired in the early years of his service. Adler, trained as a political scientist, had long held a strong passion for regulating consumer hazards. He served as an assistant to Pittle and another committed commissioner for nine years before being appointed counsel to the Subcommittee on Health and the Environment of the House Committee on Energy and Commerce, which had been transformed from a corporate lapdog to a legislative leader. In 2008, he served on the Obama transition team and coauthored a report on the CPSC for the Obama administration. President Obama nominated Adler to the commission in March 2009.

### A Worthy Raising of Standards—with a Caveat

Shortly after Nixon's reelection in 1973, we decided to try something that was to my knowledge unprecedented: we prepared the committee to reject a nominee to a regulatory agency who was undeniably competent but had represented the regulated industry aggressively for many years. We reasoned that even a well-intentioned regulator, after so many years, would have absorbed his clients' strongest arguments against regulation and would find it difficult to be neutral on issues affecting them.

The nominee was Robert Morris, a corporate lawyer who, as counsel to the Standard Oil Company of California (SOCAL), had spent nearly twenty years in combat with the Federal Power Commission (FPC) over its regulatory initiatives. Nixon nominated Morris to the commission, which then exercised their authority to regulate natural gas prices and related industry practices. Before Nixon even sent this nomination to the Senate, Morton Mintz had written an article in the *Washington Post* sharply criticizing the appointment of an oil company advocate to the FPC.[2]

That was enough for us. We had no doubt that Morris was competent and that his intentions were honorable. He may have believed he could be an impartial regulator and not an agent of the oil industry. But Merlis, with one of our most tenacious Magnuson Fellows, Henry Lippek, and I believed that no one who had spent almost two decades committed to the economic interests of SOCAL could shed himself of bias toward their interests in favor of those of the public. We determined to do what we could to persuade Magnuson and a committee majority to oppose Morris's nomination. We did, despite Morris's insistence at his hearing that he would faithfully carry out the duties of an FPC commissioner. In committee, Magnuson led a vote to report the nomination to the Senate floor without a recommendation of confirmation. With the weight of Magnuson's disapproval and a majority vote of the committee, the Senate voted against confirmation of Morris. After the vote, exercising the procedural rule we forgot when Byington was nominated, Magnuson offered a motion to table further consideration of the nomination. Morris's nomination was rejected.

To the best of my knowledge, this was the first time that the Senate had rejected a nomination on the sole basis that no regulator who had represented a regulated industry could be relied on to regulate that industry in the public interest. We were very proud of that advance in the evaluation of regulatory nominees. But there was a catch. The defeat of Morris's nomination was followed by the committee's confirmation of William Springer, a retired member of Congress from Illinois, to another vacancy on the FPC. The committee lackadaisically succumbed to the self-serving practice of favoritism to former members of Congress. Springer was confirmed. The outcome, according to Merlis, was that the Senate confirmed Springer, an "undistinguished former congressman," whereas it had not confirmed Morris. "It should have been vice versa," he says, "because while Morris may have been an energy lawyer, he actually had a brain."

The principle of questioning the objectivity of a regulator who had long represented the regulated industry was fundamentally sound, and implementing it showed an advance in the vigor of Senate responsibility. Still, it should not have become a rigid rule. This caution is reinforced by our experience with Peter Hutt. We initiated the purloined oversight hearing of Hutt because we were convinced that a corporate lawyer representing the food and drug companies regulated by the FDA could not be impartial in his role as regulator. In the end, Hutt proved faithful to his assignment as general counsel of the FDA and was responsible for toughening the FDA's regulatory processes. Morris was an honorable man and almost certainly would have been a more conscientious FPC commissioner than his political hack co-nominee. I was also wrong about Elizabeth Hanford. I had assumed that having embraced the Nixon White House's antipathy to federal regulation, Hanford could not reverse course. She did, and she remained faithful to her pledge to consumer advocacy groups and the committee.

Ironies abounded in the nomination process, including when Carter nominated me for FTC chairman. When I went before the committee I had served for so many years, my two close friends, Merlis and Allison, made sure I went through the full process Merlis had developed. Later, when Sharon Percy Rockefeller, wife of Jay Rockefeller, West Virginia's Democratic governor, was nominated by Carter to the board of the Corporation for Public Broadcasting, Merlis and Allison required her to make a full financial disclosure, which, by our rules, we made public. The storied millionaire governor, Merlis recalls, was not happy with our forcing this disclosure. Thirty-five years later, however, when he was chairman of the Commerce Committee, Rockefeller applied an elaborate process for regulatory nominees similar to the one he had resented when his wife was asked to go through it.

### An Abused Legacy

We made mistakes in developing a system for treating presidential regulatory nominees, who would be a critical link in our efforts to ensure the effectiveness of public interest regulation. Our judgment sometimes undermined the nomination of an exceptional individual who had once served corporate interests. Furthermore, we added to the laborious and time-consuming process to which nominees are now uniformly subjected, discouraging able potential candidates from agreeing to serve. Worse, the elaborate process we developed was later twisted into the tool of a corporate-directed Senate that added unending delays in an effort to discourage presidential nominees too strong for senators hostile to regulation.

Early in 1975, I was forced to participate, against my will, in just such an abuse of Senate power. It was initiated in a naked vendetta by the newly seated New Hampshire Democratic senator John Durkin, one of the most vindictive committee members I ever encountered from either party.

Durkin's election still bears the distinction of taking the longest time in Senate history from Election Day to his seating in the Senate. The vote count on November 5, 1974, had favored his Republican opponent, former representative Louis Wyman, by 355 votes. Durkin requested a recount, which resulted in his victory by 10 votes. Governor Meldrim Thomson then certified Durkin as the winner. Wyman, however, requested a second recount, in which he prevailed by 2 votes. After a record-breaking seven-month squabble among senators, the Democratic Senate declared the seat vacant. Durkin eventually won it in a special election.

Although he had succeeded in finally winning the election, Durkin proved relentless in avenging a perceived slight. He was convinced that the New Hampshire attorney general, Warren Rudman, had intervened in the second recount to misread enough votes to elect the Republican by two. No evidence came forth to support this charge. Moreover, Rudman was widely respected by both Democrats and Republicans in New Hampshire for his probity as attorney general. On February 4, 1976, President Ford nominated Rudman to be a member of the Interstate Commerce Commission, with the expectation that he would be chairman. Rudman had played a role in studying and recommending reform in rail and trucking regulation, and he was well qualified. Shortly after his nomination, Rudman came to see me. I interviewed him extensively and concluded that he was a uniquely prepared candidate for the position, regardless of party.

Then Senator Durkin summoned me to his office. He demanded that we engineer the rejection of Rudman's nomination, candidly confessing that his demand had nothing to do with Rudman's qualifications and everything to do with his own illusory mistreatment at Rudman's hands as state attorney general. I told him I could not do that. He said he would talk to Magnuson, and he did. Magnuson had little interest in whether Rudman was confirmed or not; but he was inclined to defer to Durkin's request, though he harbored little regard for Durkin. He was simply responding to the traditional deference among senators to oppose any nominee who is opposed by either senator from the nominee's state—in effect, a right of blackball.

I resisted, arguing that Rudman seemed well qualified and highly regarded, but I agreed to unleash the committee staff's most persistent investigator, John Dale, to go to New Hampshire and investigate everything he could find that might incriminate Rudman so the committee would have a just reason for opposing his nomination—at least enough to threaten to discredit him sufficiently to force him to withdraw his name.

Off went John Dale to spend several weeks in New Hampshire ferreting out every possible flaw in Rudman's behavior. I met with Rudman and told him about the investigation, and he responded that he was ready to provide any data Dale asked for. At the end of several weeks, Dale came back. He had found only one minor lapse: Rudman had taken a business deduction for his personal law library at a time when he was not in private practice. I told Durkin that if Rudman offered an explanation or even an apology and promised to revise his tax statement, this lapse alone might not justify a rejection.

"I don't care," said Durkin. "I want his nomination killed."

I arranged another visit with Rudman. I leveled with him, "There is no way in hell that the committee is going to approve your nomination."

Rudman thanked me graciously and said, "I'm going to withdraw. I'm then going back to New Hampshire, and I'm going to run against him for the Senate in 1980." He did, and he took Durkin's seat and served a distinguished career as a moderate Republican in the Senate from 1980 to 1993, when he retired, rejecting offers to become a Republican leader in presidential campaigns in order to pursue nonpartisan advocacy for economic and social justice.

Durkin disappeared from politics. He had wrought his own defeat. To the best of my knowledge, no former chairman of the publicly obscure Interstate Commerce Commission has ever subsequently run successfully for the Senate.

Our legacy in strengthening the Senate's role to give advice or withhold consent can be abused by partisan bullies. But the serious examination of presidential regulatory nominees to ensure their competence and commitment to the goals Congress has legislated remains essential. In the hands of a responsible Senate, they are still available to serve the common good.

# 11

# Pushing the Boundaries

While Richard Nixon and Gerald Ford were in office and Democrats continued to lead Congress, the more entrepreneurial of the Democratic senators (served by their entrepreneurial staff) transformed the oversight function. The Senate Commerce Committee, more than any other committee, expanded its oversight strategies to achieve the complementary goals of weakening the impact of special interest lobbies and prodding underachieving regulators. We developed a range of tactics to prod regulators into regulating and to intimidate or shame wrongdoers into voluntary reform.

## A Bumblebee's Gall

Of all the members of our committee whom I respected and enjoyed working with throughout my service to the committee, Senator Philip A. Hart stands out. He was gracious, scrupulously ethical, and deeply dedicated to the interests of the poorest and most neglected of his Michigan constituents. By 1969, he had gained sufficient seniority on the committee to be eligible for a subcommittee chairmanship. Hart had developed an early concern about the deterioration of the environment. No other committee held jurisdiction over environmental issues, so Jerry and I suggested to him that we create a new subcommittee on the environment. Magnuson approved.

Staffing such a subcommittee, however, would be a challenge. Though I had sought every opportunity to work with Hart, he had kept his distance. I had not been able to assuage his concern that Magnuson's staff would always put Magnuson's interest ahead of that of any other committee member. Magnuson had too often been a roadblock to Hart's consumer protection initiatives.

Then, as I was struggling to find the right staff member to work with

Hart on the new Subcommittee on the Environment, Leonard Bickwit showed up. Unlike the other Bumblebees, he came to see me bearing classic Eastern Seaboard legal credentials: a Harvard law degree and a stint with a premium New York law firm. He looked the part, handsome and well-groomed. He told me he had turned down several offers on the Hill because he greatly admired Senator Hart and was eager to work for him. I thought Bickwit might break the ice, so I hired him and arranged for him to meet with Hart as staff for the proposed subcommittee. My strategy worked. Hart told Bickwit that members of the committee staff had not previously had a strong relationship with him, but, "if that's what you want, we'll do something about that."

Meanwhile, Bickwit and I had been searching for an initiative that would meet Hart's determination to challenge human abuses to the environment. I found it by accident, in an investigative report by Thomas Whiteside in the *New Yorker*: a well-documented exposé of the risks to vulnerable communities of the herbicide 2,4,5-T, which the US military had used in Vietnam to destroy crops and denude forests. It had also created widespread sickness, including among US soldiers. Yet the Agriculture Department, with no regulatory bent, listed 2,4,5-T, an ingredient in Agent Orange, among permissible herbicides, and it was being widely spread along US roads to contain overgrowth.

Whiteside was married to my cousin, Marie, and we were close friends. Because of that, I had advance notice of his article. I realized that it could be the foundation for oversight hearings. I alerted Bickwit, and he immediately contacted Whiteside. Whiteside's article had been scrupulously researched and was temperate and balanced, despite its horrifying implications. Yet, when the two men met, Bickwit recalls, Whiteside shed his balance and spoke passionately about the need to ban Agent Orange. Bickwit remembers Whiteside's outrage in recalling tests of the impact of exposure to the herbicide on laboratory baby chicks: "[He said that] those that had experienced no exposure to 2,4,5-T were very healthy. But those who were exposed to the chemical either in the embryo stage or later were really sick. They were 'sick chicks,' as he put it. He saw no humor at all in his description of things—consistently expressing only resentment and outrage."

Whiteside led Bickwit to the scientists who would make the most effective witnesses in establishing the extensive risks of 2,4,5-T. Bickwit then suggested to Hart that holding oversight hearings on the Agriculture Department's failure to curb the widespread use of Agent Orange as an herbicide would be a fitting job for the new subcommittee. Hart readily agreed. The hearings were set for 1970.

Counseled by Whiteside, Bickwit recruited the scientists as witnesses. On the first day of the hearings, they made a strong case for banning the domestic use of 2,4,5-T. Bickwit had not scheduled any industry witnesses or Agriculture Department representatives that first day to rebut or obscure the experts' testimony. The hearing, Bickwit confesses, was by no means balanced, but it triggered great publicity: "It was televised on the evening news. The *Washington Post* actually had a picture of Hart holding up one of these chicks."

The next week, however, the industry witnesses and Agriculture Department spokespersons had their day. Hart turned to Bickwit to question them. Prepared by Whiteside, he was ruthless in his challenges. The industry people, Bickwit recalls, were upset that Hart did not ask the questions and that Bickwit "was acting like a prosecutor."

"It was clear," he adds, "what side I was on."

Their complaints were understandable. Magnuson had not been in the habit of delegating the questioning of witnesses to a mere staff member. But it worked. When the assigned witness for the Agriculture Department appeared, he quickly announced that 2,4,5-T would immediately be banned. Though the department never acknowledged that the ban was directly related, as Bickwit remembers, "There was no doubt that the ban was prompted by the hearing."

### The Virtues—and Hazards—of Poaching

Hart's subcommittee was finished with herbicides, but Bickwit was not. Though, under the Environmental Protection Agency's (EPA) jurisdiction, the Commerce Committee had jurisdiction over chemical products swallowed or inhaled, herbicide legislation was administered by the Agriculture Department and had always fallen within the jurisdiction of the Agriculture Committee. Hearings, however, were unrestricted, so Bickwit got busy organizing hearings to which he summoned EPA executives to testify on the environmental dangers of approved, environmentally destructive herbicides beyond 2,4,5-T. As he admits, he was far less gentle in his inquisitions and follow-up questions than Hart was inclined to be. Soon he developed a reputation for ferocity among fellow Senate staffers. As a staffer, he felt free, he says, to be "obnoxious" in a way no senator would be to a fellow senator, and he was able to pose follow-up questions because, as a staffer, he had more time than the senators to become familiar with the subject of a hearing.

Occasionally Hart felt the need to rein Bickwit in. In his determination to go after the deputy EPA administrator, John Quarles, for example, Bickwit asked him point-blank whether he had done such and such, "based on all of what we've just been talking about." When Quarles answered yes, Bickwit replied, "Don't you think that's *outrageous*?" After a bit of sparring ("I wouldn't say that." "I don't want to put words in your mouth." "I'm not going to let you."), Hart whispered to Bickwit, "Try *unfortunate*."

Bickwit remained undaunted by Hart's restraint. Among Senate committee staff members who had taken note of the Commerce Committee's cavalier disregard for respecting established committee jurisdictions was the able but timorous staff director of the Senate Agriculture Committee, Harker Stanton. While Bickwit could not find a way to develop herbicide regulatory legislation that would be referred to the Commerce Committee, Stanton became wary of arousing Bickwit's wrath if his committee developed an herbicide improvement bill that was weak. Bickwit did not disabuse him of this concern. Thus, in an act of intercommittee reach none of us had tried before, Stanton agreed to allow Bickwit to participate in the development of the Agriculture Committee's herbicides bill.

Bickwit ardently advocated stronger provisions. Once, when he proposed an amendment, Stanton responded, "We can't go there. The industry won't buy it." To which Bickwit said, "Why don't we have the industry come into our discussions? I'd just as soon talk to the people who are actually making the decision than talk to you." Stanton backed down. "We did move the legislation," Bickwit recalls, "in a way that was more environmentally sound."

### A Little Help from His Friends
Bickwit also worked with Hart and other Commerce Committee members to develop and promote the advancement of the subcommittee's mandate by introducing bills regarding food inspection, toxic substances control, safe drinking water regulation, and protection of the environment and ocean mammals. Some of these bills became laws, some did not, but all generated considerable public interest as they progressed through the system. Their progress followed the course of other Bumblebee-managed bills, with the addition of one innovative expansion of the Bumblebees' reach: the informal recruitment of volunteers to help ensure that the committee bills Bickwit was working on would succeed once they reached the

Senate floor. Bickwit told me that he knew a lot of people in town who viewed what they were working on as "exciting" and that "they were dying to volunteer."

"I learned from you," he added, "that when you had a floor amendment, it was a good idea to just call as many offices as possible, and see if you could talk them into voting for it. Most people weren't that thorough. That was one of the principal activities of the volunteer groups." Those volunteer groups consisted mainly of restless, able young women who, despite their evident skills, were virtually barred from professional staff committee jobs.

### Not So Fast, but Planting Seeds

Hart and Bickwit had achieved the legislative objective of banning the domestic use of herbicides containing 2,4,5-T after a single hearing with no legislative labyrinth. Ed Merlis and Ed Cohen, in contrast, working for the Consumer Protection Subcommittee, would require of its chairman, Senator Frank Moss, exhaustive, frustrating efforts either to achieve timely legislation or to shame industry and stimulate public concern until their efforts yielded regulatory legislation.

Perhaps foremost among Cohen's initiatives was the airbag crusade. By 1970, Ralph Nader and others were frustrated by the Nixon administration's chokehold on the National Highway Safety Administration, which included a clampdown on any efforts it might make to mandate airbags in all automobiles. Nonetheless, in 1971 Moss introduced legislation that would mandate an airbag in every new car and truck. Detroit automakers objected, claiming airbags would raise costs and depress sales. Despite their opposition, Moss held extensive hearings that included compelling testimony that airbags would save thousands of lives. With Magnuson's backing, the bill passed the Senate but lay buried in the House committee until 1972, when a critical group of active public safety advocates who had gained seniority on the House committee pushed it through and prevailed on the full House to pass an identical bill, leaving it only for the Senate to act again.

Detroit, however, was not to be foiled. While the most aggressive progressive on the House committee, John Moss, and his supporters again voted for the bill and sent it to the House floor, the automobile lobby successfully persuaded Senate members (doubtless some with their hands out) to re-refer the bill to the Judiciary Committee. That committee reported it back to the Senate floor so weakened by industry amendments that Magnuson and Frank Moss let it die. Moss later wrote, in sadness:

I mourn the loss of that simple bill because it was all ready to be passed and was a much needed consumer safety bill. If those airbags had been installed in accordance with the bill, more than 100,000 deaths a year and many times that number in injuries could have been prevented. I think of it every time I read about someone hitting the windshield and breaking up his face or dying. . . . My older brother, Wayne Moss, was killed in an automobile accident, when he was slammed into the steering wheel when a truck skidded head on into his car. I believe he would have lived had there been airbags then.[1]

Still, Detroit was shaken by the near passage of the bill and the likelihood that they would eventually be forced to adopt airbags. General Motors experimented with airbags in a thousand Chevrolet Impalas in 1973, planning to install them in some Oldsmobiles, Buicks, and Cadillacs the next year. But the Impalas did not sell, and there were flaws in the technology that set development back. It was not until twenty years after the Moss hearings that Congress, in 1990, passed a law that required that all cars sold in the United States be equipped with either an airbag or automatic seat belts. Because automatic seat belts were often viewed as a nuisance by the public, automakers often chose the airbag. In 1991, Congress enacted the Intermodal Surface Transportation Efficiency Act, which ordered the National Highway Safety Administration to require both driver-side and passenger-side airbags in all new vehicles by 1998. It was far too long in coming, but at least we had helped lay the foundation twenty-six years earlier.

### Making Toast of Empty Cereals

Even more tortuous was the path of Merlis and Moss's initiative to publicly shame the cereal manufacturers for their aggressive marketing to children of cereals made up of highly processed grains and loaded with sugar. Merlis had been lobbied by a skillful public interest advocate named Robert B. Choate. Choate gave evidence before a Moss hearing in July 1970 that the most popular brands of dry breakfast cereal had been denuded of vitamins, dietary minerals, and protein. Many of the most popular cereals, he rated as "empty" calories, which "fatten but do little to prevent malnutrition." The hearings generated some media coverage, but nothing changed.

By 1971, Merlis had worked with Moss to develop two more bills to police deceptive advertising, a truth-in-advertising bill and a companion bill to create the National Institute of Marketing Science. Choate saw Moss's hearings on these bills as an opportunity for more public shaming of the cereal companies. He told Merlis about a science experiment by an eleven-year-old middle school student from Melbourne, Florida, named Dawn Ann Kurth. Kurth had fed a selection of the most prominent cereals to one group of mice and the ground-up cardboard boxes in which the cereals had been packaged to a control group. The mice that ate the ground-up cereal boxes thrived, while those who ate the contents were sickened. In June 1972, she was invited to testify before the Consumer Protection Subcommittee on her findings. After describing her experiment, Kurth excoriated the deceptive advertising directed toward children, which promoted one such cereal as "the breakfast of champions."

Moss was delighted by the media coverage of the hearing, especially a laudatory story on the front page of the *Washington Post*. "His only frustration," Merlis recalls, "was that the front page picture of him in the *Washington Post* was below the fold."

"Part of what we did to encourage our senators," he adds, "was to get them media accolades, which made them much more willing to do some of the down and dirty work that was necessary."

The effort to ensure that mass-marketed cereals are healthful proceeds at a snail's pace even now.

## Expanding the Power—and the Ease—of the Chastening Letter

Almost as effective as oversight hearings was the deployment of letters and questionnaires to regulators and resistant industries. These commanding letters and questionnaires, usually signed by Magnuson or a subcommittee chairman, were not easily stonewalled. The stonewalling was an implicit confession that could become, with help from our media friends, a public relations headache. It was easy for us to prepare letters and to persuade our senators to approve them—letters allowed them to intimidate the recipient organizations without having to take on the burden of a hearing.

Sluggishness in the agencies we had created drew our special oversight, especially in their start-up years. For example, to enforce our Poison Prevention Packaging Act, the FDA was required to organize an advisory committee of experts to recommend the most effective designs for the child safety caps they would mandate through their regulatory powers. The agency took more than a year just to organize the advisory committee. Merlis drafted a scathing letter to the FDA (over Magnuson's signature) in which he pointed out that since the act had passed, approximately 150 children had died because they had not appointed the advisory committee. The letter moved them.

Letters to the agencies, Merlis recalls, had a healthy secondary impact. The agency heads would normally refer letters to the staff who had done the groundwork on the activity our letter was challenging with a request that they draft a response. Whereas agency heads would "try to sugarcoat" the agency's formal response, the working staff were usually conscientious and just as frustrated as we were. "They'd surreptitiously give us a call to let us know what really was going on," especially "when higher levels in an agency were condoning something" that should not have been condoned.

When several of our corporate friends complained that all we ever did was criticize business, Merlis recalls, we sent a letter to the top two hundred *Fortune* 500 companies and invited them to tell us in their own words what they had done to better the environment, to benefit consumers, or to advance social goals. About half responded and we compiled the responses, with some editorializing, and printed the compilation as a committee report titled *Initiatives in Corporate Responsibility*. It silenced some and shamed others into doing more.

### Undermining the Tobacco Lobby's Juggernaut

For four years after Magnuson's 1965 Cigarette Labeling and Advertising Act was signed into law, the tobacco lobby carried out unceasing efforts to amend it to permanently eliminate the Federal Communications Commission's (FCC) and the FTC's authority to regulate cigarette advertising. They failed. So devastating were the proposed regulations that the two commissions were poised to enforce that the industry pleaded for legislation allowing them to simply cease all television advertising.

In the end, the House Commerce Committee members who were friends of the tobacco lobby extracted one concession in finalizing the tobacco industry's forced retreat. In conference with the House Commerce Committee members, Magnuson agreed to set the effective date of the TV ban for the night of January 1, 1971, rather than December 31, 1970, thus giving the companies and the broadcasters the perverse gift of allowing cigarette commercials on the one day of the year in which most families, with children assembled, turned on their television sets to watch the popular New Year's Day college football bowl games. The ban on cigarette advertising on television holds to this day.

We Bumblebees became a collaborative resource for the now formidable anti-tobacco advocacy organizations to draw on. Beginning with the initial hearings on the cigarette act, we continually developed activities to help strip "controversial" from the media's characterization of the science behind the indictment of smoking and to expose the mendacity of the tobacco companies. To our quiver of tactics that began with the letters, we added press releases and floor statements by our senators, all loaded with scientific data. We promoted them with follow-up calls to responsive journalists, and we broadened the design of committee hearings, all in an effort to undermine the tobacco industry's arguments for Congress to save them from the unleashing of FTC and FCC advertising constraints.

We scheduled hearings to ensure publicity for the anti-tobacco message. On February 23, 1966, for example, Magnuson convened a Commerce Committee hearing we had scheduled in which officials from the Department of Agriculture—we had no jurisdiction—were summoned to account for a film the department, in its traditional role as international promoter of US agricultural products, had commissioned. A colleague of Ed Merlis's in the Department of Health, Education, and Welfare had alerted him to the glossy film, funded by the Department of Agriculture and produced by Hollywood's Warner Bros. It was to be squeezed between feature films in movie theaters around the world.

The hearing opened with a viewing of the film. It is a bizarre, unintended parody of a travelogue, entitled *The World of Pleasure*. It bears no disclosure that it is US government–funded tobacco propaganda. It is presented as a celebration of the shimmering wonders of Hollywood in which—none too subtly—a half dozen or so romantic couples are smoking ecstatically. The finale opens with a chorus line of women leaning over with their backsides turned prominently to the camera. When they twirl around in unison and straighten to face the camera, each has a glowing cigarette dangling from her mouth. Magnuson, as chair, excoriated the hapless departmental officials who had been sent to take the rap. The witnesses pledged that such promotions would cease.

After the hearing, Magnuson received a telephone call from his friend Orville Freeman, secretary of agriculture, who expressed outrage that a fellow Democrat would so publicly embarrass a member of his own administration. Magnuson, wary of offending the highly regarded cabinet member, feigned ignorance, blaming Merlis and me as rogue staffers. But Magnuson—along with Jerry—was buoyed by the media coverage, especially the television clips of the film and Magnuson's display of righteous indignation.

To undercut the tobacco industry's campaign to maintain the illusion that there remained a scientific controversy over the safety of tobacco, we hatched a plot and recruited Daniel Brewster, a new committee member and recently elected senator from Maryland, who was eager to make a name for himself. During the 1965 hearings on the cigarette labeling bill, Brewster wrote a letter to each of the thirty-seven witnesses named by the Tobacco Institute's legal team, asking whether and how much they had been paid to testify that the scientific evidence against smoking was unproven. He released their answers at an opportune moment during the hearings. They had all been paid, quite handsomely for academics, and some had received additional funds for their research. Though the practice of paying witnesses was common, the public admissions helped to undermine the objectivity of the industry's witnesses and generated the media coverage we sought.

Even hearings on a bill that was otherwise going nowhere provided a platform. The introduction of a new bill authored by Magnuson and co-sponsored by Senators Robert Kennedy and Frank Moss on May 17, 1967, provided the opportunity for three days of hearings the following August. Although these hearings were ostensibly designed to hear testimony on the efficacy of tar and nicotine warnings, which the bill proposed to enact, we structured them so that the first two days were dedicated to testimony by the most credentialed, prestigious, and eloquent scientists, who presented overwhelming evidence that smoking is a cause of death and disease. We called them in an effort to take revenge against the tobacco lobby for stacking the 1965 hearings on the first labeling bill with witnesses who offered pseudoscience to challenge the evidence against smoking.

To encourage media advocacy, we generated press releases announcing floor statements. On March 7, 1969, for example, Senator Moss delivered a statement on the floor of the Senate to an audience that included sympathetic journalists. The content of the floor statement was not news, but it highlighted a new FTC report demonstrating that the cigarette manufacturers had been artificially raising the nicotine levels yielded by their cigarettes to hook smokers more deeply.

More newsworthy was a floor statement Magnuson had delivered the previous year excoriating a Tobacco Institute scam: an agent of the Tobacco Institute had paid a financially hard-pressed journalist, Stanley Frank, to write a purportedly independent review of the science in the January 1968 issue of *True* magazine under the title, "To Smoke or Not to Smoke—This Is Still the Question." As I remember, the article concluded with a patently false statement on the order of, "At the moment, all we can say for sure is that the cause of cancer isn't known and that there is absolutely no proof that smoking causes human cancer."

By the mid-1970s, we began to note the invisible hand of the media: none of the tobacco industry's counterarguments against the dangers of tobacco was legitimate. The scientific case against smoking was no longer "controversial."

### Sometimes They Simply Gave Up Quickly

Soon after the ban on broadcast cigarette advertising went into effect in January 1971, tobacco companies started sending free samples of single and double packs of twenty cigarettes in the mail. A month later, when Magnuson and Moss started getting complaints about these mailings, we put together a bill to ban the unsolicited mailing of sample cigarettes. When Merlis and I were ready for Moss to introduce it in the first week of March, I called the chief tobacco lobbyist, Earle Clements, to tell him what Moss—with Magnuson's blessing—was going to do. Clements invited us to lunch at the International Club.

As soon as we were seated, Clements summoned the waiter with a flamboyant signal and asked imperiously, "Do you have some eggs back there?" The waiter said yes and, as Merlis recalls, Clements, holding his thumb and forefinger about three-fourths of an inch apart, ordered the waiter to "cut me a slice of Virginia ham about this thick. Then," he continued, "fry up three eggs easy and put them on top of the ham. I'll pay you whatever you want to charge."

Once our orders came, we told Clements about the Moss bill and the travesty of sending cigarettes in the mail, clearly labeled so children home from school would know what they were and take them. He asked us to wait before introducing the bill. We waited a week. The day after *Advertising Age* published an article by Stanley Cohen about the practice and the anticipated legislation, Moss introduced the bill. Clements called about a day later. After reminding me that he had asked us to wait on the bill's introduction, he predicted that the companies would voluntarily refrain from sending unsolicited mail-order samples. They did.

As Merlis recalls, the companies' ready agreement was probably based on fear of our holding hearings and undermining their plans through legislation or regulation. "It was probably too successful an effort on our part. Had we held hearings we might have been able to identify and explore their plans and create an environment which contained the redirection of their advertising dollars."

# 12

## *Pushing Open the Closed Door*

When I approached Senator Magnuson in 1969 with a proposal that we transfer a particular one of his able office staff members to the Commerce Committee, he would have none of it: "We can't have a woman in the Senate meeting room. We won't be able to talk freely with women in the room." What totally escaped his consciousness was that there were already two or three women in attendance at every committee session. They were not just present; they often performed critical tasks to support the Bumblebees.

Arlene Sidell, for example, who was educated as a political scientist at the University of Washington, was already "in the room" as mark-up clerk for committee votes. She told me:

> I would often get frantic calls from the staff counsels who were never totally sure of the actual votes of senators on the committee on amendments and bills being voted out of the Commerce Committee. They would challenge me that I might have made a mistake, but I was always right and I saved them from giving their bosses the wrong count. They would even ask me to explain what the amendments said because they were not paying attention. They would refer the press to me since they did not want to be inaccurate.

Only two stories in this book so far feature the leadership of women, and neither of those women was a Senate Commerce Committee Bumblebee. One was Senator Maurine Neuberger, the fourth woman ever elected to the US Senate—and one of only two women serving at the time. The other was Joan Claybrook, the lowly intern who had as much impact on the strength of automobile safety legislation as any senior male staffer.

Why were there no female Bumblebees?

In the 1970s, the door to professional status in the United States, whether in business or government, was overwhelmingly closed to women. In 1950 there were no women in my class at Yale College. Yale Law School, among the most progressive law schools in the country, had just hired its first female law professor when I entered with the class of 1959. Of the 150 or so students in that class, only 9 were women. The University of Washington law school was equally inhospitable to female students. Until 1975, no women had ever been chosen from the graduating class for the Magnuson Fellowship.

During the 1970s, I interviewed many young people, including many women, eager to work in the Senate or in similar offices where they might make a difference. Often they asked, "What kind of education or training would help me?" My answer to the women was always the same: "If you have a law degree, you won't be asked to get the coffee."

As the feminist movement progressed and more and more people awoke to the inequities between men and women in compensation and promotion, Magnuson remained among the laggards. I worked below his radar, bringing to the committee a succession of solidly able female summer interns, a few of whom stayed on for a year or two. Gradually, I began to hire female professional staffers for some of the subcommittee chairmen, but always behind Magnuson's back. None of these staffers, however, was assigned primary responsibility for managing a subcommittee or an important bill. Even as professional staff members, they remained in supportive roles.

Most of the female interns, legislative assistants, and subordinate professional staff members whom Magnuson employed, however, later moved into leadership roles in government, nonprofit advocacy groups, and law or lobbying firms that were at least as challenging as those of the men they worked for. Today there are few distinctions between male and female senior staff members, but it took until 1974 before Magnuson would accept female lawyers as professional staffers. He did so involuntarily—when the Magnuson Fellowship program finally chose its first graduating woman.

### Mary Schuman

Mary Schuman was chosen in the fall of 1975. Like many of the rest of us, Schuman was an accidental Bumblebee. Until she was selected as a Magnuson Fellow, she had never heard of the internship program, nor was she interested in government service. She was prepared to begin a career as a practicing lawyer. Nonetheless, she was delighted to accept the internship and leave Seattle. During the sixteen months she served as a committee staff member, Schuman exhibited ideal Bumblebee qualities: wit, innate ability, and a taste for strategic mischief. Her brief service on the committee staff opened doors that led her to a top position in the White House, where her decisions had a national impact.

As a new Magnuson Fellow, Schuman was housed in an office with Ed Merlis and Ed Cohen. "They welcomed me," she recalls. "They wanted to help me get situated in Washington. I could tell right away that I had landed in the right place. They were smart, hardworking, and dedicated, and I loved them all instantly." But she did not escape their inaugural rite. At first she was given minor tasks involving noncontroversial presidential nominations to secondary positions at the Commerce Department, of little interest to the Commerce Committee members. Then she was given an assignment that seemed significant: she was to be counsel to the Aviation Subcommittee and prepare for three weeks of hearings on what was then the central issue in transportation—deregulation of the airline industry.

Deregulation was a hot topic at the time among conservatives, who were chronically antithetical to government interference in the "free market," and liberals, who generally favored regulation when it served the public interest but who were wary of the many industry-inspired regulations that served industry at the expense of consumers. Aviation regulation would be the test case. The aviation industry had effectively written Civil Aeronautics Board (CAB) regulations giving the existing companies monopoly protection against competition and guaranteeing profits based on the costs—not the efficiency—of providing passenger service. Some deregulation supported by liberals benefited consumers, but the CAB regulations would have benefited only the companies.

Aviation regulation was solidly housed in the Commerce Committee, but an even more aggressive team than us made a bold grab for investigative jurisdiction over the issue: the Administrative Practice Subcommittee, an obscure subcommittee of the loosely defined Government Operations Committee. Its chairman was Senator Edward Kennedy, who was evolving into an effective entrepreneurial political leader. His subcommittee staff, I have to acknowledge, outshined us in both brilliance and aggressiveness. Because they were enchanted by the possibility of unmasking the flaws in aviation regulation, they had begun to hold highly publicized investigative hearings marking the CAB for destruction.

The chairman of the Commerce Committee's Aviation Subcommittee, Howard Cannon of Nevada, was outraged by Kennedy's poaching on his legislative territory and equally appalled at the thought of deregulation.

Cannon was the airlines' champion. He was determined to challenge Kennedy's jurisdictional theft and his deregulatory apostasy by scheduling his own hearings on airline regulation, with his own witnesses, heavily tilted toward friends of the Air Transport Association (ATA).

Knowing only that she was responsible for preparing Cannon and the other members of the subcommittee, Schuman "labored for weeks, writing opening statements, questions, answers to questions, follow-up questions." Soon she had "a nice little stack of documents prepared." But something was awry, she recalls with chagrin. Merlis and Cohen were "snickering and giggling" about the work she was doing. "I could tell," she says, "they thought it was amusing that I was working as hard as I was." She found out why. A few days before the hearings were scheduled to begin, she received a large brown envelope that contained "a complete set of staff work for the hearing—opening statements for everybody, questions, answers, follow-up questions, follow-up answers." There was no indication of where it had come from.

When her officemates stopped laughing, they told her the envelope was from the ATA and that all the work she had been doing was unnecessary. Sure enough, Cannon and the other committee members discarded all of Schuman's laborious work and read faithfully from the ATA playbook. The hearings tilted heavily against deregulation, and Cannon introduced a bill artfully drafted to change nothing.

But Schuman had the last snicker. Her hard work provided her with a solid grounding in airline regulation and its flaws. It would not be wasted. In late November 1976, shortly after Jimmy Carter was elected president, Schuman received a call from Harrison Welford, who was managing planning on domestic policies for the Carter transition. Welford had been borrowed from Senator Philip Hart's office, where, as legislative assistant, he had grown to respect Schuman's depth and judgment on aviation regulation. He invited Schuman to join the transition team. As Schuman recalls, "They wanted somebody to write what we then called an 'option paper' to the president-elect, saying there is interest in airline regulatory reform, and you need to decide, are you for it, are you against it? Do you want to have your own bill? Do you want to let the Senate and the House write their bills?"

Schuman joined the team and soon became Carter's White House policy expert on transportation deregulation. Reform was needed, she believed, because the regulations were good for the airline industry but not for the traveling public. "The only competition among airlines," she says,

"was for better meals and better silverware and linen napkins and magazines and all sorts of things that travelers didn't want and were paying very
dearly for." But Schuman could not support the radical deregulation that
Kennedy's team advocated. She shunned the label "deregulation" and stuck
with "regulatory reform." She understood that Kennedy's staff proposals
could create fear among the public that "planes would fall out of the sky
and they would become unsafe and small towns would lose all air service
and the whole system would be so disruptive that the public would suffer."
Her idea was to reassure people that nothing was being taken away.

Regulatory reform was her goal in drafting the options memo, but she
did not come out with a firm recommendation of this middle ground.
She had learned from her Commerce Committee experience that when
presented with an options memo, "the decider" always picks the middle
option. So she followed the formula of putting one extreme option to the
left, one extreme option to the right, and the one she liked she would phrase
to "look like the moderate, reasoned, wise approach" so it would be "the
obvious approach for the person who's reading that memo."

That her opinion paper was appreciated was affirmed by a call she received, just as her work for the transition team was ending, from Stuart
Eisenstadt, Carter's assistant in charge of developing his domestic policy
agenda. Eisenstadt invited Schuman to continue her work on airline regulation and help the new administration look into the economic regulation
of trucks, railroads, and maybe telecommunications.

Fearing that if she stayed any longer in the political world she would be
unable to start fresh as a lawyer "in the real world practicing law," Schuman
said no. Then Eisenstadt invited her to join him on a visit to the Old Executive Office Building next to the White House. There he walked her down
a "magnificent, palatial hallway" and showed her the room that would be
her office. It had twenty-foot ceilings, a desk, sconces, chandeliers, and
couches and armchairs upholstered in red brocade. The draperies too were
red brocade. Schuman decided it would be a good place to work and accepted the job.

"It's clear in retrospect," she says, "that that office had to go to a woman,
because no man was going to work in a red bordello. But I was perfectly
happy there."

Not just happy; Schuman proved tough and strategic. With other
White House staff, she drafted the proposed airline regulation reform bill
that President Carter submitted to Congress. When she was given the role
of White House lobbyist on the bill, she successfully persuaded Cannon,

Magnuson, and other committee members—who varied widely in their attitudes and their coziness with the ATA—that the bill was the soundest and most politically expedient solution to the need for regulatory reform.

At the same time she needed to persuade the new staff director for the Senate Antitrust Subcommittee to support the bill. That would be harder; the subcommittee staff had convinced Kennedy that radical deregulation was called for. To her dismay, Schuman learned that the new subcommittee staff director, David Boies, was a Wall Street lawyer who was famed for taking no prisoners as a litigator. But when she met with Boies, rather than allow herself to be intimidated, she aggressively lectured him: "We're the president. If this industry is destroyed, it's on his watch. So we've got to make sure that doesn't happen." Boies resisted, but Schuman wore him down. Kennedy did not oppose the bill, and it passed essentially as Carter had proposed it. Boies and Schuman were later married.

Schuman was not finished getting her way as far up the line as the president's chief of staff, Hamilton Jordan. The regulatory reform bill had to be properly enforced, and that task would fall to the members of the CAB, whose three-member majority Carter needed to nominate. Jordan asked Schuman for her advice on two of the members, but said he reserved for himself the selection of nominee for chairman.

Schuman diligently pursued her assigned task and came up with two qualified candidates, as Jordan had requested. Still, she was not finished. The key appointment would be the chairman of the CAB. She ignored Jordan's injunction and set out to find the ideal candidate. Everyone she called for advice directed her to a Cornell professor named Alfred Kahn, saying, she recalls, "He's written on the subject; he ran the New York Public Services Commission; he understands regulation; he's smarter than everybody."

She submitted her memo with recommendations for all three CAB vacancies. The next day she received a curt phone call from Jordan's assistant, who told her Jordan was not interested in who she thought should be chairman because he was going to make that decision. He wanted choices, not her view. So she wrote a revised memo, in which she said she had three candidates for chairman: Alfred Kahn, A. E. Kahn, and Fred Kahn (the name by which Alfred Kahn was known among his friends). She wrote a few sentences about each one of them and sent the memo to Jordan. This time he called her himself and thanked her, adding, "Finally, you did what I asked. I'm picking the second one."

"That's fantastic," Schuman replied. "You know, Hamilton, he would have been my choice, but I knew you weren't interested in my choice."

## Sharon Nelson

Unlike Schuman, Sharon Nelson was determined early on to find a means of serving the public interest. "I wanted to do good in the world," she says. At Carleton College she was mesmerized by the charismatic Marxist historian Karl Weiner, who revealed to her the sorrows of the world from the Middle Ages to the Nazi Holocaust. She decided she wanted to teach college history as he did. But like so many other women in the 1960s, her ambition was suppressed. The department chairman at Carlton told her that no female applicant was likely to get scholarship funding for a PhD, though she could get funding for a master's degree to qualify her for teaching high school. She was accepted, with a full scholarship, to the Master of Arts in Teaching program at the University of Chicago, where she was a close witness to the 1968 Democratic Convention demonstrations. "It awakened all my civil liberties instincts," she recalls. After completing her degree, she started teaching in a racially and economically mixed high school on the border between Chicago and neighboring Gary, Indiana.

A short time later Nelson moved with her husband to Seattle, where, following her desire to "do service in the public interest," she volunteered in the juvenile justice system, then for the Washington State Judicial Council, which was dedicated to law reform, and for the Kennedy-era Office of Economic Opportunity (OEO). Inspired by her work for the OEO, Nelson became determined to "make law more accessible to poor people," and in 1972 she entered the University of Washington law school. There, at the encouragement of a friend, she applied for the Magnuson Fellowship and was accepted.

Nelson's assignments as an intern were modest and her time with the Commerce Committee was short, but she believes that the informal training she received, the support of her colleagues, and the Bumblebee methods she absorbed helped her find her life's calling—consumer protection—and armed her for achieving much of her later success. Like Schuman, Nelson was housed with Merlis and Cohen in a cluttered and noisy office. Also like Schuman, she exclaims, "They were great! I was really given first-rate skills by those guys. They were warm and helpful. They were looking out for me."

Soon after she started her internship, Nelson was delighted to become part of the process of writing a conference report on the Toxic Substances Control Act. The House-Senate conference committee had come to an agreement, and, she recalls, "the staff had all this power to fill in, explain, construe, what this legislative language meant. That was fun. And I thought, 'Wow, that is a lot of power!'"

Nelson also relished the independence she had in developing oversight hearings. Among those were the radiation and safety oversight hearings. At first, the hearings were designed to expose the risks of radiation leakage from household appliances like microwave ovens. But as Nelson and her Bumblebee colleagues burrowed deeper into the hazards of radiation, they went well beyond the jurisdiction of the Commerce Committee. Even the Department of Defense, which was jurisdictionally the domain of the Senate Armed Services Committee, became their prey when Nelson learned that the department was experimenting with low-frequency radar off the shores of Cape Cod. That discovery led her and her colleagues to look into which other agencies of the federal government were using this new technology and to ask them what they were doing to ensure that the American public was not being overexposed to untested health risks.

When they drew in epidemiologists and other scientists from the National Academy of Health, they learned that Vietnam veterans were subject to testicular cancer because they had navigated their helicopters by following radar signals, which exposed them to huge doses of radiation. By then, Nelson had to get a top-secret clearance to do the oversight hearings, which had started with a narrow focus on consumer protection issues but had evolved into a far broader inquiry. Nelson has no recollection of which senator held the hearings that she and her colleagues had structured and scripted because, she says, "we owned these hearings. We didn't let anybody else conduct them. They were our hearings. We set them up, and we asked the questions."

Nelson acknowledges that the hearings did not produce actionable evidence that all product radiation should be subject to new regulation. There was sufficient testimony, however, and broad enough publicity to put pressure on microwave oven manufacturers to take steps to ensure the safety of their products. Though the committee took no further action, like Schuman on aviation, Nelson inadvertently emerged as a respected expert on the effects of radiation on health. When she left the committee staff, she joined the Washington office of Consumers Union as a lobbyist for consumer protection, with acknowledged expertise in radiation hazards. Later, she was invited to become a public member of a national commission investigating the effects of nonionizing radiation on the human body. She also had the cherished opportunity to work with Senator Hollings, who had recently ascended to the chairmanship of the Commerce Committee's Communication Subcommittee, where she developed valuable knowledge in telecommunications technologies.

In the early 1980s, Nelson moved to Washington State, where she was selected by the state legislature to coordinate a joint select committee to rewrite the state law on telecommunications regulation. The Regulatory Flexibility Act was passed in 1985 with only two votes against it in the state House. (One of those dissenting votes was cast by Jack Metcalf, a Republican who had run unsuccessfully against Magnuson.) During the next two decades, Nelson chaired the Washington Utilities and Transportation Commission and served as the volunteer chair of Consumers Union; she created and directed the work of the Shidler Center for Law, Commerce, and Technology at the University of Washington law school; and she headed the Consumer Protection Division of the state attorney general's office.

As a leader in public service, Nelson adopted the leadership transparency style she had seen in the Commerce Committee. She told her staff at the Consumer Protection Division that this style of leadership, the Bumblebee practice, would be her model. "They got it; they loved it," she says. She had also learned "how to get staff to be really excited and working with me" in her Commerce Committee days.

"I enjoyed the work so much," she told me, "because I had learned from you how to be a head of an agency."

## Maggie Finally Gets It

Magnuson's political star was dimmed in his defeat for reelection in 1980—the era of Ronald Reagan's ascendancy. He retired gracefully and returned to Seattle, where he and Jermaine regularly welcomed to their home the high proportion of Bumblebees who had also resettled in the area. His wit had not escaped him. At a gathering of the Bumblebees to celebrate his eightieth birthday, Magnuson offered a wry toast. His long-term colleague and friend Senator "Scoop" Jackson had died of a heart attack several years earlier. The irony of his death at the age of seventy was that he had been a faithful practitioner of a healthy lifestyle, swimming and exercising every day. Magnuson, by contrast, had lived in early carousing style, maintaining his vigor with the daily imbibing of at least a quart of vodka. At that birthday celebration, he proclaimed to the faithful Bumblebees, "I stand before you a testament to clean living."

Magnuson's mellowness at last encompassed a female Bumblebee, Sharon Nelson, whose political star had risen brightly in Washington State, as recounted earlier. As chair of the state regulatory commission, Nelson had run into heavy corporate resistance to her regulatory restraints on behalf of the state's consumers, especially the telecommunications and private electric power companies. She told me that she had been invited along with a couple of fellow Bumblebees to Magnuson's house for dinner in 1985. He opened up to them in a way only a few of us male staff members had experienced when we worked for him.

"He was sitting in his chair," she said, "and he had his vodka in his hand, and his cigar." The others were "chatting away, and I'm just being quiet, 'cause he really hadn't paid much attention to me ever."

> And he goes, "Sharon!"
> And I answered, "Yes, Senator, what?"
> He said, "Did you see that ad on TV?"
> I said, "Which one?"
> He said, "The one for GTE Squirt."
> I said, "Oh you mean, GTE Sprint?" (General Telephone had just bought the Sprint Company.)
> He said, "Squirt? Sprint? Who can tell the difference between telephone companies and soda pop companies anymore?"
> What he meant was, "Why should these companies who have all the earmarks of monopolies be advertising on television? It's just a waste of the ratepayers' money." That was his attitude. And it was the right attitude at that time.

Nelson also ran into hostile resistance from corporations she had regulated as chair of the Washington Utilities and Transportation Commission. In an article from the July 2, 1989, *Seattle Post-Intelligencer*, Shelby Scates (who had faithfully covered Magnuson from Washington, DC, for many years), describes Nelson as a former "staffer for Senator Warren Magnuson" with "a keen sense of humor and knowledge of the utilities," who is "too good for the sake of utilities whose appetite for more profit at the expense of ratepayers, as described by federal judge Harold Green, 'isn't deep; it's bottomless.'" He adds, "In the past, utility moguls making significant salaries have tongue lashed Nelson for her attention to the needs of consumer budgets. Apparently that's not sufficient. They aim to have her fired."

Magnuson readily shared with Nelson the experience he had gathered over a half-century of confronting unhappy regulatees. He told her that the best way to bring the power companies to heel was to get the city council to threaten to expand the city's existing publicly owned and operated electric utility, thereby swallowing up a larger portion of the area served by the private utility.

"Then," he said to her, "they'll come and talk to you." She did. They did.

### Not Even Halfway There

Despite the successes of women like Mary Schuman and Sharon Nelson, who got their starts in the 1970s, not all of us fully internalized the cultural changes taking place around us. One day, still in the early 1970s, I was sitting at my desk during lunchtime, and one of our professional women staffers, working for a senator other than Magnuson, burst into my office, enraged and upset. She and the senator, her friend and colleague, had scheduled a business meeting downtown with corporate lobbyists advocating for a bill that she was deeply involved with. The meeting was scheduled at the Metropolitan Club, which, like most private clubs of the time, barred women. When the two of them reached the door, the steward told them simply that she could not be admitted. The senator turned to her and said, "You better go back to the Hill." He went in. I immediately issued a memorandum to all the staff forbidding any more staff meetings to be held at any place at any time that did not allow women to participate.

The Civil Rights Act had been passed for more than a decade before our committee began to recruit women. To our lasting shame, however, we recruited no black, Latino, or Asian committee professional staff members. Nor, I believe, did any of the other congressional committees. The country, the Congress, and the committee still had a long way to go in eradicating racial and ethnic discrimination. We still do.

# 13

# *Time to Move On*

One evening in mid-December 1976, I came home feeling high on the events of the day. I told my partner, Anna—soon to become my wife—that that morning had begun with breakfast in the Senate cafeteria. I had sat alone, reviewing the day ahead. One by one, a coterie of Senate staff people had approached my table to pay their respects or to ask favors. I boasted to Anna that I had felt like a mafia don. I was a power in the Senate.

Her reaction was forceful. It went something like this: "Look at you. You're all puffed up, just resting on your laurels. You've delegated most of the hands-on committee staff work that once energized you. You've stayed too long."

She was right. After thirteen years, I was stale and smug. Meanwhile, other Bumblebees had flourished. Lynn Sutcliffe, Ed Merlis, and Tom Allison, in particular, had taken on leadership roles within the committee. I was basking in their light.

Furthermore, the election of Jimmy Carter had opened an opportunity for me. In a change of administrations from one party to the other, it is common for the newly elected president, seeking potential nominees to head government agencies, to turn to congressional staff members of his own party who are knowledgeable about the agencies overseen by the committees they worked for. I had daydreamed about the chairmanship of the FTC, which administered many of the consumer protection laws we had worked on. But I had held back. Working for Magnuson, I had been sheltered by a strong leader—I was not sure that I could become one. I had persuaded myself, instead, that I could still play an important role by staying. I could help ensure that the new president nominated experienced candidates to the regulatory agencies, candidates with strong public interest commitments.

Now that excuse seemed like a cover for my timidity. I awoke from my torpor and called a friend who was serving on the Carter transition team, Anne Lewis, to express my interest in the FTC chairmanship. Lewis was among the most politically skillful liberal Democrats I knew. She encouraged me to launch a quiet campaign for the position and promised to make certain that I was seriously considered. I told Magnuson that I was going to try for the position. As I expected, he expressed no enthusiasm; he didn't like change, and I didn't ask him to take any action on my behalf. I later learned that he had given his unstinted approval in response to a call from the Carter White House. Meanwhile, Senator Fritz Hollings, having heard of my interest from other staff people, wrote a warm letter to the president urging my appointment. When Carter telephoned Ralph Nader, seeking suggestions for consumer regulatory agencies, Nader suggested me for the FTC. A few business lobbyists offered their support; far more were troubled by the prospect.

The good fortune that sealed my nomination, however, had little to do with me. Leaks from the White House that I was being considered were picked up by the business press. So was the rumor that the president was also considering Bella Abzug, a fiery member of Congress from New York City. Abzug was an outspoken progressive activist who had made many enemies among corporate lobbies and inspired unease among more timid ideological allies who had not yet embraced leadership by a woman. She was seen as uncontrollable.

After Carter took office and began to fill his most important posts, I heard nothing. Then, one day in mid-February, I received a telephone call from Hamilton Jordan, Carter's White House chief of staff.

"Have you got your shoes polished?" Jordan asked me. "The president wants to see you."

I didn't stop to polish my shoes. I rushed to the White House and was ushered into Jordan's office.

"Last night," Jordan said, "I told the president that we had two candidates for FTC chairman, Bella Abzug and you." The president, he continued, was appalled. "'We can't appoint *Bella Abzug* to the FTC!'"

That left me. I left the Commerce Committee and was sworn in on April 22, 1977.

### The Depletion of the Bumblebees

For a while, the Bumblebees carried on without missing a beat. Magnuson wisely appointed the proven troika of Merlis as staff director, Allison as the committee's chief counsel, and James P. "Bud" Walsh as general counsel.

Walsh had played a strong, innovative role as counsel for the Oceans and Fisheries Subcommittee, whose central role in the prosperity of Washington State was political bread-and-butter to Magnuson. As a result, he had also earned Magnuson's trust.

During the first few years of the Carter administration, these three and other staff members continued to strengthen existing laws and develop others, despite the ongoing opposition of the targeted industries. They did so with high energy. But the ranks of seasoned Bumblebees had begun to erode. I've already chronicled the career leaps of our first two female staff members. After only a year with the committee, Mary Schuman had joined the Carter transition team and then catapulted to a high level of Carter's White House staff. Sharon Nelson stayed on the committee, enriching her skills, through 1977. She carried those skills and her passion for consumer protection to the Washington office of Consumers Union and the potent Washington Utilities and Transportation Commission. She was so well respected by her fellow regulators across the country that they elected her president of the National Association of Regulatory Utility Commissioners.

The Carter election was an invitation for others to move on as well. Several of my colleagues on the committee staff had served the committee and Magnuson for six years or more. Armed with impressive portfolios of work they had done on the committee, and their dedication to the public interest, they were also appointed to senior Carter administration positions. A few others were drawn to the more traditional path for accomplished congressional staff members: the private practice of law in DC, invariably involving lobbying. Even then, most of them also found ways to honor the public interest orientation they had developed in their Commerce Committee work.

Ed Cohen, for example, was appointed deputy to the president's consumer adviser, Esther Peterson. When Reagan replaced Carter as president, there was no place for a committed consumer advocate in the White House, but Cohen found a role in the private sector consistent with his values: lobbying for the Honda Corporation.

Why Honda? That choice was the reflection of an event that had occurred while Cohen, who had begun taking primary responsibility for bills, was staffing a bill to fill gaps in the automobile safety law. The law would mandate safety airbags. Lobbyists for the US car makers and others used their political influence to express their grievances to the committee's senators. One day, while the bill was in process, Honda Sōichirō, the founder and CEO of Honda Corporation, came to visit Cohen and me, accompanied by a team of his associates. His US colleagues understood and respected the key role of staff. Honda told us that he was not opposed to the legislation; he simply wanted to know when and how he could prepare his company to meet the proposed law's mandates.

Thereafter, the Honda representatives in Washington consistently distanced the company from the rest of the automobile lobby, continuing to support stronger regulatory rules and never attempting to undermine them. When Cohen prepared to leave government service, he joined Honda's Washington office and soon became the company's chief US lobbyist. "It's the only company that would hire me," Cohen told me, "and it was the only company I would work for. It's very progressive in its thinking."

Lynn Sutcliffe had been drawn to low-cost energy conservation for consumers through his work with Senator Hollings on the Commerce Committee. When a former classmate and friend at Princeton, Bill Bradley, was elected to the Senate, Sutcliffe left the committee to counsel Bradley in developing early legislative support for economic energy conservation legislation. Later, he joined with other like-minded congressional staffers to create a law firm that promised to dedicate itself to clients promoting environmental protection, especially energy conservation. When the law firm fell short of realizing that ambition in its effort to serve paying clients, Sutcliffe, ever a driving force, moved on to join a private company whose promise was also to serve the public interest. He soon discovered that the firm's lust for profit outweighed its commitment. Again he moved on, seeking a new way to serve the public interest without compromise.

Manny Rouvelas, who also remained committed to the public interest, became the managing director of a law firm that lobbied on behalf of Washington State's maritime interests. In the late 1970s, he helped form and co-lead Lawyers and Lobbyists for Campaign Financing Reform. He lobbied for public financing of congressional campaigns, affirming that the gushing river of campaign money flowing from corporate lobbyists was poisoning the integrity of their profession.

The largest contingent of departing Bumblebees, especially those who had joined the committee staff as Magnuson Fellows, returned to Washington State to practice law. Most of their practices left DC behind. Many, such as Dan O'Neal, found ways to involve themselves in nonprofit good works. O'Neal founded and helped lead a volunteer coalition of citizens working to preserve the environmental safety of Puget Sound, the pride of Seattle and other cities on its shores.

Not every Bumblebee devoted himself to doing good after leaving the committee, though most did well. One former Bumblebee, who had been among the most radical advocates on the committee staff in pursuing the public interest, acknowledged to me that, as a member of a law firm, he did not discriminate between clients seeking the public interest and those resisting it. He brought to all clients the same gift: the strategies that he had absorbed through his work on the Commerce Committee.

### "People Like Me Don't Leave Legacies"

When I asked Jerry Grinstein, the prime moving force behind the creation of Magnuson's Bumblebees, "What do you consider your legacy?" he demurred.

"People like me," he said, "don't leave legacies."

Most of us had been convinced that as he continued to play a powerful, though informal, leadership role in the politics of Washington State, Jerry would one day choose to run for the Senate or the governorship. And that he would win.

We were wrong about his seeking elected office but not in our judgment that in whatever course Jerry chose, he would excel. If any of us can lay claim to a worthy legacy, it is Jerry. Soon after joining what was perhaps the most distinguished law firm in Seattle, he was made partner. He took great interest in serving as general counsel of Seattle's successful but stormy horse racetrack organization, where he filled far more than the usual lawyer's role. He became the turn-to guy, called on to calm internal conflicts. He was still a leader.

Among his more needy clients was Western Airlines, which was a hundred million dollars in debt. When there seemed no way to avoid bankruptcy, the airline's board (of which he was a member) turned to Jerry with the unstated message, "You're so smart, why don't you try to save the airline?" He did, by negotiating a merger with Delta Airlines, which saved most of Western's employees their jobs but left him without one.

He was soon recruited to become CEO of Burlington Northern, one of the nation's largest railroads. He also served on the board of Delta Airlines, which had swallowed Western. When Delta faced bankruptcy, that board turned to Jerry to serve as CEO to save the company from collapse. This time he saved the company by negotiating it through an inevitable bankruptcy. Again, his efforts saved many jobs. On a recent visit with Jerry and his wife, Carolyn, I came across a Christmas greeting from one of his close colleagues at Delta, Cathy Cone. With her permission, I quote excerpts from her letter to Jerry:

> When I received a Christmas card today from a Delta retiree thanking me for her pension, I could not help but reflect on the days when we were all on the same team, working to keep the pensions of tens of thousands of Delta people that would not be near as well off today, if it had not been for you. I told the retiree that you are the one she needs to be thanking! Without your work and know how, it would never have been possible. . . .
>
> You made such a difference in the lives of so many that don't even realize it. . . . You have been such a blessing to so many and I just wanted to let you know how often I think about our dinners with the Board Council, the laughs we had and the work we did together to help so many. It would have been a much different outcome without you in the driver's seat!

Characteristically, Jerry dismisses his efforts as no more than pragmatic business: "A company can't work unless its employees feel they are respected. There is no way that thousands of employees serving the public can be supervised during their daily work. They need to feel that they are trusted, and their loyalty needs to be earned."

These words reveal what all the stories in this book with Jerry at the center illustrate: his boundless caring for those who needed his help, beginning with Magnuson and including a great many of the Bumblebees he recruited and watched over. I was one of them.

By 1980, the "liberal hour" nation, Washington, and Senate Commerce Committee we had known had passed. In 1981, newly elected president Ronald Reagan replaced me as FTC chairman with a conservative Republican whose unstated motto was, "Government regulation, bad; untethered free market, good." I remained for three more years as a commissioner. Because I had little to do but dissent from the new commission's refusals to regulate, I had time to write my first book, *Revolt against Regulation: The Rise and Pause of the Consumer Movement*. That period of hopeful resistance to effective consumer protection regulation has lasted nearly half a century. I have faith, now, that the "liberal hour" will return.

## *More Than Ever, We Need Now a New Generation of Bumblebees*

Featured in the stories in this book have been corporate lobbyists who were politically influential, richly funded, and deeply skilled in their advocacy. My greatest pleasure in writing this book has been chronicling how, as Magnuson's Bumblebees, we built the counterforce to those lobbies. In doing so, I have avoided describing the quantum leap in the number of corporate lobbyists operating in Washington over the past thirty years and the consequent political dominance they have gained over all phases of the legislative process. Every politically sentient American is aware that Washington lobbyists are the powerhouse of the plutocracy.

An extraordinary book published in 2015 by Lee Drutman, *The Business of America Is Lobbying*, however, shocks even my professional awareness of the extent to which corporate lobbying has captured government.[1] One particular aspect of Drutman's study offers a coda to this book: the business lobbies' takeover of every staff function we performed.

Citing a recent survey, Drutman writes:

> Two-thirds of current staffers described lobbyists as "necessary to the process" as either "collaborators" or "educators." Staffers also frequently referred to lobbyists as "partners." Occasional pieces of investigative reporting reveal what most lobbyists will probably acknowledge—that they are deeply involved in the developing and drafting of legislative policy. . . .
>
> Often, lobbyists do more than just share expertise. They also help congressional offices to draft legislation, develop the talking points and explanations for why the legislation makes sense, write speeches and letters in support of it, seek out cosponsors and supporters both within and outside of government, and generally see a bill through from start to finish.[2]

None of what Drutman describes is entirely new. A scattering of the stories that appear here refer to similar takeovers under lobby-friendly senators. But the lobbyists were never so omnipresent, and they were more often than not outwitted by resistant entrepreneurial senators and their Bumblebees.

When progressive senators and representatives recapture power in the Senate and House, no matter how deeply committed to social justice they may be and how entrepreneurial their ambitions, the new chairs and members of congressional committees will never achieve their goals without a team of Bumblebees at their backs. In this regard, the Magnuson Bumblebees provide a model: only the dogged insistence of a committee or subcommittee chair to build a full complement of strategically skilled and substantively expert staff members serving the committee majority can adequately empower the legislators to counteract the smothering grip of the corporate lobbyists. More than ever, we need now a new generation of Bumblebees.

# Interviewees

Leonard Bickwit
Joan Claybrook
David Cohen
Edward Cohen
Stanley Cohen
Philip Elman
David Freeman
Gerald "Jerry" Grinstein
Charles LeMaistre
Michael Lemov
Terry Lierman
Edward Merlis
William Meserve
Ralph Nader
Sharon Nelson
Daniel O'Neal
Manny Rouvelas
William Ruckelshaus
Mary Schuman
Arlene Sidell
Lynn Sutcliffe

# *Acknowledgments*

So many to thank! I started this book as a memoir of the good years I served on the staff of Senator Warren Magnuson, chairman of the Commerce Committee. I soon realized, however, that my stories were thin gruel for a book, and so I reached out to my former colleagues on the staff, seeking their stories about how they helped our boss and other committee senators succeed in enacting legislation to serve the public interest against the power of the vested-interest lobbyists. Their stories and mine fill this book. The staff members and other colleagues and mentors from those days whose stories and insights are recounted here are listed as Interviewees. But even those I interviewed who do not appear here contributed to my awareness of the range of creative advocacy that fueled the Senate, and especially Magnuson's Commerce Committee, in those years.

I owe a debt of gratitude to Michael Ames, director of the Vanderbilt University Press and the overseeing editor and publisher of this book. Michael shepherded me through two earlier books. He is not a nitpicking editor, but in essential broad strokes he set the focus and parameters of the book, then kept me from wandering away from them.

Throughout, Debby Smith, developmental editor, disciplined my draft of each chapter. She was invariably encouraging. She entered the tone and spirit of the book, putting herself in my place as narrator and offering wise suggestions. Thanks to Debby, the book morphed, as if by magic, from rambling early drafts into a far more engaging, tighter final manuscript with nothing essential missing. To keep my sensitive ego from deflating, her suggestions were almost always accompanied by her heartening pleasure in at least some words and phrases in every draft.

Many of the Bumblebees were ready at the call, but Ed Merlis became the third limb of my team. Early in the evolution of the book, knowing that he has a nearly photographic memory and infinite patience, I called on Ed to fill the gaps and repair the lapses in my forty- to fifty-year-old memories and those of our fellow Bumblebees. Ed plunged in and reviewed every chapter through multiple progressions. His memory is uncanny. He made one correction that defies belief, soberly noting that a meeting that took place nearly forty years ago, and that I had described as occurring on a Wednesday, had actually taken place on the previous Monday. His judgment in critiquing my prolix drafts kept me focused on the book's goals. His memory enlightened me to Bumblebee exploits I had known little about, such as those of one of our more mischievous staff members, Tom Allison. Sadly, Tom died before I could interview him. Thanks to Ed, I am able to give Tom the special credit as a strategist that he deserves.

Another critical partner was Kay Carlson, the intrepid transcriber of the interviews that make up the core of the book. Her patience is unlimited, her counsel wise: Don't conduct interviews in the middle of a noisy restaurant. Don't talk while your interviewees are talking. Don't move the recorder too far away from or too close to your interviewee. Despite my continual lapses, she always managed to produce a flawless transcript.

I am indebted to a succession of resourceful political science graduate students who undertook the challenging tasks of checking facts, ensuring the accuracy of citations, and confirming the veracity of stories I thought I remembered. I found these researchers through the help of American University's renowned political science professor James Thurber, who recommended students whom he deemed most capable. As students do, each moved on. Each time, Thurber filled the vacuum. Those who unraveled the most challenging enigmas were Vivien Leung, Rory Jackson, and Kristen Miano.

When I submitted the final manuscript to Vanderbilt, I quickly discovered that work on the book was hardly finished. I am indebted to Joell Smith-Borne, Vanderbilt's managing editor, for expertly guiding it through the complicated process of production, and to Betsy Phillips, manager of sales and marketing, for enthusiastically and creatively publicizing the book. In the final stage of the book, the copy editor, Zachary Gresham, who fully respected my objectives, uncovered my lapses in precision with eagle eyes and offered wise remedies.

I am grateful, too, to the volunteer reviewers of the chapters, whose commentaries proved insightful and encouraging. Particular among them are David Cohen, Laura Tracy, and our children, Daniel Sofaer, Mark Pertschuk, and Amy Pertschuk.

Finally, I thank my wife, Anna, for her love and constant support. More than once, she gently challenged my judgment and always turned out to be dead right.

# Notes

## Introduction

1. James Q. Wilson, *Bureaucracy: What Government Agencies Do and Why They Do It* (New York: Basic Books, 1989), 76–77.
2. Ira Shapiro, *The Last Great Senate: Courage and Statesmanship in Times of Crisis* (New York: Public Affairs, 2012).
3. *The Commerce Committees: A Study of the House and Senate Commerce Committees*, Ralph Nader Congress Project, David E. Price, director (New York: Grossman, 1975), 30.
4. David E. Price, *Who Makes the Laws? Creativity and Power in Senate Committees* (Cambridge, MA: Schenkman, 1972), 100.
5. We appropriated the term *children's hour* from President Franklin Roosevelt, who used it to describe the late afternoons when he convened his closest advisers for informal talk.
6. This is my first confession: no record has been found of Ehrlichman's complaint about overzealous staff members or his use of the word "bumblebees," despite the efforts of my successive graduate research assistants in Washington, DC, and despite my desperate broadcast plea to the whole Bumblebee e-mail list. Though Shelby Scates, a Washington-based journalist for the *Seattle Post-Intelligencer* who closely covered Magnuson for many years, devotes a whole chapter to the role of Magnuson's Bumblebees in his political biography *Warren G. Magnuson and the Shaping of Twentieth-Century America* (Seattle: University of Washington Press, 1997), his single source for the term is me. I insist, however, that I did not make it up. I could not have hoodwinked all the Bumblebees who anointed themselves as such, and Magnuson's Bumblebee of the Week award could not have rested on my word alone. Finally, there was Jermaine's bumblebee pillow, which, alas, has also disappeared. Ah, well.

## 1  An Accidental Bumblebee

1. 108 Cong. Rec. 3677 (1962) (statement of Sen. Maurine Neuberger).
2. Quoted in Richard Kluger, *Ashes to Ashes: America's Hundred-Year Cigarette War, the Public Health, and the Unabashed Triumph of Philip Morris* (New York: Vintage Books, 1997), 21.

3. Quoted in ibid., 223.

4. Charles A. LeMaistre, "The Untold Story of the 1964 Report on Smoking and Health" (unpublished manuscript, 2013), in the author's possession.

5. Walter Sullivan, "Cigarettes Linked to Cancer, U.S. Report Concludes," *New York Times*, January 12, 1964.

## 2 *Jerry and Maggie*

1. Staff director was Jerry's functional title. His formal title, as he is listed in the Commerce Committee calendars, was "Chief Counsel."

2. *The Commerce Committees: A Study of the House and Senate Commerce Committees*, Ralph Nader Congress Project, David E. Price, director (New York: Grossman, 1975).

3. Shelby Scates, *Warren G. Magnuson and the Shaping of Twentieth-Century America* (Seattle: University of Washington Press, 1997).

4. Minority staff director was Kenney's functional title. His formal title, as he is listed in the Commerce Committee calendars, was "Assistant Chief Clerk."

## 3 *A Bumblebee's Crucible*

1. James Ridgeway, "Underground War on Auto Industry," *New Republic* 155 (December 3, 1966): 21, quoted in Timothy Joseph McMannon, "Warren G. Magnuson and Consumer Protection" (Ph.D. diss., University of Washington, 1994), 1.

2. Richard Kluger, *Ashes to Ashes: America's Hundred-Year Cigarette War, the Public Health, and the Unabashed Triumph of Philip Morris* (New York: Vintage Books, 1997), 288.

3. Robert C. Hockett, "Cigarettes: Why More Research?" MS prepared for *Yale Scientific*, n.d.

4. "Health Warning Required on Cigarette Packs," *CQ Almanac 1965*, 21st ed., 344–51, Washington, DC: Congressional Quarterly, 1966.

5. Kluger, *Ashes to Ashes*, 291.

6. The reports to Congress were actually issued by the US surgeon general, who operated within HEW.

7. Editorial, *New York Times*, July 9, 1965.

## 4 *A Triumph of Passionate Truth over Power*

1. Quoted in Justin Martin, *Ralph Nader: Crusader, Spoiler, Icon* (New York: Basic Books, 2002), 47.

2. *Federal Role in Traffic Safety: Hearings before the Subcommittee on Executive Reorganization of the Committee on Government Operations*, United States Senate, 89th Congress, 1st sess. (1965), pt. 2, 781.

3. Elizabeth Drew, "The Politics of Automobile Safety," *Atlantic Monthly*, October 1966.

4. Doris Kearns Goodwin, *The Bully Pulpit: Theodore Roosevelt, William Howard Taft, and the Golden Age of Journalism* (New York: Simon and Schuster, 2013).

5.  Ralph Nader, *Unsafe at Any Speed: The Designed-in Dangers of the American Automobile* (New York: Grossman, 1965).

6.  Quoted in Martin, *Nader*, 47.

7.  Ibid., 53.

8.  Drew, "Politics of Automobile Safety," 99.

9.  Ibid., 100.

10. Michael R. Lemov, *Car Safety Wars: One Hundred Years of Technology, Politics, and Death* (Madison, NJ: Fairleigh Dickinson University Press, 2015).

11. Drew, "Politics of Automobile Safety," 101.

### 5  High Spirits and High Gear

1.  111 Cong. Rec. 3235 (1965) (statement of Sen. Warren Magnuson).

2.  Quoted in Timothy Joseph McMannon, "Warren G. Magnuson and Consumer Protection" (Ph.D. diss., University of Washington, 1994), 142.

3.  112 Cong. Rec. 12819 (1966) (statement of Sen. Mike Mansfield).

4.  Quoted in David E. Price, *Who Makes the Laws? Creativity and Power in Senate Committees* (Cambridge, MA: Schenkman, 1972), 31.

5.  Lyndon B. Johnson, "Special Message to the Congress on Consumer Interests," March 21, 1966, online by Gerhard Peters and John T. Woolley, American Presidency Project, www.presidency.ucsb.edu/ws/?pid=27505.

6.  Child Protection Act of 1966, Public L. No. 89-756, 74 Stat. 375 (1966).

7.  Quoted in McMannon, "Magnuson and Consumer Protection," 292n176.

8.  *Flammable Fabrics Act Amendments of 1967: Hearings on S.1003, Before the Senate Committee on Commerce*, 90th Cong., 57 (1967) (statement of Peter Hackes).

9.  Ibid., 77 (statement of Dr. Abraham Bergman).

10. Ibid., 95 (statement of William M. Segall).

11. Quoted in McMannon, "Magnuson and Consumer Protection," 290.

### 6  Jerry's Juggernaut

1.  Product list provided by one of the staff members working on Magnuson's campaign in Seattle, who prefers to remain anonymous.

### 7  Colonizing the Bumblebees

1.  Michael R. Lemov, *People's Warrior: John Moss and the Fight for Freedom of Information and Consumer Rights* (Madison, NJ: Fairleigh Dickinson University Press; Lanham, MD: Rowman and Littlefield, 2011), 85.

2.  Steven Greenhouse, "Evelyn Dubrow, Labor Lobbyist, Dies at 95," *New York Times*, June 22, 2006.

### 8  The Flights of the Bumblebees

1.  *Washington Merry-Go-Round: The Drew Pearson Diaries, 1960–1969* (Lincoln: University of Nebraska Press, 2015), entry for Sunday, October 25, 1964, 263.

2.  Glenn Robertson, "Hollings 'Angered' by Tour of Slums," *Charleston [SC] Evening Post*, January 11, 1968, 12.

3.   Rudolph A. Pratt, "The Beginning of a . . . Rennaissance [sic] in Dixie?"
     Charleston [SC] Evening Post, February 23, 1969, 15.

**9** *Finishing Unfinished Business*

1.   Timothy Joseph McMannon summarizes the commission's report in "Warren G.
     Magnuson and Consumer Protection" (Ph.D. diss., University of Washington,
     1994), 298.
2.   Michael R. Lemov, *People's Warrior: John Moss and the Fight for Freedom of
     Information and Consumer Rights* (Madison, NJ: Fairleigh Dickinson University
     Press; Lanham, MD: Rowman and Littlefield, 2011), 90.
3.   Ibid., 93.
4.   120 Cong. Rec. 31321 (1974) (statement of Rep. John E. Moss).

**10** *Advise and Dissent*

1.   James S. Turner, *The Chemical Feast: Ralph Nader's Study Group Report on the
     Food and Drug Administration* (New York: Grossman, 1970).
2.   Morton Mintz, "Nixon Nominee to FPC Faces Stiff Opposition," *Washington
     Post*, May 17, 1973, A16.

**11** *Pushing the Boundaries*

1.   Quoted in Richard R. Hart, *A Sense of Joy: A Tribute to Ted Moss* (Springville,
     UT: Bonneville Books, 2003), 211.

**13** *Time to Move On*

1.   Lee Drutman, *The Business of America Is Lobbying: How Corporations Became
     Politicized and Politics Became More Corporate* (New York: Oxford University
     Press 2015).
2.   Ibid., 40.

# Index

Numbers appearing in bold refer to pictures.